ACTIVITIES AND RESOURCES FOR GUIDING YOUNG CHILDREN'S LEARNING

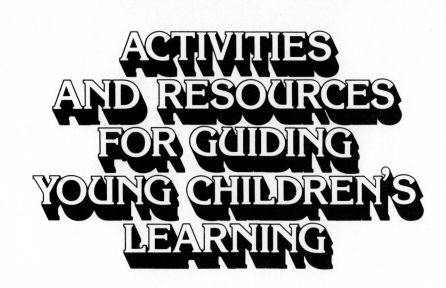

ACTIVITIES AND RESOURCES FOR GUIDING YOUNG CHILDREN'S LEARNING

Norma Bernstein Tarrow
Professor
California State University, Long Beach

Sara Wynn Lundsteen
Professor
North Texas State University

With **Sandye Schneider Dinato** • **Margaret Van Fleet** • **Michael Carr**

Illustrations by Margaret Van Fleet,
with the assistance of Sandye Schneider Dinato

McGraw-Hill Book Company
New York St. Louis San Francisco Auckland Bogotá Hamburg
Johannesburg London Madrid Mexico Montreal New Delhi
Panama Paris São Paulo Singapore Sydney Tokyo Toronto

To Irv, Alex, Mark, Harriet,
and especially Dani and Michael

ACTIVITIES AND RESOURCES FOR GUIDING
YOUNG CHILDREN'S LEARNING

1 2 3 4 5 6 7 8 9 0 WCWC 8 9 8 7 6 5 4 3 2 1

This book was set in Century by ECL Art Associates, Inc.
The editors were Phillip A. Butcher and Susan Gamer;
the design was done by Caliber Design Planning;
the cover illustration was done by Margaret Van Fleet;
the production supervisor was John Mancia.
Webcrafters, Inc., was printer and binder.

Library of Congress Cataloging in Publication Data

Tarrow, Norma Bernstein.
    Activities and resources for guiding young
children's learning.

    Includes bibliographies.
    1. Creative activities and seat work—Handbooks,
manuals, etc.   2. Activity programs in education—
Handbooks, manuals, etc.   3. Lesson planning—Hand-
books, manuals, etc.   I. Lundsteen, Sara W.
LB1537.T34   372.13   81-1843
ISBN 0-07-039108-4   AACR2

Contents

Section 4
Language Development: Activities and Resources

Section 5
Affective Development: Activities and Resources

Section 6
Multicultural Approaches to the Curriculum

Section 7
Education of Children with Special Needs

Preface

Teachers and caretakers of young children are always looking for new ideas. We hope that whether you are an experienced teacher, a beginning teacher, or a student of education, you'll find in this book some useful, practical, and interesting ideas for working with children from infancy to age nine. In a sense, this book is a companion to our textbook *Guiding Young Children's Learning* (McGraw-Hill, 1981); the two books can certainly be used independently of each other, but we believe that they will also work very well in conjunction. The textbook provides a theoretical basis for work with young children; it answers the question "Why?" This book of activities and resources provides concrete, practical examples; it answers the question "How?"

In this preface, we will be explaining the way *Activites and Resources for Guiding Young Children's Learning* works. But before we do so, let us explain something about our approach to early childhood education, and in particular to the formulation of objectives and activities for young children.

We are developmental-interactionists. What this means, briefly, is that we believe that as children interact with the environment, they develop simultaneously in different areas; that the different aspects of their development are closely interrelated; that the sequence of development is universal; that activities for children should be developmentally sound, growing out of certain processes and aimed at certain generalizations and skills; and that it is useful and rewarding to approach the traditional subject areas as aspects of the developmental processes. Bear with us now, while we expand somewhat on each of these thoughts.

The developmental areas are usually identified as follows: psycho-physical-motor (which includes perception, small- and large-muscle skills, mental health, and physical growth); cognitive (which has to do with the growth of thought processes); language (which has to do with the processes and skills of communication); and affective (which has to do with socialization, creativity, and the self—emotions, personality, self-concept, and attitudes). As we've just noted, we believe that development in these areas is simultaneous and interrelated and that, as a result, activities designed to foster development in one area will tend to foster development in other areas as well.

In these areas, we believe, all children go through the same sequence of development; that is, they all go through the same stages. This is not to say, of course, that all children develop identically; obviously, they do not. They differ in the rate at which they go through the stages—and this means that anyone working with young children must have a large and varied repertoire of objectives and activities, to meet the needs of individual children. It also means that categorizing activities and objectives precisely by age level or grade level is unwise—instead, activities and objectives should be seen as covering rather broad, loose age ranges.

A corollary of this is that activities and objectives need to be related to children's development. We can compare guiding children's learning to building a house. In both cases, we need a solid foundation and a sturdy framework—when these are in place, we can go on to the exterior and interior arrangements and furnishings. In early childhood education, then, we need a foundation based on what we know about development, and a framework based on objectives that are matched with children's development. We can then confidently go on to build our day-to-day activities, which constitute the curriculum.

When we approach teaching and learning in this way, how do we think about the traditional subject areas? We believe that any subject area—science, mathematics, reading, and so on—can be approached from the standpoint of any of the developmental areas. That is, each subject area involves each kind of development—psycho-physical-motor, cognitive, linguistic, and affective. In this book, we have distributed the subject areas among the developmental areas so as to give you *examples* of how the subject areas can be approached developmentally. For instance, consider music. If you think about it, you will see that music is a psycho-physical-motor subject (because children sing and dance and play instruments), and a cognitive subject (because children learn many new concepts), and a language subject (because it has a vocabulary of its own), and an affective subject (because it is so greatly involved with attitudes and emotions). We have chosen to treat music as a part of the affective curriculum, and that certainly is appropriate; but we realize that it could also be treated appropriately as a part of any of the other areas. So it is with each of the subjects. We have matched up subject areas and developmental areas as follows:

Psycho-physical-motor: Expressive and objective movement; nutrition; safety; physical and mental health.
Cognitive: Science and mathematics.
Language: Oral communication; reading; writing.
Affective: Social studies; art; music.

Our purpose in this arrangement is to *illustrate* how each subject "looks" when it is approached from the perceptual-motor area, the cognitive area, the language area, or the affective area. Our readers may find it interesting, and instructive, to move each subject from the area where we've placed it to the other areas, and see how it looks from each new viewpoint.

How This Book Works

Having introduced our theoretical stance, we'll now explain how our book is put together.

There are seven sections. The first provides general resources; the second, third, fourth, and fifth provide objectives, activities, and specific resources for the four developmental areas (psycho-physical-motor, cognitive, linguistic, and affective); the sixth is a special section on multicultural approaches; the seventh is a similar section on special education. In the following paragraphs, we give you a preview of each of these sections.

Section One This is our section of general resources—resources which cut across all the developmental and subject areas. It's rather unusual to *begin* with resources—most books of this nature (at least the ones we have seen) tend to put the resources last. We have placed them at the beginning so that you will start right away to become familiar with sources of helpful materials. As you work with our activities in the later sections, or make up activities of your own, remember these resources—and *use* them. (You will find that they also give you ideas for discovering other resources.) No teacher or caretaker needs to work in isolation—a wealth of information, ideas, and materials is out there waiting for you.

Sections Two, Three, Four, and Five These are our developmental sections. Each has the same format: after a brief general introduction, we discuss objectives and activities for infants and toddlers (that is, youngsters through age 3) and then give a table of objectives and activities for this age group. We then discuss our objectives for older children (ages 4 to 9) and list major objectives in a table or tables, followed by detailed sample activities. Finally, we give resources for each subject area.

The relationship between the objectives and the activities is of the utmost importance. For infants and toddlers, activities are so simple that they can be described in a line or two, and thus we have been able to present them in tabular form: each activity is aligned with the objective it is designed to foster. For older children, our activities take a more elaborate form (explained below), and our objectives are more numerous and more complex. Consequently, the simple visual match-up is not practical; instead, we have a "key" to match each activity with its objective. The point we want to stress is that each activity has a specific objective; as you use the activities, you should be very much aware of the objectives.

The tables of objectives for older children may look formidable at first, but we have found them practical and easy to use. The objectives take various forms; in some subject areas they are generalizations, in some they are skills, and in some they are processes. For each subject area, the table of objectives presents a progression from the most simple to more complex generalizations, skills, or processes and thus may be considered as forming a framework for that subject. The objectives are grouped by what we call "curriculum areas"—that is, subdivisions of subject areas—and by age levels. (Sometimes, to make things clearer or more precise, we identify some additional categories—but curriculum areas and age levels are always our major ones.)

For the activities for older children, we have used a basic format with some slight variations. We begin by stating a description of the activity; a playful title to be used in presenting it to the children; the curriculum area; and the age level. We then state the objective, giving the "key" to the table of objectives; list the materials you'll need for the activity; and go through the steps you and the children will follow in doing the activity. Last, we note appropriate variations or follow-up activities, or suggest ideas for different activities aimed at the same objective. Most of our activities are quite flexible as regards the number of children that can participate—they can generally be adapted for use with the whole class, one or more groups (of varying sizes), pairs of children, and individual children. (Occasionally, however, we do give suggestions about this, noting—for example—that an activity is a class project, or that the class is divided into groups, or that the children work with partners.)

We'd like to make four points about the activities, one minor and three major.

First, the minor point. The "title for children" is, as we've mentioned, playful. These titles often include figures of speech, puns, alliteration, and so on. We like them, because we've found that children like them. But if they don't appeal to you or your children, don't hesitate to drop them altogether, change them, or substitute titles of your own.

Second, a major point. The "age range" noted for each activity—and for each set of objectives in the tables—is a suggestion only. We've already pointed out that children develop at different rates; it's impossible, therefore, to be very precise about age levels for which the activities are appropriate. We have deliberately made our ranges rather wide; and you'll notice that the age levels on the tables of objectives overlap. We give objectives and activities at four levels: level A corresponds to ages 3 to 5; B, to ages 4 to 6; C, to ages 5 to 7; and D, to ages 7 to 9. In choosing activities for individual children or groups, you'll want to consider not only the children's ages but also their developmental level. For example, both level B and level C include age 6; but for a precocious 6-year-old, you'd probably want to choose activities from level C rather than level B.

Third, another major point. We are firm believers in the importance of concrete, firsthand, "hands-on" experiences for children; and our activities reflect this belief. Developmental objectives are reached by exploration and manipulation of many kinds of objects, substances, and materials, and by exposure to many kinds of immediate, personal experiences; keep this in mind as you work with our activities and as you formulate your own.

And fourth, another major point. To arrive at any skill, process, or concept, several—often many—activities are needed. We have not attempted to present all possible activities leading to any of our objectives. The activities we provide are examples—*not* a script to be followed word for word, and not a manual of lessons. We believe that teachers will want to use their imagination and creativity to build on our samples, creating a file of activities— ours and their own—keyed to specific objectives and suited to their own purposes and their own children.

Although we have used the word "file," by the way, you need not take it literally. The activities have been designed typographically so that they can be removed from the book, reproduced, and cut apart to fit into a file box; and many of our readers will probably want to do this. But of course each teacher must come up with his or her own retrieval system for materials like this—you may prefer to use looseleaf notebooks, spring binders, or folders, for example.

Following the activities, we give some specific resources. These lists of resources, like the activities, are not meant to be exhaustive. Our goal has been to help you discover how and where to find resources that you can use effectively. Remember that early childhood education is a fluid area—knowledge, literature, and materials are all expanding and changing.

Section Six This is our section on multicultural approaches, an area we consider especially significant in today's world. As in the developmental sections, we give some important objectives; here, however, these take the form of a list of concepts. Following the objectives are sample activities illustrating the multicultural approach—again, we stress the importance of concrete, "hands-on" experiences for children—and some useful multicultural resources.

Section Seven This is our section on special education. It is different from the developmental sections. Because we believe strongly in the principle of mainstreaming—that is, bringing "special" children into the regular classroom and treating them as much as possible like "normal" children—we have not listed any specific objectives and activities for special children. Instead, we simply give some ideas and guidelines for teachers and caretakers, in the hope that these will help you discover how best to make your special children a part of all your classroom goals and activities. We end with some specific resources for special education.

Appendix Our appendix consists of blank activity forms. We hope that you will find them useful for creating your own activities, and that they will serve to remind you that you can continue the process we've begun in this book— finding activities that will enhance children's development and learning.

Acknowledgments

For their creative ideas, their constructive criticism, their time and efforts, and their interest and supportiveness, we gratefully acknowledge the invaluable assistance of our colleagues in California and Texas. The "California crew": Erline S. Krebs, lecturer, California State University, Fullerton; Betty L. Perez, teacher, early childhood and special education, Wakeham School, Garden Grove, California; and Dorothy Rubin, preschool teacher, Horace Mann Elementary School, Anaheim, California. The "Texas team": Bertha W. Kingore, Hardin Simmons University, Abilene, Texas; Mary Glenn Peery, assistant professor, North Texas State University; Jacquelyn Smith, principal, Spring Valley Elementary School, Richardson, Texas; and Carol Mason Wolfe, senior research scientist, Institute for Creative Studies, Dallas, Texas.

Our thanks also go to Dani and Michael Dinato, on whom we tried out many of our ideas.

Finally, this book would never have come to be without the continuous and prolific efforts of Sandye Dinato, educational consultant and former director of the Tuvia Preschool, Redondo Beach, California; Margaret Van Fleet, teacher, Hacienda-La Puente Unified School District, California; Michael Carr, teacher, Los Alamitos School District, California; and Susan Gamer, our editing supervisor at McGraw-Hill, who helped put the whole thing together.

Norma Bernstein Tarrow
Sara Wynn Lundsteen

Section 1
GENERAL RESOURCES

In this opening section we present general resources for early childhood education. We've divided these into three major categories: a bibliography for teachers (books and periodicals); a bibliography for children (again, books and periodicals); and sources and suppliers of learning materials. Under "sources and suppliers" we have specific sections on commercial sources, free (or inexpensive) materials, audiovisual materials, and community resources.

In Sections 2 through 7, we give specific resources for developmental and curriculum areas. In these later sections, there is some variation in the way resources are presented, but basically we'll be using the categories introduced in this first section: bibliography for teachers; bibliography for children; and learning materials.

Remember that our lists of resources are not meant to be definitive. As we noted in the Preface, our goal is to give you ideas about where and how to find useful sources; and you will want to remember, too, that both sources and published materials are constantly changing.

Bibliography for Teachers of Young Children: Books and Periodicals

Books:

Caney, S. *Play book*. New York: Workman, 1975. (Clear, lively directions and photographs of seventy ingenious activities for children. A good resource for parents and preschool and elementary teachers.)

Croft, D., & Hess, R. *An activities handbook for teachers of young children*. Boston: Houghton Mifflin, 1972. (Excellent coverage of activities in language, science, the arts, mathematics, and cooking is provided by this resource book. Bibliographies are well annotated, and a special feature is the extensive listing of literature for children in a variety of categories.)

Danoff, J., Breitbart, V., & Barr, E. *Open for children*. New York: McGraw-Hill, 1977. (Curriculum sections of this resource book show how activities for young children extend into the more traditional subject-oriented curriculum and how these subjects form an integrated whole.)

Directory of resources on early childhood education. Urbana, Ill: ERIC, 1971. (A directory listing early childhood education organizations, major publications, centers, and laboratories, to serve as a resource to educators seeking information or services.)

Early childhood education: How to select and evaluate materials. New York: EPIE Educational Institute, 1972. (43 W. 61st St., 10023. This report lists educational materials and kits available commercially. Suggestions are provided for selecting and evaluating materials and for matching them to educational philosophy.)

Eliason, C., & Jenkins, L. *A practical guide to early childhood curriculum*. St. Louis: Mosby, 1977. (Designed for in-service and preservice teachers, this resourceful book contains a concrete curriculum approach based on the concepts being developed in children 3 to 6 years of age. Major concepts are identified, units and lesson plans provided, and resources suggested for such areas as size and seriation, weather and temperature, language arts, and plants.)

Flemming, B., Hamilton, D., & Hicks, J. *Resources for creative teaching in early childhood education*. New York: Harcourt Brace Jovanovich, 1977. (Poorly organized but exceedingly valuable materials for the classroom teacher; lists curriculum areas with everything from finger plays to community resources and background for the teacher.)

Hyman, R. *Paper, pencils, and pennies: Games for learning and having fun*. Englewood Cliffs, N.J.: Prentice-Hall, 1977. (An excellent guide to simulation games that includes word games, role-playing activities, values-education exercises, and simulations of social and physical situations.)

Jones, S. *Good things for babies.* Boston: Houghton Mifflin, 1976. (A consumer guide to more than 250 products used during the baby's first two years and a valuable resource for parents and caretakers. Products listed were chosen on the basis of maximum safety, convenience, and helpfulness.)

Jones, S. *Learning for little kids: A parent's sourcebook for the years 3 to 8.* Boston: Houghton Mifflin, 1979. (Superb resource book for parents—or teachers—containing information and suggestions for activities and learning materials relating to areas such as art, nature, fantasy, language, and mathematics, as well as value-laden subjects such as sex, birth, death, illness, divorce, adoption, and moving.)

Kaplan, S., Kaplan J., Madsen, S., & Gould, B. *A young child experiences.* Santa Monica, Calif.: Goodyear, 1975. (Independent and group activities and ideas for learning centers and task cards are clearly described and illustrated in this practical and creative sourcebook for teachers of young children.)

Kaplan, S., Kaplan J., Madsen, S., & Taylor, B. *Change for children.* Santa Monica, Calif: Goodyear, 1973. (Ideas and activities for individualizing learning in this excellent sourcebook deal with room environment and organization, the development and use of learning centers, planning, record keeping, and evaluation. Detailed illustrations and a section of worksheets make it relatively easy for the uninitiated to implement the ideas.)

Linderman, C. *Teachables from trashables.* St. Paul, Minn.: Toys 'n' Things Training and Resource Center, 1979. (906 N. Dale St., 55103. This book is designed as a catalyst for new ways of turning "junk" into unique toys. Stress is placed on creating safe, educational toys that develop skills and knowledge.)

Lorton, M. *Workjobs: Activity-centered learning for early childhood education.* Menlo Park, Calif.: Addison-Wesley, 1972. (A superb collection of teacher-made activities designed to foster specific concepts and skills for the elementary school child. Also included is a section on how to prepare for activity-centered teaching, how to begin such a program, how to keep records, and how to evaluate progress. Clear descriptions and photographs accompany each activity.)

Malehorn, H. *Encyclopedia of activities for teaching grades K–3.* Englewood Cliffs, N.J.: Prentice-Hall, Parker, 1975. (A collection of early childhood instructional ideas for all principal areas of the curriculum. Nearly 2,000 suggestions in 700 short citations.)

Pitcher, E., Lasher, M., Feinburg, S., & Braun, L. *Helping young children learn* (3d ed.). Columbus, Ohio: Merrill, 1979. (This new version emphasizes children's own experimentation, self-direction, and self-expression, and the importance of play to enhance learning. A cognitive-developmentalist approach suggests that teachers provide appropriate challenges to stimulate the child's successive mastery of certain concepts. Excellent bibliographies and lists of curriculum materials are provided for each curriculum area.)

Schmidt, V. *Early childhood development: Helping the three-, four-, and five-year-old child learn in day care, nursery school, and kindergarten.* Dallas: Hendrick-Long, 1976. (A straightforward description of the components of an early childhood program, including suggested equipment and activities. Extensive bibliographies cover general and specific areas of program planning. Also included are lists of journals, publishers, organizations, and materials sources relevant to early childhood programs.)

Stein, S., & Lottick, S. *Three, four, open the door.* Chicago: Follett, 1971. (Hundreds of activities suitable for the young child's home or school are

provided. Most of them are quite creative and clearly described, although more illustrations would be helpful.)

Taetzsch, S., & Taetzsch, L. *Preschool games and activities.* Belmont, Calif.: Fearon, 1974. (This book provides a variety of basic activities and games designed to help children develop skills and concepts to ease the transition from preschool to elementary school.)

Watrin, R., & Furfey, P. *Learning activities for the young preschool child.* New York: Van Nostrand, 1978. (This is a practical "how-to" book that provides preservice and in-service teachers with play activities for teaching toddlers from ages 1 to 3. Recipes and directions for constructing simple teaching materials are included.)

Journals:

Child Development. (Published by the University of Chicago Press for the Society for Research in Child Development, 5750 Ellis Ave., Chicago, Ill. 60637.)

Childhood Education. ACEI, 3615 Wisconsin Ave., NW, Washington, D.C. 20016.)

Children. (Children's Bureau. Subscriptions through Superintendent of Documents, U.S. Government Printing Office, Washington, D.C. 20402.)

Elementary School Journal. (University of Chicago Press, 5750 Ellis Ave., Chicago, Ill. 60637.)

Merrill-Palmer Quarterly. (71 E. Ferry Ave., Detroit, Mich. 48202.)

Young Children. (NAEYC, 1834 Connecticut Ave., NW, Washington, D.C. 20009.)

Periodicals:

Early Years. (Box 1223, Darien, Conn. 06820.)

Instructor. (7 Bank St., Dansville, N.Y. 04437. Many classroom ideas and activities.)

Learning Magazine. (530 University Ave., Palo Alto, Calif. 94301. New approaches, new materials available. Excellent magazine.)

Teacher. (7 Bedford St., Stamford, Conn. 06901. Formerly *The Grade Teacher.* Packed with ideas and resources.)

Professional organizations:

Association for Childhood Education International (ACEI), 3615 Wisconsin Ave., NW, Washington, D.C. 20016.

Child Study Association of America, 9 E. 89th St., New York, N.Y. 10028.

Day Care and Child Development Council of America, Inc. (DCCDCA), 1401 K St., NW, Washington, D.C. 20005.

Educational Resources Information Center/Early Childhood Education (ERIC/ECE), 805 W. Pennsylvania Ave., Urbana, Ill. 61801.

National Association for the Education of Young Children (NAEYC), 1834 Connecticut Ave., NW, Washington, D.C. 20009.

Play Schools Association, 120 W. 57th St., New York, N.Y. 10019.

U.S. Department of Health, Education, and Welfare (now U.S. Department of Education), Office of Child Development, Children's Bureau, Washington, D.C. 20201.

Newsletters:

Day Care and Early Education. (Published five times a year by Behavioral Publications, 72 Fifth Ave., New York, N.Y. 10011.)

ERIC/ECE Newsletter. (805 W. Pennsylvania Ave., Urbana, Ill. 61801.)

Interracial Books for Children. (Published eight times a year by Council on Interracial Books for Children, 1841 Broadway, New York, N.Y. 10023.)

Report on Preschool Education. (Capitol Publications, Inc., Suite G-12, 2430 Pennsylvania Ave., NW, Washington, D.C. 20037.)

Today's Child. (Roosevelt, N.J. 08555.)

Voice for Children. (Newsletter of the Day Care and Child Development Council of America. Included in membership in the organization.)

Encyclopedias:

American peoples encyclopedia. (Sears, Roebuck and Co., 925 South Homan Ave., Chicago, Ill. 60624.)

Collier's encyclopedia. (P. F. Collier and Son, 640 Fifth Ave., New York, N.Y. 10019.)

Encyclopaedia Britannica. (Encyclopaedia Britannica Educational Corp., 425 N. Michigan Ave., Chicago, Ill. 60611.)

Encyclopedia Americana. (Grolier Educational Corp., 845 Third Ave., New York, N.Y. 10022.)

Encyclopedia international. (Grolier Educational Corp., 845 Third Ave., New York, N.Y. 10022.)

Lincoln library of essential information. Also *Lincoln library of social studies.* (Frontier Press, Lincoln-Le Veque Tower, Columbus, Ohio 43215.)

Negro heritage library. (Buckingham Learning Corp., 160–08 Jamaica Ave., Jamaica, N.Y. 11432.)

Negro in American history. (Encyclopaedia Britannica Educational Corp., 425 N. Michigan Ave., Chicago, Ill. 60611.)

New Caxton encyclopedia. (Pergamon-Chambers' Library Service, Maxwell House, Fairview Park, Elmsford, N.Y. 10523.)

World book encyclopedia. (Field Enterprises Educational Corp., Merchandise Mart Plaza, Chicago, Ill. 60654.)

Bibliography for Children: Books and Periodicals

Reference books:

Book of knowledge. New York: Grolier Educational Corp. (845 Third Ave., 10022).

Britannica junior. Chicago: Encyclopaedia Britannica Educational Corp. (425 N. Michigan Ave., 60611).

Childcraft and *Childcraft annual.* Field Enterprises Educational Corp., Merchandise Mart Plaza, Chicago, Ill. 60654.

Compton's picture encyclopedia. (Reference Division, Enclycopaedia Britannica Educational Corp., 425 N. Michigan Ave., Chicago, Ill. 60611.)

Compton's young children's precylopedia. Chicago: F. E. Compton and Co., 1971.

Golden Book encyclopedia. New York: Western Publishing Co., Inc., Golden Press (ordering address 1220 Mound Ave., Racine, Wis. 53404).

New wonder world. New York: Parents Magazine Education Press (52 Vanderbilt Ave., 10017).

Our wonderful world. New York: Grolier Educational Corp, 1971.

Periodicals:

American Girl. Girl Scouts of America, 830 Third Ave., New York, N.Y. 10022.

American Junior Red Cross News. American Red Cross, National Headquarters, Washington, D.C.

Boys' Life. Boy Scouts of America, New Brunswick, N.J.

Child Life. Saturday Evening Post Co., 1100 Waterway Blvd., Indianapolis, Ind. 46206.

Children's Digest. Better Reading Foundation, Inc., Bergenfield, N.J. 07621.

Children's Playmate. Mueller Printing and Lithograph Co., 6529 Union Ave., Cleveland, Ohio 44105.

Geographic School Bulletin. National Geographic Society, 17th and M Sts., Washington, D.C. 20036.

Golden Magazine. Golden Press, Inc., 1220 Mound Ave., Racine, Wis. 53404.

Highlights for Children. 2300 W. Fifth Ave., Columbus, Ohio 43215.

Jack and Jill. Curtis Publishing Co., Independence Sq., Philadelphia, Pa. 19106.

National Geographic. National Geographic Society, 17th and M. Sts., Washington, D.C. 20036.

Natural History. American Museum of Natural History, Central Park West at 79th St., New York, N.Y. 10024.

Plays. Plays, Inc., 8 Arlington St., Boston, Mass. 02116.

Ranger Rick's Nature Magazine. 381 W. Center St., Marion, Ohio 44302.

Sports. McFadden Publications, 205 E. 42d St., New York, N.Y. 10014.

Wee Wisdom. Unity School of Christianity, Unity Village, Mo. 64065.

Young Miss. Parents Magazine Enterprises, Inc., 52 Vanderbilt Ave., New York, N.Y. 10017.

Zoonooz. Zoological Society of San Diego, San Diego, Calif.

Sources and Suppliers of Learning Materials

Commercial Sources

A note or postcard to most of these companies should get you a catalog:

ABC School Supply, Inc., 437 Armour Circle NE, Box 13084, Atlanta, Ga. 30324.

Afro-Am Publishing Co., Inc., 1727 S. Indiana Ave., Chicago, Ill. 60616.

American Science and Engineering, 20 Overland St., Boston, Mass. 02215.

American Guidance Service, Inc., Publisher's Bldg., Circle Pines, Minn. 55014.

American Speech and Hearing Assn., 9030 Old Georgetown Rd., NW, Washington, D.C. 20014

Angeles Nursery Toys, 4105 N. Fairfax Dr., Arlington, Va. 22203.

Bailey Films, Inc., 6509 De Longpre Ave., Hollywood, Calif. 90028.

Binney and Smith, Inc., 380 Madison Ave., New York, N.Y. 10017.

Bowmar, 622 Rodier Dr., Glendale, Calif. 91201.

CBCO Standard Publishing, 9 Kulick Rd., Fairfield, N.J. 07006.

Child Guidance, Questor Education Products Co., 200 Fifth Ave., New York, N.Y. 10010.

Childcraft Education Corp., 20 Kilmer Rd., Edison, N.J. 08817.

Childhood Resources, 5307 Lee Hwy., Arlington, Va. 22207.

Children's Book and Music Center, 2500 Santa Monica Blvd., Santa Monica, Calif. 90404.

Community Playthings, Rifton, N.Y. 12471.

Constructive Playthings, 1040 E. 85th St., Kansas City, Mo. 64131.

Creative Playthings, Division of CBS, Inc., Princeton, N.J. 08540.

Creative Publications, P.O. Box 10328, Palo Alto, Calif. 94303.

Dennison Manufacturing Co., 67 Ford Ave., Framingham, Mass. 01701.

Developmental Learning Materials, 7440 Natchez Ave., Niles, Ill. 60648.

Education Activities, Inc., P.O. Box 392, Freeport, N.Y. 11520.

Ed-U-Card/Ed-U-Card Corps., Subsidiaries of Binney and Smith, 60 Austin Blvd., Commack, N.Y. 11725.

Educational Developmental Laboratories, McGraw-Hill Book Co., 1221 Avenue of the Americas, New York, N.Y. 10020.

Educational Performance Associates, 563 Westview Ave., Ridgefield, N.J. 07657.

Educational Teaching Aids Division, A. Daigger and Co., Inc., 159 W. Kinzie St., Chicago, Ill. 60610.

Eureka Resale Products, Dunmore, Pa. 18512.

Fisher-Price Toys, Division of Quaker Oats Co., East Aurora, N.Y. 14052.

Follett Publishing Co., 1010 W. Washington Blvd., Chicago, Ill. 60607.

GAF Corporation, Consumer Photo Products, View-Master, 140 W. 51st St., New York, N.Y. 10020.

Gryphon House, 1333 Connecticut Ave., NW, Washington, D.C. 20036.

Hayes School Publishing Co., Inc., 321 Pennwood Ave., Wilkinsburg, Pa. 15221.

Holcomb's, 3000 Quigley Rd., Cleveland, Ohio 44113.

Ideal School Supply, 11000 S. Lavergne Ave., Oak Lawn, Ill. 60453.

Information Center on Children's Cultures, Administrative Offices, 331 E. 38th St., New York, N.Y. 10016.

Instructo Corp., Cedar Hollow Rd., Paoli, Pa. 19301.

Interstate Printers, Inc., 1927 N. Jackson, Danville, Ill. 61832.

Judy Instructional Aids, The Judy Co., Sales Office, 250 James St., Morristown, N.J. 07960.

J. B. Lippincott Co., Educational Publishing Div., East Washington Sq., Philadelphia, Pa. 19105.

Lauri Enterprises, Phillips, Maine 04966.

Lakeshore Equipment Co., P. O. Box 2116, 1144 Montague Ave., San Leandro, Calif. 94577.

Lego Systems, Inc., P. O. Box 2273, Enfield, Conn. 06082.

Mab-Graphic Products, Inc., 310 Marconi Blvd., Copiague, N.Y. 11726.

Macmillan Co., School Div., Front and Brown Sts., Riverside, N.J. 08075.

Mead Educational Services, B and T Learning, 5315-A Tulane Dr., Atlanta, Ga. 30336.

Media Projects, Inc., 201 E. 16th St., New York, N.Y. 10003.

Milton Bradley Co., 443 Shaker Rd., East Longmeadow, Mass. 01028.

Monterey Learning System, 99 Robles, Monterey, Calif. 93940.

Parker Brothers, Inc., Division of General Mills Fun Group, Inc., Salem, Mass. 01970.

Playskool, Inc., Milton Bradley Co., Springfield, Mass. 01100.

Practical Drawing Co., P. O. Box 5388, Dallas, Tex. 75222.

Reader's Digest Assoc., Pleasantville, N.Y. 10570.

Romper Room Toys, Hasbro Industries, Inc., Pawtucket, R.I. 02861.

Scholastic Early Childhood Center, 904 Sylvan Ave., Englewood Cliffs, N.J. 07632.

Shindana Toys, Division of Operation Bootstrap, Inc., 6107 S. Central Ave., Los Angeles, Calif. 90001.

Society for Visual Education, Inc. (SVE), 1345 Diversey Pkwy., Chicago, Ill. 60614.

Teaching Resources, 100 Boylston St., Boston, Mass. 02116. (617-357-8446)

Sources of Free and Inexpensive Materials

Many sorts of catalogs are published, including:

Salisbury, G. *Catalog of free teaching materials.* (P.O. Box 1075, Ventura, Calif. 93003.)

Textbooks in print, including teaching materials. New York: R. R. Bowker. (1180 Avenue of the Americas, 10036. A catalog and price list published annually.)

Wagner and Christopher. *Free Learning Materials for Classroom Use.* (State College Extension Service, Cedar Falls, Iowa 50613.)

The following are published by Educators' Progress Service, Randolph, Wis. 53956:

Educators' guide to free films.
Educators' guide to free filmstrips.
Educators' guide to free social studies materials.
Educators' guide to free teaching aids.
Educators' index of free materials.

Other printed sources:

Publishers' catalogs.
Magazines and newspapers.
Sales catalogs.
Discarded textbooks.
Reader services sections of most education-oriented magazines.

Government sources:

Child Nutrition Division, U.S. Department of Agriculture, Washington, D.C. 20250.

Office of Child Development, U.S. Department of Health, Education, and Welfare (now U.S. Department of Education), 400 Sixth St., SW, Washington, D.C. 20201.

Superintendent of Documents, U.S. Government Printing Office, Washington, D.C. 20402.

Community sources:

Libraries.
Museums.
Chambers of commerce.
Utility companies.
Private interest groups.
Service organizations.
Local businesses and clubs.

Embassies.
Consulates.
Medical organizations.
Recreational businesses.
Radio and television stations.
Insurance companies.
Parents of students.

Try these sources for new items, discards, promotional items, or handouts:

Retailers (local and national).
Manufacturers.
Commercial industries.

Visit other classrooms. If you see something you like, you maybe able to:

Build one yourself.
Buy a less expensive version at the dime store.

Audiovisual Materials

What Are Audiovisual Materials?

"Audiovisual materials" means just about anything children can learn from by watching and listening. With the following devices, you can make your own audiovisual materials:

Cameras.
Tape recorders (reel-to-reel or cassette).
Videotape recorders.

All kinds of projectors can be used:

Movie projectors.
Slide projectors. (Use these with slides, or just make shadows on a screen.)
Loop projectors.
Overhead projectors. (The children can make their own pictures for these.)
Opaque projectors.

Things to listen to or with:

Radio.
Records.
Cassettes.
Headsets. (Each child can listen privately.)

Things to look at:

Posters.
Charts. (Express an idea in visible form.)
Watch and learn with television.

And the basics have lasting value:

Musical instruments (whistles, toy trumpets, miniature percussion instruments).
Books to read.
Books to write in.

Where Can You Get Audiovisual Materials?

Types of sources:

Film rental companies.
Film and record producers.
Publishers.
Photographers.
Music stores and bookstores.
Nonprofit and service organizations.
Industry.
Government.
Libraries (public, private, school, college).
Curriculum laboratories.

The film industry.
Discarded texts.
Theaters.
High schools and colleges.
Travel agents.
Self-improvement groups.
Toy stores and teachers' supply stores.
Garage sales.
Private productions (your own recordings, home movies).

Where to find out about audiovisual materials:

Magazines.
Film review catalogs.

Some publications:

Children are centers for understanding media. Washington, D.C.: ACEI, 1973. (3615 Wisconsin Ave., 20016. Produced with Center for Understanding Media, New York. Shows how to involve children in filming and taping. Includes bibliography of resources.)

Schwann children's record and tape guide. (W. Schwann, Inc., 137 Newbury St., Boston, Mass. 02116.)

Film libraries; record suppliers; audiovisual centers; free or inexpensive rentals—listed by state or territory (U.S.) or province (Canada):

Auburn University, Cooperative Extension Film Library, Auburn, Ala. 36830.

Division of Libraries, Pouch G, Juneau, Alaska 99801.

University of Arizona, Bureau of Audiovisual Services, Tucson, Ariz. 85721.

University of Arkansas, Cooperative Extension Film Library, P.O. Box 391, Little Rock, Ark. 72003.

Center for Cassette Studies, Inc., 8110 Webb Ave., North Hollywood, Calif. 91605.

Disneyland Records, 800 Sonora Ave., Glendale, Calif. 91200.

Filmfair Communications, 10900 Ventura Blvd., P.O. Box 1728, Studio City, Calif. 91604.

GB Media, Ed Siegel or Georgia Brown, 333 North Flores, Los Angeles, Calif., 90048.

Handel Film Corp., 8730 Sunset Blvd., West Hollywood, Calif. 90069.

Higgins, Alfred, Productions, Inc., 9100 Sunset Blvd., Los Angeles, Calif. 90069.

Raht, John, Box 591, San Clemente, Calif. 91200.

Rhythms Productions, P.O. Box 34485, Los Angeles, Calif. 90034.

U.C. Agricultural Extension, Visual Aids, 1422 S. 10th St., Richmond, Calif. 94804.

Colorado State University, Office of Educational Media, Film Library, Fort Collins, Colo. 80521.

Argosy Music Corp., Motivation Records, 101 Harbor Rd., Westport, Conn. 06880.

University of Connecticut, Audiovisual Center, Storrs, Conn. 16268.

University of Delaware, Cooperative Extension Film Library, Agricultural Hall, Newark, Del. 19711.

Southeast Media Services, Jim Wall, P.O. Box 13237, Orlando, Fla. 32859. (305-855-2243 or 305-855-1748.)

University of Florida, Gainesville, Fla. 32601. Motion Picture Service, Florida Cooperative Extension Service, Editorial Dept.

ABC School Supply, 437 Armour Circle NE, Box 13084, Atlanta, Ga. 30324.

University of Georgia, Athens, Ga. 30601. Cooperative Extension Service, Film Library.

University of Hawaii, College of Tropical Agriculture, Cooperative Extension Service, Film Library, 2500 Dole St., Rm. 108, Honolulu, Hawaii 96822.

University of Idaho, Audio Visual Center, Moscow, Idaho 83843.

Encyclopaedia Britannica Educational Corporation, Sales Service, Department 8-X, 425 N. Michigan Ave., Chicago, Ill. 60611.

Sanders, Carroll, 2343 Emert, Granite City, Ill. 62040.

Scott, Foresman and Co., 1900 E. Lake Ave., Glenview, Ill. 60025.

University of Illinois, Visual Aids Service, 1325 South Oak, Champaign, Ill. 61820.

Purdue University, Audio Visual Center, Stewart Center, West Lafayette, Ind. 47907.

Iowa State University, Media Resources Center, Pearson Hall, Ames, Iowa 50010.

Kansas States University, Umberger Hall, Cooperative Extension Service, Film Library, Manhattan, Kan. 66502.

University of Kentucky, Audio Visual Services, Scott St., Lexington, Ky. 40506.

Louisiana State University, Cooperative Extension Service, Film Library, Knapp Hall, University Station, Baton Rouge, La. 70803.

University of Maine, Instructional Systems, Orono, Maine 04473.

University of Maryland, Audiovisual Service, Rm. 1, Annapolis Hall, College Park, Md. 20742.

Boston University, Abraham Krasker Memorial Film Library, 765 Commonwealth Ave., Boston, Mass. 02215.

Rankin, Richard J., 20 Pearl St., Marblehead, Mass. 01945.

Michigan State University, Instructional Media Center, East Lansing, Mich. 48823.

University of Minnesota, Agricultural Extension Service, Film Library, St. Paul, Minn. 55101.

Mississippi State University, Cooperative Extension Service, Film Library, Mississippi State, Miss. 39762.

University of Missouri, Audio Visual and Community Services, 203 Whitten Hall, Columbia, Mo. 65201.

Montana State University, Campus Film Library for Cooperative Extension Service, Bozeman, Mont. 59715.

University of Nebraska, Instructional Media Center, 901 North 17th, Rm. 421, Lincoln, Nebr. 68508.

University of Nevada, Audio Visual Center, Reno, Nev. 89507.

University of New Hampshire, Hewitt Hall, Audio Visual Center, Durham, N.H. 03824.

Childcraft Education Corp., 20 Kilmer Rd., Edison, N.J. 08817.

Kimbo Educational, P.O Box 246, Deal, N.J. 07723.

Rutgers University, Communications Center, College of Agriculture and Environmental Science, New Brunswick, N.J. 08903.

New Mexico State University, Cooperative Extension Service Film Library, Drawer 3A1, Las Cruces, N.M. 88003.

AA Records, 250 W. 57th St., New York, N.Y. 10019.

Anti-Defamation League of B'nai B'rith, 823 United Nations Plaza, New York, N.Y. 10017.

Children's Record Guild, 225 Park Avenue South, New York, N.Y. 10003.

Cornell University Film Library, 31 Roberts Hall, Ithaca, N.Y. 14850.

Folkways Records, 43 W. 61st St., New York, N.Y. 10023.

KTAV Publishing House, Inc., 75 Varick St., New York, N.Y. 10013.

RCA Records, 1133 Avenue of the Americas, New York, N.Y. 10036.

Syracuse University Film Rental Center, 1455 E. Colvin, Syracuse, N.Y. 13210. (315-479-6631.)

Tikva Records, 22 E. 17th St., New York, N.Y. 10003.

UNICEF, U.S. Committee for UNICEF, 331 E. 38th St., New York, N.Y. 10016.

United Synagogue Book Service, 155 Fifth Ave., New York, N.Y. 10010.

Young People's Records (YPR), 225 Park Avenue South, New York, N.Y. 10003.

North Carolina State University, Department of Agricultural Information, P.O. Box 5037, Raleigh, N.C. 27607.

North Dakota State University Cooperative Extension Service, Film Library, State University Sta., Fargo, N.D. 58102.

Ohio State University, Extension Service Film Library, 2120 Fyffe Rd., Columbus, Ohio 43210.

Oklahoma State University Audiovisual Center, Stillwater, Okla. 74074.

Orange Films Limited, 32 Howden Rd., Scarborough, Ont., Canada M1R3E4.

Audiovisual Instruction, DCE Bldg., P.O. Box 1491, Portland, Oreg. 97207.

Hartman, Ira, Candy Road, R.D. #1, Box 319, Mohnton, Pa. 19107.

Westminister Press, Witherspoon Bldg., Rm. 905, Philadelphia, Pa. 19107.

University of Puerto Rico, Agricultural Extension Service, Mayaguez Campus, Rio Piedras, P.R. 00928.

University of Rhode Island, Audiovisual Center, Kingston, R.I. 02881.

Clemson University Extension Agricultural Communications Dept., Service Rm. 92, Plant and Animal Science Bldg., Clemson, S.C. 29631.

University of South Carolina, Instructional Services Center, Columbia, S.C. 29208.

South Dakota State University, Cooperative Extension Service Film Library, Brookings, S.D. 57006.

University of Tennessee Teaching Materials Center, Div. of Continuing Education, Knoxville, Tenn. 37916.

Texas A & M University, Agricultural Communications, Rm. 201, Services Bldg., College Station, Tex. 77843.

Utah State University, Audio Visual Services, Logan, Utah 84321.

University of Vermont, Audio Visual Center, Ira Allen Chapel, Burlington, Vt. 05401.

Horner, Jack, P.O. Box 29732, Richmond, Va. 23229.

Virginia Polytechnic Institute Media Services, Patton Hall, Blacksburg, Va. 24061.

Washington State University, Audio Visual Center, Pullman, Wash. 99163.

West Virginia University, Cooperative Extension Service, 215 Coliseum, Morgantown, W.V. 26506.

University of Wisconsin Extension, Bureau of Audio Visual Instruction, P.O. Box 2093, Madison, Wis. 53701.

University of Wyoming, Audio Visual Services, Laramie, Wyo. 82070.

How Can You Evaluate Audiovisual Materials?

Ask other users.
Read producers' literature.
Talk to sales representatives.
Read professional reviews.
Examine the actual product.
Talk to colleagues.

Questions to ask about kits or sets:

What are the main materials?
Why is the product sold as a kit rather than as individual materials?
Must all components be purchased or used as a unit?
Are supplemental materials available?
What's the cost, per pupil and for the class?
Is there a teacher's manual? What's in it?
Is there a training program for use of the materials?
Are there diagnostic or evaluative materials?
What other services are available?

How much time and supervision are needed?

What learned skills does the material exercise? What developmental view does it reflect?

How is this kit different from others?

For reviews on multimedia resources, read these periodicals:

Instructor. (Instructor Publications, 7 Bank St., Dansville, N.Y. 14427.)

Reading Teacher. (International Reading Assoc., Inc., 800 Barksdale Rd., Newark, Del. 19711.)

Scholastic Teacher. (Scholastic Magazines, 50 W. 44th St., New York, N.Y. 10036.)

School arts. (Davis Publications, Inc., 50 Portland St., Worcester, Mass. 01608.)

Teacher. (Macmillan Professional Magazines, Inc., 1 Fawcett Pl., Greenwich, Conn. 06830.)

Community and Other Resources

How to Get Help, Speakers, Information, Etc.

For a start, there's printed material:

U.S. government publications. (Superintendent of Documents, Government Printing Office, North Capitol St., NW, Washington, D.C. 20402.)

Yellow Pages of Learning Resources: Resources Directing Area Code 800) (Cambridge, Mass.: M.I.T. Press. Shows how the community can be a source for learning.)

Newspapers.

Publishers. (Books and periodicals)

Governments are good providers of speakers and information:

Local government. (Representives from the courthouse, the police and fire departments, and just about any agency.)

Federal government. (The FBI, NASA, the Postal Service, and the armed services are a few suggestions.)

Write to these national organizations:

American Association for Jewish Education, 114 Fifth Ave., New York, N.Y. 10011.

American Indian Historical Society, 1451 Masonic Ave., San Francisco, Calif., 94117.

Association for Childhood International (ACEI), 3615 Wisconsin Ave., NW, Washington, D.C. 20016.

B'nai B'rith, 1640 Rhode Island Ave., NW, Washington, D.C. 20036.

Day Care and Child Development Council of America (DCCDCA), 1012 14th St., NW, Washington, D.C. 20005.

National Association for the Advancement of Colored People (NAACP), 1790 Broadway, New York, N.Y. 10019.

National Association for the Education of Young Children (NAEYC), 1834 Connecticut Ave., NW, Washington, D.C. 20009.

National Association for Retarded Citizens (NARC), 2709 Avenue E East, Arlington, Tex. 76011.

National Congress of American Indians (NCAI), 1765 P St., NW, Washington, D.C. 20024.

National Council for Black Child Development (NCBCD), 490 L'Enfant Plaza East, SW, Suite 3204, Washington, D.C. 20024.

Office of Early Childhood Development (OECD), Office of Education, Department of Health, Education, and Welfare (now U.S. Department of Education), 1200 19th St., NW, Washington, D.C. 20506.

Other organizations can be approached at the local level:

American Red Cross.
Braille Institute.
Sierra Club.
Religious organizations.

There are many sources in the community:

Industry. (Manufacturers, oil companies, public utilities, airlines, and assembly plants.)
Businesses. (Supermarkets; retail stores; moving companies, large and small; bakers; florists; car dealerships; and car washes.)
Clubs.
Service organizations.
Chamber of commerce.
Small business administration.
Community workers.
Private agencies.
Speakers' bureaus.
Colleges. (Childhood development departments.)
The medical professions. (Pediatricians, pediatric nurses; dentists, dental hygienists; speech and hearing clinicians; mental health workers.)

There are several kinds of arts and cultural organizations:

Museums.
Symphony orchestras.
Dance studios.
Arts councils (federal, state, and local).
Bookstores.
Little theater groups.
Libraries.

And there are individual persons who can demonstrate or speak about their own interests:

Musicians.
Actors.
Stamp and coin collectors.
Politicians.

How to Get Ideas for Field Trips Some businesses and institutions are directly concerned with interesting things to do:

Hotels and motels. (Free brochures are available from most.)
Travel agencies. (Don't overlook the local affiliate of the American Automobile Association.)
Convention centers.
Chambers of commerce.

Try some of these printed sources:

Newspapers. (The "where to go" section.)
The Yellow Pages. (Look under "Manufacturers," for example.)
Road maps. (Many show points of interest.)
Curriculum guides. (present, past—even outdated.)

Others in business:

Real estate brokers. (They know the community.)
Public relations departments.

Many ideas are passed by word of mouth. Speak to:

Librarians.
Museum curators.
Other teachers.
Parents of pupils.

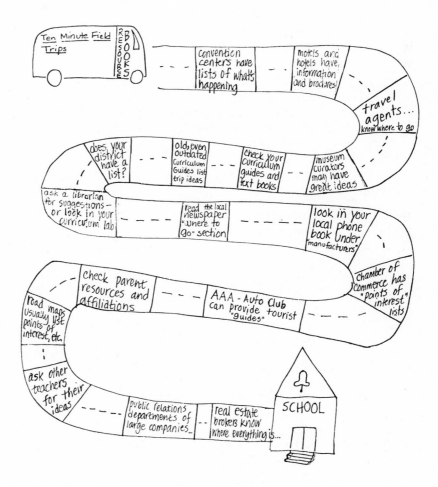

Section 2

PSYCHO-PHYSICAL-MOTOR DEVELOPMENT: ACTIVITIES AND RESOURCES

By "psycho-physical-motor" development we mean development having to do with growth and maturation, movement, and integration of mind and body. To foster growth and maturation, we concentrate on physical health, nutrition, and safety; to foster the development of movement, we concentrate on both expressive and objective movement; to foster integration of mind and body, we concentrate on principles and practices of mental health.

In this section, we identify objectives for psycho-physical-motor development and provide sample activities to help achieve them. We begin with objectives and activities of a global nature for infants and toddlers, and then go on to objectives, activities, and resources for older children (preschool through the primary years).

Our objectives and activities for older children are in the curriculum areas noted above: objective and expressive movement, nutrition, safety, and physical and mental health. As we've noted, all these areas are important in psycho-physical-motor development. It's necessary to understand, however, that each of them also has cognitive, linguistic, and affective components. To take just one example, nutrition involves new concepts (the cognitive element), new vocabulary (the linguisitic element), and sound attitudes (the affective element). We also need to realize that other subject and curriculum areas have a psycho-physical-motor component—for example, creation in all the media of art and instrumentation in music involve movement, as does writing. Movement, nutrition, safety, and health illustrate the psycho-physical-motor domain, but they do not define it.

Objectives and Activities for Infants and Toddlers

For the first 18 months of life, infants are absorbed in trying out their sensory apparatus and physical capabilities, while achieving a balance among bodily activity, rest, and nourishment. For the next 18 months, toddlers are improving large- and small-muscle control, coordination, and locomotor skills.

Objectives and activities that foster infants' and toddlers' psycho-physical-motor development are suggested in the following table, which stresses manipulative skills, coordination, balance, and the like. These—combined with meeting young children's need for adequate rest, nutrition, safety, and medical care in a calm and secure environment—will help prepare children for the more advanced objectives and activities of preschool and primary school.

Sequential Objectives and Activities for Psycho-Physical-Motor Development: Birth to 36 Months

LEVEL	OBJECTIVE	ACTIVITY
Birth to 1 month	1. To allow freedom of movement and encourage kicking and arm waving.	1. Place child on a firm mat (the fewer clothes, the better).
	2. To encourage head turning.	2. Hang objects on the sides of the crib (objects that make noise encourage turning toward sounds).
	3. To encourage tightening of grasp.	3. Place a finger in the child's palm.
	4. To encourage grasping and muscle development (especially of the neck).	4. Gently pull the child's arms.
1 to 3 months	1. To exercise the extremities.	1. Let the child splash in warm water.
	2. To encourage total body movement.	2. Hang a "cradle gym" in the crib.
	3. To encourage total body movement and crawling.	3. Place a toy in front of the child.
	4. To strengthen muscles and teach neck control.	4. As the child grasps your fingers, pull the child up to a sitting position.
3 to 6 months	1. To encourage movement and and strengthen neck and arm muscles.	1. Place a pillow under the child's stomach.
	2. To stimulate creeping or crawling.	2. Place toys just outside the child's reach.
	3. To teach adjustment of grasp.	3. Have the child hold toys of different sizes.
	4. To encourage use of arm muscles to grasp and pull forward.	4. Attach a set of gymnastic type rings to the head of the crib.

(Continued)

Sequential Objectives and Activities for Psycho-Physical-Motor Development: Birth to 36 Months (continued)

LEVEL	OBJECTIVE	ACTIVITY
6 to 9 months	1. To encourage crawling and stimulate development of motor skills.	1. Play a game of chase on the floor—possibly through an obstacle course of pillows, chairs, boxes, etc.
	2. To help develop small-muscle coordination.	2. Hang a "busy box" in the crib.
	3. To help develop large-muscle coordination.	3. Let the child push a stroller, pull a wagon, or lift light but bulky objects.
	4. To encourage movement.	4. Dance with the child or let the child dance alone.
	5. To encourage manipulation.	5. Place a different object in each of the child's hands.
9 to 12 months	1. To encourage large-muscle activity.	1. Roll balls with the child.
	2. To stimulate movements and develop arm and leg muscles. (*Note:* Movements are easier in water.)	2a. Let the child experiment with swimming in the tub. b. Let the child help wash himself or herself at bath time. c. Let the child take swimming lessons.
	3. To develop small-muscle coordination.	3a. The child builds block towers. b. The child "combs" a doll's hair.
	4. To encourage walking and develop leg muscles.	4. The child uses a small chair to stand up.
	5. To stimulate use of fingers and development of eye-hand-mouth coordination.	5. Let the child feed himself or herself.
12 to 18 months	1. To help develop large-muscle control, motor skills, and a sense of purpose.	1. Allow the child to walk around pushing large objects: boxes, a wagon, a tricycle, a chair.
	2. To help develop small-muscle control, manipulation, and eye-hand coordination.	2a. The child drops pennies into a bank. b. The child picks up tiny objects. c. The child scribbles with crayons.
	3. To help develop gross body movement and control.	3. Have the child dance, tumble, and climb on stacked mattresses.
	4. To encourage movement with purpose and more refined use of muscles than in free movement.	4a. Play catch with the child, using a foam rubber ball. b. Blow bubbles for the child to "catch."
18 to 24 months	1. To develop small muscles.	1. Have the child imitate you as you do the following: fold a piece of paper; draw a straight line; screw a jar lid on and off; play with small plastic animals and human figures.
	2. To improve large-muscle control and development.	2. The child marches forward and backward (with or without music).
	3. To encourage creativity and exercise large and small muscles.	3. The child builds a fort from large boxes or a table or chairs and blankets or sheets.
	4. To develop balance and body movement.	4. The child follows a "trail" of stepping stones or large cutout footprints.
	5. To improve manipulation.	5. The child stacks blocks or construction toys.
24 to 36 months	1. To develop aim and concentration.	1. The child shoots for a target (bean-bag toss, ring toss, etc.).
	2. To develop aim, concentration, and ability to grasp and release.	2. The child drops clothespins into a bottle.
	3. To improve balance and gross body control.	3. The child walks on a board or beam between two long pieces of string (or along a wall with the walking space defined by one long piece of string).
	4. To improve small-and large-muscle development, timing. coordination, and balance.	4. Have the child engage in gymnastics.

Objectives and Activities for Older Children

Introduction: Objectives

The objectives and activities we have listed for infants and toddlers suggest a "global" approach to psycho-physical-motor development. As children mature, objectives and activities can become more specialized, as is reflected in our table of objectives for older children.

We have divided our psycho-physical-motor objectives for children in preschool and primary school into six curriculum areas, as follows.

For movement:

1. **Expressive movement.** Here, both amount and quality of effort change as children use the body and relate it to objects and other persons. Gymnastics and dance evolve from these experiences.
2. **Objective movement.** In this area, perceptual-motor, large-muscle, small-muscle, and locomotor skills are refined. Participation in rule-governed games and in fitness activities and stunts represents a culmination of such development.

For growth and maturation:

3. **Nutrition.** Here, children are introduced to various foods and gain awareness of both principles and practices of good nutrition, including preparation of food and planning of meals.
4. **Safety.** Obviously, physical safety is essential for growth and maturation. In this area, awareness of hazards, preventive and protective measures, and practical applications are stressed.
5. **Physical health.** Here, children gain awareness of the nature of physical well-being and how it is achieved. Preventive and curative measures are introduced; attention is given to hygiene, dental health, first aid, and disease.

For integration of mind and body:

6. **Mental health.** In this area, we emphasize attending to mental states, dealing with stress, and achieving "centeredness."

On the table of objectives, these six curriculum areas form the horizontal axis; the general age levels from the vertical axis. The objectives, then, are classified by area and age level. On this table, to make orientation easier, we also provide some subheadings describing the objectives (e.g., "body awareness," "spatial awareness"); and at each age level the objectives progress from "awareness" through "problem solving" to "integration and adaptation"—the indication that real and lasting learning has taken place.

Following the table of objectives are our sample activities for older children, grouped in the six curriculum areas we have just described. Each of the activities is aimed at a specific objective from the table. As we explained in the Preface, for each activity the objective is stated, and a key is provided so that you can find it on the table. The key is to be read as "curriculum area, age level, objective"; thus "1-A-1" means "area 1, level A, objective 1."

Remember that the age levels are only approximate; teachers will need to use their own judgment and be flexible in working with these objectives and activities. Remember, too, that the activities are meant to serve as a model: adapt them to your own children's needs and interests, and add some of your own, being sure that they are aimed at specific objectives. The result should be a rich and balanced developmental curriculum.

Turn the page for the table of objectives. . . .

CURRICULUM AREAS			
	(1) EXPRESSIVE MOVEMENT	(2) OBJECTIVE MOVEMENT	(3) NUTRITION
LEVEL A (AGES 3 TO 5) — AWARENESS	**Body awareness:** 1. Locate and identify body parts. 2. Move body parts freely.* **Spatial awareness:** 3. Orient oneself with respect to others. 4. Use directional vocabulary.	**Perceptual-motor awareness:** 1. Develop sensory discrimination (visual, auditory, kinesthetic, figure-ground).* 2. Develop eye-hand and eye-foot coordination.* 3. Develop small- and large-muscle control.*	**Identifying and tasting food:** 1. Sample ingredients. 2. Taste new foods in different states.* 3. Name foods.
LEVEL A (AGES 3 TO 5) — PROBLEM SOLVING	**Relationships (to persons and objects):** 5. Move in relation to objects. 6. Perform stunts with a partner. 7. Interrelate body parts in movement. **Quantitative or qualitative adjustment:** 8. Use and change degrees of speed and force.	**Skills practice:** 4. Nonlocomotor: push; pull. 5. Locomotor: walk; run; crawl; turn.* 6. Manipulative: bounce; kick; toss; catch.	**Fundamentals of nutrition:** 4. Identify origins and characteristics of food. 5. Develop healthful eating habits.
LEVEL A (AGES 3 TO 5) — INTEGRATION AND ADAPTATION	**Gymnastics:** 9. Balance on balance beam. 10. Perform body and tumbling stunts. **Dance:** 11. Move rhythmically and creatively to music.*	**Fitness:** 7. Respond with body to oral commands. 8. Strengthen hand grip and leg muscles. 9. Develop muscular strength and coordination. **Games:** 10. Play freely and spontaneously. 11. Participate in low-organization games.	**Food preparation:** 6. Help prepare snacks. **Meal planning:** 7. Select healthful foods.
LEVEL B (AGES 4 TO 6) — AWARENESS	**Body awareness:** 1. Locate and identify body parts. 2. Move body parts in response to directions (music optional).* **Spatial awareness:** 3. Orient and position oneself with respect to others, objects, and space.	**Perceptual-motor awareness:** 1. Continue development of discrimination, coordination, and control. 2. Improve finger dexterity. 3. Improve balance, strength, agility, coordination, and flexibility.	**Identifying and tasting food:** 1. Experience food through all the senses (e.g., see, taste, smell). 2. Categorize food.
LEVEL B (AGES 4 TO 6) — PROBLEM SOLVING	**Relationships (to persons and objects):** 4. Move in relation to objects and equipment. 5. Perform group stunts. 6. Interrelate body parts in movement.	**Skills practice:** 4. Nonlocomotor: bend; twist; reach. 5. Locomotor: march; hop; jump; tiptoe; gallop; slide. 6. Manipulative: slide; climb; swing on apparatus; roll; catch.	**Fundamentals of nutrition:** 3. Identify origins and characteristics of food.* 4. Develop healthful eating habits.
LEVEL B (AGES 4 TO 6) — INTEGRATION AND ADAPTATION	**Gymnastics:** 7. Climb on apparatus. 8. Do stunts and tumbling with a partner. **Dance:** 9. Move rhythmically and creatively to music.	**Fitness:** 7. Exhibit advanced small- and large-muscle control and 8. Perform calisthenics for agility and flexibility. 9. Use appropriate posture and stance. **Games:** 10. Participate in low-organization games (e.g., jumping rope). 11. Join in simple relays.*	**Preparation of food:** 5. Clean, cut, mix, and cook food. 6. Convert raw food to a different edible product. (E.g., convert wheat to bread.) **Planning meals:** 7. Plan snacks.

*Asterisk indicates that an activity has been provided for this objective.

		CURRICULUM AREAS		
		(4) SAFETY	(5) PHYSICAL HEALTH	(6) MENTAL HEALTH
LEVEL A (AGES 3 TO 5)	AWARENESS	**Identification of hazards:** 1. Note hazards at home and in the classroom. 2. Identify unsafe places and things in the environment.	**Recognition of health needs:** 1. Develop good habits for using toilet. 2. Learn about body hygiene and dental care.* 3. React appropriately to hunger and thirst.	**Recognition of mental states:** 1. Express both positive and negative feelings. 2. "Read" expressions as clues to feelings.
	PROBLEM SOLVING	**Prevention of accidents:** 3. Understand and follow safety rules (e.g., wheeled toys, water, playground equipment).* **Protection of the body:** 4. Dress appropriately. 5. Learn how to fall safely. 6. Learn when to walk and when to run.	**Prevention of disease:** 4. Dress appropriately. 5. Develop good habits with regard to rest and nutrition. 6. Cooperate during medical check-ups and immunizations.*	**Dealing with stress:** 3. Rest at nap time. 4. Use various emotional outlets. 5. Practice simple relaxation exercises.*
	INTEGRATION AND ADAPTATION	**Adjustment of behavior or environment:** 7. Learn how to get help. 8. Learn to avoid trouble.	**Restoration of health:** 7. Follow doctors' orders. 8. Support the healing process in cases of, e.g., scratches, cuts, scrapes, and sores.	**Feeling "centered":** 6. Allow oneself and others to express a variety of emotions.
LEVEL B (AGES 4 TO 6)	AWARENESS	**Identification of hazards:** 1. Note hazards at home and school. 2. Identify fire hazards.	**Recognition of health needs:** 1. Develop good habits when using the toilet. 2. Understand body hygiene and 3. dental care.* React appropriately to changes in the weather.	**Recognition of mental states:** 1. Express feelings as they develop. 2. Use words to describe feelings.* 3. Use oral and bodily cues to recognize how others feel.
	PROBLEM SOLVING	**Prevention of accidents:** 3. Understand and follow safety rules (e.g., water, fire, pedestrian). **Protection of the body:** 4. React promptly and appropriately in emergencies. 5. Learn to walk or run as appropriate.	**Prevention of disease:** 4. Dress appropriately.* 5. Develop good habits with regard to rest and nutrition. 6. Understand the purpose and be familiar with the procedure of regular checkups (eyes, ears, teeth, etc.).	**Dealing with stress:** 4. Spend an appropriate amount of quiet time, resting. 5. Recognize and acknowledge one's own emotional "ups" and "downs." 6. Discuss contemporary stories involving problem solving.* 7. Do simple relaxation exercises. 8. Use various emotional outlets.
	INTEGRATION AND ADAPTATION	**Adjustment of behavior or environment:** 6. Report emergencies.* 7. Avoid trouble.	**Restoration of health:** 7. Be a good patient. 8. Support the healing process in cases of cuts, sores, broken bones, etc.	**Feeling "centered":** 9. Freely share feelings and ideas. 10. Participate in large and small groups. 11. Like oneself.

(Continued)

		CURRICULUM AREAS		
		(1) EXPRESSIVE MOVEMENT	(2) OBJECTIVE MOVEMENT	(3) NUTRITION
LEVEL C (AGES 5 TO 7)	**AWARENESS**	**Body awareness:** 1. Discover how body parts work. 2. Coordinate body movements. 3. Move body parts to music. **Spatial awareness:** 4. Work at different levels. 5. Develop basic skills of laterality.	**Perceptual-motor awareness:** 1. Refine discrimination, coordination and control. 2. Improve small-muscle skills and balance. 3. React quickly.	**Identifying and tasting food:** 1. Recognize relationship between ingredients and prepared food products.
	PROBLEM SOLVING	**Relationships to persons and objects:** 6. Move in relation to objects, equipment, and gymnastic apparatus.* 7. Perform group stunts. 8. Work out with a partner. **Quantitative or qualitative adjustment:** 9. Increase strength and stamina. 10. Use and change speed, force, and direction.	**Skills practice:** 4. Nonlocomotor; fall; raise; lower. 5. Locomotor: leap; skip; march; jog. 6. Manipulative: climb a rope; roll; bat; kick; catch.	**Fundamentals of nutrition:** 2. Understand and explain our food needs. 3. Develop healthful eating habits.
	INTEGRATION AND ADAPTATION	**Gymnastics:** 11. Climb on ladders. 12. Work out on balance beam. 13. Do stunts and tumbling with a partner. **Dance:** 14. Move creatively to music.	**Fitness:** 7. Further refine muscle development and coordination. 8. Do calisthenics for agility, flexibility, and endurance. 9. Use appropriate posture and stance. **Games:** 10. Play cooperative and circle games.* 11. Participate in relays and games involving small-muscle control.	**Preparation of food:** 4. Help prepare simple meals.* **Meal planning:** 5. Plan a meal.*
LEVEL D (AGES 7 TO 9)	**AWARENESS**	**Body awareness:** 1. Discover how body parts work. 2. Control and coordinate body movements. 3. Move body parts in response to instructions or music. **Spatial awareness:** 4. Vary orientation and position. 5. Practice skills of laterality and bilaterality.	**Perceptual-motor awareness:** 1. Refine basic perceptual-motor skills and balance and control. 2. React quickly and accurately.	**Identifying and tasting foods:** 1. Classify foods. 2. Taste unusual foods.
	PROBLEM SOLVING	**Relationships (to persons and objects):** 6. Move in relation to objects, equipment, and gymnastic apparatus.* 7. Work out alone and in groups. **Quantitative or qualitative adjustment:** 8. Use and change speed, force, direction, level, and focus.	**Skills practice:** 3. Nonlocomotor: turn; lift. 4. Locomotor: jog; jump hurdles. 5. Manipulative: aim; throw; catch; bounce; dribble; roll; pass; kick.	**Fundamentals of nutrition:** 3. Identify foods in basic food groups.* 4. Describe different processes of food production. 5. Understand and explain how the body uses food.
	INTEGRATION AND ADAPTATION	**Gymnastics:** 9. Hang, swing, and balance. 10. Work out on balance beam. 11. Tumble. **Dance:** 12. Move creatively to music.	**Fitness:** 6. Do calisthenics for endurance and stamina and to relieve tension.* 7. Respond precisely to verbal directions. 8. Control posture and weight. **Games:** 9. Play organized (e.g., team) games. 10. Learn rules of games.	**Preparation of food:** 6. Participate in the preparation of a complete meal. **Planning meals:** 7. Plan menus.

*Asterisk indicates that an activity has been provided for this objective.

		CURRICULUM AREAS		
		(4) SAFETY	(5) PHYSICAL HEALTH	(6) MENTAL HEALTH
LEVEL C (AGES 5 TO 7)	**AWARENESS**	**Identification of hazards:** 1. Note hazards at home, at school, and in recreation areas. 2. Identify fire hazards. 3. Identify unsafe areas and activities.	**Recognition of health needs:** 1. Develop good habits and practices of body hygiene (e.g., wash hair) and dental care.* 2. React appropriately to fatigue.	**Recognition of mental states:** 1. Notice one's own reactions to different situations and stimuli. 2. Explain one's own feelings. 3. Show awareness of and concern for the different feelings of others.
	PROBLEM SOLVING	**Prevention of accidents:** 4. Understand and follow safety rules (water, fire, bicycle). **Protection of the body:** 5. React promptly and appropriately in an emergency. 6. Wear appropriate clothing.*	**Prevention of diseases:** 3. Dress appropriately. 4. Understand the need for medical and dental checkups (measuring, weighing, innoculations, x-rays, etc.) and for vitamins.	**Dealing with stress:** 4. Identify stressful situations. 5. Allow oneself to have and express both positive and negative feelings. 6. Do breathing and relaxing exercises.* 7. Use various emotional outlets.
	INTEGRATION AND ADAPTATION	**Adjustment of behavior or environment:** 7. Report emergencies. 8. Help to clean up and make the environment safe. 9. Learn and use basic first aid.	**Restoration of health:** 5. Be a good patient. 6. Support the healing process in cases of cuts, sores, broken bones, etc. 7. Learn basic first aid. 8. Understand the importance of rest and sleep.	**Feeling "centered":** 8. Freely share feelings and ideas. 9. Participate in activities with groups and individuals. 10. Be aware of the need for rest and the need to talk. 11. Like oneself.
LEVEL D (AGES 7 TO 9)	**AWARENESS**	**Identification of hazards:** 1. Identify hazards throughout the environment. 2. Identify unsafe play areas, activities, and toys.*	**Recognition of health needs:** 1. Have good habits of body hygiene. (e.g., care for hair and nails) and dental care. 2. Control weight. 3. React constructively to pain.	**Recognition of mental states:** 1. Anticipate emotional reactions to various situations. 2. Describe the physical sensations of stress. 3. Discuss feelings—one's own and those of others.
	PROBLEM SOLVING	**Prevention of accidents:** 3. Understand and follow safety rules (fire, transportation, poisons). **Protection of the body:** 4. React promptly and appropriately to emergencies. 5. Learn basic lifesaving techniques. 6. Wear proper clothing and protective devices for certain activities.*	**Prevention of disease:** 4. Understand the need for, and the procedures of, preventive medical and dental care. 5. Respond to one's own health needs and to changes in one's own physical condition. 6. Understand contagion. 7. Notice symptoms.	**Dealing with stress:** 4. Recognize and discuss emotions and problems. 5. Do breathing and relaxation exercises. 6. Use various emotional outlets.
	INTEGRATION AND ADAPTATION	**Adjustment of behavior or the environment:** 7. Report emergencies. 8. Eliminate hazards. 9. Learn and use basic first aid.	**Restoration of health:** 8. Be a good patient. 9. Support the body's healing processes. 10. Learn about disease. 11. Respond to health emergencies.	**Feeling "centered":** 7. Recognize how mind and body work together. 8. Divide time appropriately among play, work, and rest. 9. Participate with individuals and groups.* 10. Like oneself.

Activities for Expressive Movement

Description   Exploring the ways our body parts can move to music.
Title (for children)   "Body Part Disco."
Curriculum area   Expressive movement (body awareness).   Age range   3 to 5.

What is our objective?   To move body parts freely (table: 1-A-2).
What will we need?   Large open area, covered with a rug or rugs; record or tape player; record or tape of disco music.
How will we do it?
1.   The children sit on the rug, and the teacher reminds them that it is now time to relax the body.
2.   Children and teacher do some deep breathing as a way of feeling balanced.
3.   Children and teacher do some simple stretches to loosen tight muscles, concentrating on certain body parts (e.g., hands, feet, head).
4.   The teacher starts the music and asks the children: "Show me ways to move a hand . . . a foot . . . etc." The children think of ways to move these body parts in rhythm with the music.
5.   Teacher and children end with a deep-breathing exercise.
What else can we do?   Variations: Movement of the whole body can be stressed. Direction of the movement can also be varied (up and down, back and forth, etc.). And the quality of the movement can be varied (slow and fast, quiet and loud, light and heavy, happy and sad)—for this variation, different kinds of music should be used.

Description Responding freely and individually to "mood music," using scarves as props.
Title (for children) "Scarf Dance."
Curriculum area Expressive movement (dance).   **Age range** 3 to 5.

What is our objective? To move rhythmically and creatively to music (table: 1-A-11).
What will we need? Spacious clear area; one scarf for each child, or one scarf to be used by each child in turn; record or tape of instrumental music.
How will we do it?
1. The teacher gives a scarf to each child, or to the child who'll start the activity.
2. The teacher explains that the children are to use their imaginations, letting the scarf be anything they want as they move with it in response to the music.
3. Each of the children in turn moves with the music, explaining what he or she is doing.
What else can we do? Other activities: "Animal walks" to music ("How would a bear move? An elephant? A mouse?"); simple gymnastics on a balance beam, to music.

Description Moving specific parts of the body to music.
Title (for children) "The Happy Puppet."
Curriculum area Expressive movement (body awareness).   **Age range** 4 to 6.

What is our objective? To move body parts in response to directions (table: 1-B-2).
What will we need? Spacious clear area; record or tape player; records or tapes of appropriate music. A wooden puppet or marionette, if available, makes a good model.
How will we do it?
1. The teacher tells the children what a puppet is, how it's put together piece by piece, and how it moves only in response to "orders" from the puppeteer. This exposition can be in the form of a story about a puppet. Then the teacher tells the children to imagine that they are puppets—at first incomplete, but then complete and able to respond to our puppeteer.
2. The children begin by responding to music as suggested by this little rhyme: "I am a puppet who's not complete;/ I have no arms and can't move my feet./ But my head moves and I can see./ Won't you please be happy with me?"
3. Next, arms, hands, and fingers are "added," but the feet still are "pasted to the floor."
4. Finally, the feet and legs can move; and the children respond to the music and the teacher as complete puppets.
What else can we do? Another activity: Children can use their bodies to form letters or numbers in response to directions.

Description Moving with plastic hoops.
Title (for children) "Hoopla."
Curriculum area Expressive movement (relationships to persons and objectives).
Age range 5 to 7.

What is our objective? To move in relation to objects, equipment, and gymnastic apparatus (table: 1-C-6).
What will we need? Plastic hoops; large area free of obstacles.
How will we do it?
1. Each child gets a hoop and finds a place to move without interfering with the others.
2. The teacher encourages the children to solve "problems" —e.g.:
   a. Get into a curled position inside the hoop, then into a stretched position.
   b. Find ways to move across the hoop in a curled position.
   c. Make your body into a "bridge" over the hoop.
   d. Find different curled and stretched positions—move from curled to stretched and vice versa.
   e. Roll the hoop.
   f. Curl up and jump through the hoop.
What else can we do? **Follow-up:** After doing individual hoop work, the children can do hoop work in pairs—i.e., with a partner. **Other activities:** Parachute, rope, and balance-beam stunts.

Description Keeping a balloon in the air using different body parts and positions.
Title (for children) "Balloon-Oh."
Curriculum area Expressive movement (relationships to persons and objects).
Age range 7 to 9.

What is our objective? To move in relation to objects, equipment, and gymnastic apparatus (table: 1-D-6).
What will we need? Inflated balloon for each child; plenty of space.
How will we do it?
1. Each child gets an inflated balloon and finds a place to work without bumping into the others.
2. The children follow the teacher's directions, finding different ways to keep the balloon in the air (e.g., with the right hand, with the left hand, with the one finger, with the head, with one foot; lying down, kneeling, sitting).
3. Then the children tap the balloon off three or four body parts in sequence (e.g., left hand, right hand, head, knee).
What else can we do? **Follow-up:** The children work with partners, tapping the balloon back and forth using different body parts. **Other activities:** Tin-can stilts; tiptoe tag.

32

Description Throwing Velcro balls at a Velcro target.
Title (for children) "Target Toss."
Curriculum area Objective movement.　　　　**Age range** 3 to 5.

What is our objective? To develop visual discrimination, eye-hand control, and large- and small-muscle control (table: 2-A-1, 2-A-2, and 2-A-3).
What will we need? Velcro balls and a Velcro-covered target; open space for throwing.
How will we do it?
1. The children take turns throwing the Velcro balls at the target.
2. After each turn, children and teacher count how many balls have stuck to the target.
3. Each child tries to improve on his or her second turn.
What else can we do? Other activities: String wooden or plastic beads on shoelaces; drop clothespins into jars with mouths of various sizes.

Description   Moving through an obstacle course and using relational terms ("over," "under," etc.).
Title (for children)   "Over, Under, Around, and Through."
Curriculum area   Objective movement (skills practice).   **Age range**   3 to 5.

What is our objective?   To practice locomotor skills—walking, running, crawling, and turning (table: 2-A-5).
What will we need?   For an indoor obstacle course: tables, chairs, boxes, cartons, blocks, etc. For an outdoor course: boxes, cartons, swings, slides, trees, rocks, etc. For both: clearly defined area for the course; ample room between obstacles.
How will we do it?
1. The teacher sets up the obstacle course.
2. The children go through it, verbalizing what they are doing: "I'm going UNDER the table, AROUND the chair, OVER the carton . . ."
3. When the children have gone through the course in one direction, they go back through it in the opposite direction, varying their actions and verbalizing these new actions: "OVER the table, UNDER the chair, THROUGH the carton . . ."
What else can we do?   **Follow-up:** Change the obstacles.   **Other activities:** "Follow the Leader"; a tug-o-war.

Description   Using relays for fitness and fun.
Title (for children)   "Riotous Relays."
Curriculum area   Objective movement (games).   **Age range**   4 to 6.

What is our objective?   To join in simple relays (table: 2-B-11).
What will we need?   Ample clear space; balls; sacks.
How will we do it?
1. The children are divided into two or more teams of five or six.
2. The children try the following relay races:
    a. Run one way; hop back on two feet.
    b. Bounce a ball one way; run back.
    c. Walk backwards one way; crawl back.
    d. Do scissors steps one way; hop back on one foot.
    e. Run one way; hop back in a sack.
What else can we do?   **Follow-up:** Relays can be made more difficult if the children have objects to carry and pass along—e.g., a ball, a beanbag, a stick.

Description Playing a tossing game involving group cooperation.
Title (for children) "Hot Potato."
Curriculum area Objective movement (games).   **Age range** 5 to 7.

What is our objective? To play cooperative and circle games (table: 2-C-10).
What will we need? Raw potato, or any small tossable object such as a Velcro ball or a beanbag; record or tape player; record or tape of music.
How will we do it?
1. The children form a circle and learn the rules for "Hot Potato."
2. The children pass the "potato" around the circle while the teacher plays music.
3. When the teacher stops the music, the person holding the "hot potato" must sit in the center of the circle (this can be called "mashed potatoes" or "potato salad" or "potato soup"—whatever the children find amusing) until the next person is caught with it.
What else can we do? **Other activities:** "Freeze Tag," "Statues," and hammer-and-nail relays are all good cooperative games.

Description Doing calisthenics to prepare for a trip to space as "astronauts."
Title (for children) "Astronaut Training."
Curriculum area Objective movement (fitness).   **Age range** 7 to 9.

What is our objective? To do calisthenics for endurance and stamina and to relieve tension (table: 2-D-6).
What materials will we need? Spacious open area; mats or rugs, if necessary.
How will we do it?
1. The children pretend to be astronauts training for a trip to space and a landing on the moon. Teacher and children discuss the calisthenics and relate them to space exploration.
2. The children do various exercises; e.g.:
    a. "Suiting up" (putting on helmets, space suits, and "moon boots")—head, shoulders, knees, toes.
    b. "Traveling to the moon"—running in place or around a track.
    c. "Moon bounce"—jumping up and down.
What else can we do? **Follow-up:** For children at the older end of the age range, you might set a class research project to learn what exercises are actually used in astronauts' training, and which of them can be done by the class.

Activities for Nutrition

Description   Tasting foods in various states.
Title (for children)   "Taste and Tell."
Curriculum area   Nutrition (identifying and tasting food).   Age range   3 to 5.

What is our objective?   To taste new (and familiar) foods in different states (table: 3-A-2).
What materials will we need?   Assorted foods that represent different states of the same basic foodstuffs (e.g., raw potato, baked potato, potato chips; raw apple, baked apple, apple juice, applesauce; grapes; grape juice, grape jelly); poster paper; drawing materials; magazines; scissors and paste.
How will we do it?
1. Teacher and students discuss a "food of the day," stressing the various ways it can be prepared.
2. During snack time, the children sample small portions of some of the different "versions" of the food of the day.
3. Teacher and children discuss how each "version" is related to the raw foodstuff.
4. The children prepare a "taste and tell" chart showing the original form of the food of the day, and as many versions as possible. This chart might consist of a large piece of poster paper with drawings by the children or pictures cut from magazines pasted on it, showing the foods the children have learned about.
What else can we do?   Follow-up: When the children are becoming familiar with different forms of foods, have a blindfold tasting to see if they can identify the foods by taste alone.

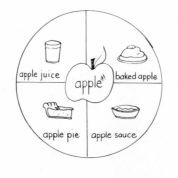

Description   Matching "processed" foods with the corresponding "unprocessed" foods.
Title (for children)   "Pick a Pair."
Curriculum area   Nutrition (fundamentals).   **Age range**   4 to 6.

What is our objective?   To identify origins and characteristics of food (table: 3-B-3).
What will we need?   Processed and unprocessed foods in pairs: e.g., orange and orange juice, peanuts and peanut butter, berries and jam, apple and applesauce.
How will we do it?
1. The teacher shows the children all the foods—the "natural" forms should be all together in one group and the "processed" forms in another group—and explains that the children are to taste and look at the processed foods and then try to tell which is the unprocessed form of each.
2. By tasting and examining, the children try to match all the pairs.
3. The children and the teacher discuss what characteristics have been used for matching pairs.
What else can we do?   Follow-up: Teacher and children discuss what happens to each of the original foods to turn it into its processed version.

Description   Preparing a simple version of a holiday meal.
Title (for children)   "Festive Feast."
Curriculum area   Nutrition (preparation of food).   **Age range**   5 to 7.

What is our objective?   To help prepare simple meals (table: 3-C-4).
What will we need?   Ingredients and utensils for cooking a simplified Thanksgiving dinner: turkey, apples, cranberries, sugar (or honey), cornbread mix, salad greens, cream, fruit punch mix, water; mixing bowls, spoons, knives, forks, etc.; oven, hotplate or range with burners; bowls, plates, and silverware for serving and eating. For this rather elaborate activity, at least one aide or volunteer is recommended.
How will we do it?
1. Beforehand, children and teacher discuss their menu (it's a nice touch to write it up formally on poster paper and display it); they may take a "field trip" to shop for some or all of the food.
2. The teacher has made arrangements for preparing and cooking the food—in the school kitchen, or with portable equipment in the classroom. (To avoid a long wait, the turkey should be partially cooked beforehand and just finished off by the children.)
3. While the turkey is finishing its roasting, the children do the following (with help as needed):
   a. Prepare the salad.
   b. Mix the cornbread batter and put it on to bake.
   c. Cook apples and cranberries to make a sauce.
   d. Make butter by shaking cream in a jar.
   e. Mix fruit punch.
4. Teacher and children serve and eat their dinner.
What else can we do?   Variation: Other holidays (e.g., Christmas, Passover, Cinco de Mayo, Chinese New Year) also lend themselves to this kind of activity.

Description   Planning a meal by cutting out and pasting up pictures of food.
Title (for children)   "Food Feast."
Curriculum area   Nutrition (meal planning).   **Age range**   5 to 7.

What is our objective?   To plan a meal (table: 3-C-5).
What will we need?   One "place setting" for each child (plate, glass, silverware, napkin, etc., drawn by the teacher on a piece of poster paper about the size of a placemat); old magazines; scissors and paste or glue; long piece of butcher paper for a "table cloth."
How will we do it?

1.   Teacher and children discuss what makes a good dinner and plan some imaginary meals. Each child gets a "place setting."
2.   The children cut pictures of foods and beverages out of magazines.
3.   Each child pastes appropriate pictures on his or her place setting.
4.   The children set their place settings on a class "table cloth" made of a long strip of butcher paper, and take turns explaining why each meal represented is good and good for us.

What else can we do?   **Follow-ups:** The children can select, prepare, and serve a simple snack; or they can prepare a picnic lunch at school—with the teacher and possibly some parents helping—and eat it outdoors (in the schoolyard, if there is a grassy spot, or in a park).

Description   Making a paper-plate mobile of the four food groups.
Title (for children)   "Foodmobile."
Curriculum area   Nutrition (fundamentals).   **Age range**   7 to 9.

What is our objective?   To identify food in basic food groups (table: 3-D-3).
What materials will we need?   For each child: four paper plates, two wire coat hangers, old magazines, scissors and paste, string.
How will we do it?

1.   Teacher and children discuss the four basic food groups.
2.   Each child gets four paper plates, and labels them "(1) MEAT, FISH, AND EGGS," "(2) FRUITS AND VEGETABLES," "(3) DAIRY PRODUCTS," "(4) GRAIN PRODUCTS."
3.   The children look through magazines and cut out pictures of foods from each group.
4.   Each child pastes pictures of different foods on the appropriate plates.
5.   The children assemble mobiles by attaching strings to the plates and tying them to the crossed wire hangers.

What else can we do?   **Variation:** If possible, it is pleasant to have a tasting of samples of foods from each group before this activity.   **Follow-up:** At snack time or lunch, have the children identify the food groups to which the foods they're eating belong.

Activities for Safety

Description Making a stoplight to illustrate safety rules.
Title (for children) "Stop and See It."
Curriculum area Safety (accident prevention).   **Age range** 3 to 5.

What is our objective? To understand and follow safety rules (table: 4-A-3).
What will we need? Black construction paper; yellow, red, and green tissue paper; scissors and glue or paste;
flashlights. The teacher prepares for each child a 12- by 6-inch rectangle of black paper, with three holes cut out.
How will we do it?
1. Each child is given a piece of black paper with three round holes cut out.
2. Either the children are given circles of red, green, and yellow tissue paper previously cut by the teacher (larger than
    the holes in the black paper) *or* each child is given some red, green, and yellow tissue paper and cuts out three circles
    himself or herself (older children can do this).
3. The children paste the colored circles in place on the black paper—the red over the topmost hole, the yellow over
    the middle hole, and the green over the bottom hole. (The result looks like a traffic light.)
4. When the stoplights are finished, the children sing this jingle, shining a flashlight through the appropriate circle:
    "Red light, red light, what do you say?/ I say stop and stop right away./ Yellow light, yellow light, what do you
    mean?/ I mean wait till the light turns green./ Green light, green light, what do you say?/ I say go—first look both
    ways." (The tune is "Twinkle, Twinkle, Little Star.")
What else can we do? **Follow-up:** After discussing when we can cross and when we can't, teacher and children go to a
corner and practice crossing with the light.

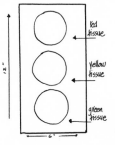

Description Practicing making telephone calls in an emergency.
Title (for children) "Emergency!"
Curriculum area Safety (adjustment or behavior).   **Age range** 4 to 6.

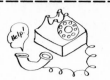

What is our objective? To report emergencies (table: 4-B-6).
What will we need? Two toy telephones. The teacher will need a list of the children's addresses, and accurate information on the community's all-purpose telephone number for reporting emergencies (most communities have one) and the minimal facts that have to be reported. (In a large city, try the police department's public information office or public relations office; in a small town, talk to the local police.)
How will we do it?
1. Teacher and children discuss what kinds of situations are emergencies and how it might sometimes happen that a child has to report such a situation.
2. The teacher, having ascertained the telephone number for reporting emergencies (e.g., 911), displays it prominently in one or more places.
3. The teacher explains—and demonstrates, using a toy telephone—how to call the number and what information to give (e.g., the address at least, and if possible the nature of the emergency—fire? injury?).
4. Then the children enact various emergencies and take turns calling the emergency number on a toy telephone. The teacher "answers" the call, using the other toy telephone, and asks for the basic information. Can each child give it? (The teacher will check each child's rendition of his or her address against the list.)
What else can we do? **Follow-up:** Make a bulletin-board display to give recognition to children who've memorized their addresses and telephone numbers. **Another activity:** The class as a whole can make a scrapbook of pictures of emergencies (frequently punctuated with the telephone number for reporting emergencies.)

Description Putting together fragments of pictures to match protective gear with appropriate sports.
Title (for children) "Scrambled Sports."
Curriculum area Safety (accident prevention).   **Age range** 5 to 7.

What is our objective? To wear appropriate clothing (table: 4-C-6).
What will we need? Sports magazines, tagboard, scissors, and paste or glue.
How will we do it?
1. Teacher and children discuss protective gear used in various sports. If possible, children should bring in samples of the protective gear they use themselves, or gear their parents or older siblings use (knee pads, chest protectors, helmets, elbow and shoulder protectors, face protectors, ski goggles, etc.).
2. The children cut out pictures of athletes wearing protective gear and paste them on tagboard. Then, each piece of tagboard is cut crosswise into three pieces, so that the athlete's head, torso, and legs and feet are separated.
3. The tagboard pieces are then scrambled, and the children put them back together again, explaining as they do so why each protector shown is important.
What else can we do? **Variation:** The children can draw their own pictures of athletes and protective gear. **Follow-up:** A "safety checkpoint" can be set up in the playground, to be sure all the children are wearing the right protective gear for sports played at school.

Description Taking a walk around the school and neighborhood to identify hazardous conditions.
Title (for children) "Danger Detectives."
Curriculum area Safety (identification of hazards).   **Age range** 7 to 9.

What is our objective? To identify unsafe play areas, activities, and toys (table: 4-D-2).
What will we need? Small DANGER signs made of construction paper (two dozen or so); butcher paper; glue or paste; crayons.
How will we do it?
1. Teacher and children take a walk around the school and through the neighborhood to look for hazards, noting the location of any they find and describing them briefly.
2. Back at school, the children draw a large map (on butcher paper) of the school and neighborhood.
3. On the map, one of the DANGER signs is pasted at each spot where a hazard was noted, with a label identifying the problem.
What else can we do? **Another activity:** Teacher and children discuss safe and unsafe toys and make up a two-column chart headed SAFE and UNSAFE; then the children cut pictures of toys out of catalogs or advertisements and paste them in the appropriate column.

Description Attaching reflective tape to clothing and bicycles.
Title (for children) "Reflecting on Safety."
Curriculum area Safety (accident prevention).   **Age range** 7 to 9.

What is our objective? To wear proper clothing and protective devices for certain activities (table: 4-D-6).
What will we need? Reflecting tape (available in automobile supply stores); scissors; needles and thread. (Optional: The teacher may make up a "cyclist education certificate"—on the order of driver education certificates—for each participating child.)
How will we do it?
1. Teacher and children discuss principles of safety for cyclists—and especially how important it is for cyclist and bicycle to be visible in darkness and twilight.
2. Darkening the room and shining a flashlight on some reflecting tape is a graphic demonstration.
3. The children bring their bicycles, cycling clothes, and protective gear to school (hats, jackets, helmets, etc.).
4. With the help of the teacher (and aides or parent volunteers, if possible), the children paste reflecting tape on their bicycles and helmets and sew it on their clothing.
5. Teacher and children review bicycle safety practices. (Optional: The teacher gives each child a "cyclist education certificate.")
What else can we do? **Other activities:** The children can make posters urging the use of reflecting tape and protective gear for cyclists, and hang them in the halls; they can also prepare and present to other classes a short program demonstrating tape and protective gear and encouraging their use.

Activities for Physical Health

Description Making a picture which demonstrates covering a sneeze or cough.
Title (for children) "Stop That Sneeze—Cover That Cough."
Curriculum Area Physical health (recognition of health needs). **Age range** 3 to 5.

What is our objective? To learn about body hygiene (table: 5-A-2).
What will we need? Construction paper; scissors and paste or glue; facial tissues; crayons. For younger children, the teacher might make patterns of a face and hand, to help the children cut out.
How will we do it?
1. Teacher and children talk about why colds are contagious—germs fly through the air when someone coughs or sneezes—and how we can keep colds from spreading by covering the mouth.
2. Each child cuts one face and one hand out of construction paper, and fills in eyes, nose, and open mouth on the face.
3. The children glue the face onto another piece of construction paper, glue facial tissue over the mouth, and finally glue the hand over the tissue.
4. The children can take their portraits home and explain to their families why it's important to cover a cough or sneeze.
What else can we do? **Another activity:** The housekeeping corner can be used for role playing—the children enact daily hygiene routines (e.g., bedtime; getting ready for school; mealtime).

Description Playing the roles of doctor, nurse, and patient at a learning center.
Title (for children) "Mini-Medic."
Curriculum area Physical health (disease prevention).   **Age range** 3 to 5.

What is our objective? To cooperate during medical checkups and immunizations (table: 5-A-6).
What will we need? Well-defined area which will become the learning center for this activity; cot; paper cups and water; chairs and magazines for the "waiting room"; toy doctor's kit including bag, stethoscope, thermometer (oral), tongue depressors, cotton balls, bandages, syringes (without needles, of course), and pad and pencil for writing prescriptions; white coats for doctors and nurses.
How will we do it?
1. The teacher sets up a special learning center called "Mini-Medic," consisting of a waiting room (chairs, magazines) and an examination room (cot, medical equipment).
2. The children "sign in" at the center—as doctor, nurse, or patient. Each child enacts the role he or she has chosen, and the children go through several kinds of medical routines: examination, innoculation, taking medicine (the water), getting a prescription, etc.
3. Later, the children take turns telling the class about their experiences in the "Mini-Medic" center, stressing cooperation with the doctors and nurses.
What else can we do? **Variation:** Have the children exchange roles. **Other activities:** A doctor or nurse can visit the class to explain common medical procedures—what they're like and why they're important—and the class can read or discuss a book or story about a trip to a hospital or doctor's office.

Description Making faces with "teeth" of black and white beans to demonstrate the importance of brushing the teeth.
Title (for children) "Brush and Beam."
Curriculum area Physical health (recognition of health needs).   **Age range** 4 to 6.

What is our objective? To understand dental care (table: 5-B-2).
What will we need? Construction paper; crayons; glue or paste; black-eyed peas; white beans; a mirror; toothbrushes.
How will we do it?
1. Teacher and children discuss brushing the teeth—why it's important, when to do it, and how to do it, and what happens to teeth that aren't brushed.
2. Children practice brushing their teeth in front of a mirror (this doesn't require water or toothpaste—but be sure the children understand that they're just "going through the motions").
3. The children get construction paper and draw two large faces with large open mouth.
4. On one face, children glue black-eyed peas into the mouth to represent teeth that haven't been brushed; on the other face, they glue white beans to show healthy, clean teeth that have been brushed.
What else can we do? **Variation:** For the practice session, use water and toothpaste—and practice as a group.
Another activity: Children can share their experiences of losing teeth, and discuss why it's especially important to take care of their new "grown-up" teeth.

I brushed my teeth today.   I need to brush my teeth.

Description Dressing up in appropriate clothing for various settings.
Title (for children) "Weather Wear."
Curriculum area Physical health (disease prevention). **Age range** 4 to 6.

What is our objective? To dress appropriately (table: 5-B-4).
What will we need? Pictures from magazines showing settings with various weather conditions (sunny beach, ski slopes, frozen pond, rainy day, mountain trail, etc.); assorted clothing (winter coats, mittens, scarves, bathing suits, sun hats, visors, galoshes, hiking boots, slickers, etc.).
How will we do it?
1. Teacher and children discuss how wearing the right clothing can help prevent some diseases—sunstroke, cold, frost-bite, etc.
2. The teacher holds up a picture and asks who has been to a place like the one shown.
3. The child who is chosen from among the volunteers is asked to explain what he or she would wear at the place shown, and why, and to choose the right clothing from the assorted samples and put it on.
What else can we do? **Variation:** Turn the activity around—have the children dress up in clothing chosen from the samples and then choose the pictures showing where it would be appropriate. **Another activity:** Dress paper dolls for different weather conditions and settings.

Description Observing what happens to a tooth soaked in cola over a period of time.
Title (for children) "Dye It Cola."
Curriculum area Physical health (recognition of health needs). **Age range** 5 to 7.

What is our objective? To develop good habits and practices of dental care (table: 5-C-1).
What will we need? Two clear glasses; a cola drink; water; two baby teeth (voluntarily donated with parents' permission).
How will we do it?
1. Teacher and children discuss why soft drinks are bad for the teeth and why you should brush after drinking one, if you drink them at all.
2. Two children have each brought in a baby tooth to be used in the experiment.
3. The teacher fills one glass with water and the other with cola, and drops one tooth into each glass.
4. Each day, the children observe what is happening to the teeth. (Older children can record their observations on a chart.)
5. At the end of several weeks, children and teacher talk about what happened to the tooth soaked in cola and why.
What else can we do? **Follow-up:** The children can learn what other foods are bad for the teeth, and what foods are good for the teeth. They can make a chart showing pictures of foods in two columns—BAD and GOOD.

Description   Doing deep-breathing and muscle-relaxing exercises.
Title (for children)   "Relax Away."
Curriculum area   Mental health (dealing with stress).   **Age range**   3 to 5.

What is our objective?   To practice simple relaxation exercises (table: 6-A-5).
What will we need?   Spacious clear area: mats or rugs.
How will we do it?
1. The lights are turned down (or shades or curtains are closed), and teacher and children lie flat on mats or rugs.
2. Teacher and children do some deep breathing, with eyes closed.
3. The teacher tells the children to tighten up and then relax various muscles, starting with the area around the eyes, then going on to the whole face, arms, hands, stomach, buttocks, legs, and feet.
4. Teacher and children discuss why it's important to be able to relax like this.
What else can we do?   **Follow-up:** When children feel tense or upset, try this exercise with them. Afterwards, discuss how they feel (better? why?).

Description Cutting out pictures of faces and discussing the way these people seem to be feeling.
Title (for children) "How Are You Feeling, Face?"
Curriculum area Mental health (recognition of mental states).   **Age range** 4 to 6.

What is our objective? To use words to describe feelings (table: 6-B-2).
What will we need? Magazines, poster or construction paper, glue or paste, scissors.
How will we do it?
1. Teacher and children discuss different kinds of feelings.
2. The children cut pictures of faces out of magazines, looking for faces that seem to express different feelings, and mount the faces on poster or construction paper.
3. In small groups, the children look at the faces and discuss how they think each person is feeling.

What else can we do? **Variation:** The children can make up a story for some of the faces, to explain why the people shown feel the way they do. **Follow-up:** In the classroom, try to recognize feelings on the faces of others—and ask people if they're feeling the way they seem to look (the teacher can ask the children; the children can ask each other or the teacher). **Other activities:** Play "feelings charades"—the teacher whispers a feeling to a child ("sad," "angry," etc.), and the child acts out the feeling for the others to guess. The teacher can also describe feelings for the children to act out in front of a mirror.

Description Creating endings for unfinished stories about conflict situations.
Title (for children) "Friendly Finish."
Curriculum area Mental health (dealing with stress).   **Age range** 4 to 6.

What is our objective? To discuss stories involving problem solving (table: 6-B-6).
What will we need? Stories about conflicts having to do with common problems of children (e.g., fighting over a toy; frustration at not being able to succeed in something)—the teacher can make these up or find them in books, or both.
How will we do it?
1. The teacher tells or reads a story about a situation involving conflict, but stops before the end. (E.g., "Heather and Annie both want to use the same jump rope. . . .")
2. The children discuss the problem and make up a "friendly finish" for the story—that is, a resolution of the conflict.
3. The children act out the ending they've made up.

What else can we do? **Variation:** The teacher finds (in books or magazines) pictures of children in conflict situations. The children in the class discuss the pictures to decide what's happening, what led up to it, and what will happen next; they can also suggest how they'd resolve the conflict themselves. (The teacher makes no value judgments here.)

Description   Reaching a relaxed state by pretending to be a marionette.
Title (for children)   "Marionette Mimics."
Curriculum area   Mental health (dealing with stress).   **Age range**   5 to 7.

What is our objective?   To do breathing and relaxing exercises (table: 6-C-6).
What will we need?   Spacious clear area (a hard surface should be covered with mats, cushions, or rugs) and, if possible, a wooden puppet or marionette to serve as a model.
How will we do it?
1. The teacher demonstrates how a marionette works—it's stiff when all the strings are held taut by the puppeteer but falls down limp if the strings are cut or the puppeteer lets them go.
2. The children start by standing stiff, like marionettes with the strings held tight.
3. Then the teacher cuts the imaginary strings, or lets go of them, and the children fall loosely to the floor.
4. The children close their eyes and breathe gently, and the teacher leads them in relaxing different parts of the body ("Your jaws are getting heavy . . .").
5. Then the teacher tells the children to relax progressively as the teacher counts backward from 10 to 1—when the teacher says "1," each child should be completely relaxed.
6. Eventually, the children are able to relax on their own whenever they want.
What else can we do?   **Another activity:** Simple Yoga exercises can help children relax.

Description   Drawing the name of a "secret pal" and doing nice little things for him or her.
Title (for children)   "Secret Pals."
Curriculum area   Mental health (feeling "centered").   **Age range**   7 to 9.

What is our objective?   To participate with individuals and groups (table: 6-D-9).
What will we need?   Name cards—in envelopes (sealed) or folded and sealed.
How will we do it?
1. Teacher and children discuss how we often feel better about doing nice things for others than about having nice things done for us.
2. The name of each child is written on a card which is then folded and sealed or put into a sealed envelope. All the envelopes are put in a box, and the children draw them out.
3. The children keep secret the name they've drawn, and during some specified period of time (say, a week or two), each child does nice things for his or her secret pal—e.g., sends little notes (unsigned) or presents; or keeps a list of nice things about the secret pal.
4. At the end of the week the children tell their secret pals who they are.
5. Teacher and children discuss how doing things for someone else made them feel.
What else can we do?   **Other activities:** Children can draw up "contracts" specifying how they intend to spend their time for one week (e.g., x hours playing, y hours sleeping, z hours working)—the teacher should check to be sure that the times are well balanced. Another good activity is a "gab group"—a few children sit in a circle, and within this circle it's "safe" to express any ideas and opinions at all.

Resources for Psycho-Physical-Motor Development

Bibliography for Teachers

American Association for Health, Physical Education and Recreation. *Foundations and practices in perceptual motor learning.* Washington, D.C.: American Association for Health, Physical Education and Recreation, 1971. (A collection of articles on motor development. Includes films, tests, and material sources.)

American Driver and Traffic Safety Education Assn. *Policies and guidelines for a school safety program.* NEA, 1974. (Discusses developing a school safety program: goals, personnel, organizing, etc.)

American Red Cross. *First aid textbook.* New York: Doubleday, 1968. (The basic reference on what to do in emergencies. A must for every classroom.)

Barlin, A., & Barlin, P. *The art of learning through movement.* Los Angeles: Ward Ritchie, 1971. (Contains examples of movement through story, fantasy, games, dramatic play, and movement with others. Includes cues for teachers and students, description of activities, ideas for lessons, and classroom activities. A 45-rpm record is included.)

Barlin, A., & Barlin, P. *Dance-a-folk-song.* Los Angeles: Bowmar, 1974. (Folk songs that are set to dance and movement are included. Although dances are staged and structured for performance purposes, there is freedom within the structure for individual expression.)

Bentley, W. *Learning to move and moving to learn.* New York: Scholastic, 1970. (This book focuses on movement education: a program of activities that help children develop balance, agility, muscle strength, coordination, stamina, and good motor skills. No expensive equipment or special training is required. Classroom teachers and parents will find it easy to introduce these games and activities.)

Blotner, J., & Pugh, J. *Hop, skip, jump, and READ.* Long Beach, Calif.: Christian Press, 1971. (An excellent aid to persons working with preschool and elementary children in the area of perceptual-motor activities. Activities in this book provide various experiences encouraging the child to be creative and to solve problems at his or her own level, and involve the use of the whole body.)

Carr, R. *Be a frog, a bird, or a tree.* New York: Harper and Row, 1977. (Excellent book! Children are encouraged to explore Yoga through mimicry, such as pretending to be a jumping frog, a flying bird, etc. Material is for children in preschool and elementary grades.)

Cherry, C. *Creative movement for the developing child.* Belmont, Calif.: Fearon, 1971. (Book uses music and finger plays as a basis for movement. Included are songs for walking, running, posture, catching, galloping, kinesthetic awareness, etc. Especially good for nonmusical teachers.)

Cratty, B. *Learning about human behavior: Through active games.* Englewood Cliffs, N.J.: Prentice-Hall, 1975. (Games intended to make children more aware and understanding of different aspects of human behavior: friendship, cooperation, motivation, and individual differences. Games from other nations are also included.)

Cratty, B. *Perceptual and motor development in infants and children.* New York: Macmillan, 1970. (This is an excellent source for understanding perceptual and motor development from infancy to age 12.)

Dauer, V., & Pangrazi, R. *Dynamic physical education for elementary school children.* Minneapolis: Burgess, 1975. (Good basic text for elementary physical education. Very useful chapter on movement education. Includes activities for perceptual-motor competency, gymnastics, and classroom games.)

Diem, L. *Children learn physical skills* (Vol. 2). Washington, D.C.: American Alliance for Health, Physical Education and Recreation, 1974. (An excellent book in helping kindergartners develop motor skills. Balancing dexterity, carrying one's own weight. Emphasizes children's choosing and inventing activities to accompany others. Needs a lot of equipment. Some can be improvised.)

Diskin, E. *Yoga for children.* New York: Arco, 1976. (Simple Yoga exercises divided into beginning, intermediate, and advanced levels help children develop a clear understanding of their bodies, breathing, and relaxation. Photographs and drawings are helpful in duplicating the positions.)

Fluegelman, A. *The new games book.* New York: Doubleday, 1976. (This is an anthology of games emphasizing *cooperation*, learning, and fun. There are descriptions of games that may be played in pairs, small groups, large groups, and *very* large groups of all ages. Excellent!)

Frostig, M., & Maslow, P. *Movement education: Theory and practice.* Chicago: Follett, 1970. (Sequences for the development of movement skills are provided for the regular classroom teacher, as well as the special educator. Suggestions for facilities, equipment, and management of movement education programs are offered.)

Gallahue, D. *Motor development and movement experiences for young children.* New York: Wiley, 1976. (For teachers of preschool through grade 3. Theory and activities. Integrates movement with curriculum as well as activities for enhancing auditory rhythmic abilities, manipulative abilities, etc.)

Gerhardt, L. A. *Moving and knowing.* Englewood Cliffs, N.J.: Prentice-Hall, 1973. (Theoretical approach to movement that involves thinking and problem solving. Includes a chapter to help the classroom teacher design a curriculum that will facilitate the child's conceptualization of space through body movement.)

Gilliom, B. *Basic movement education for children: Rationale and teaching units.* Reading, Mass.: Addison-Wesley, 1969. (Highly recommended as a basic text for the teacher interested in starting a movement education program. Teaching units for three consecutive difficulty levels are included.)

Greenberg, J. *Student-centered health instruction: A humanistic approach.* Reading, Mass.: Addison-Wesley, 1971. (Group-process skill-building activities to help build trust and communication. A values-clarification approach to mental health, drug education, sex and family-life education, environmental health, nutrition, physical-health education and ethical issues in health.)

Hendricks, G., & Roberts, T. *The second centering book.* Englewood Cliffs, N.J.: Prentice-Hall, 1977. (Transpersonal approach to education with special chapters on movement, physical education, and centering exercises.)

Hendricks, G., & Willis, R. *The centering book.* Englewood Cliffs, N.J.: Prentice-Hall, 1975. (This book provides the core of curriculum for the development of affective, intuitive, and creative processes in students. Special chapter on movement and dance is included.)

Kirchner, G., Cunningham, J., & Warrell, E. *Introduction to movement education: An illustrated program of activities for kindergarten through grade six.* Dubuque, Iowa: W. C. Brown, 1978. (General text that discusses theories of physical education and movement as well as methods for teaching skills in a creative and exploratory manner. Includes lesson plans, photographs, and charts.)

Moss, S. *Your child's teeth.* Boston: Houghton Mifflin, 1979. (A practical, informative guide to dental care. This book provides information on preventive dental care and emergency treatment suggestions from infancy through adolescence.)

Orlick, T. *The cooperative sports and games book.* New York: Pantheon, 1978. (Focus on noncompetitive games and activities with cooperation the goal. Excellent book!)

Schneider, T. *Everybody's a winner.* Boston: Little, Brown, 1976. (Subtitled "A kid's guide to new sports and fitness." This book contains descriptions of activities for individual and group participation in breathing exercises, relaxing exercises, Yoga, running, and twenty-one "new" games.)

U.S. Department of Agriculture, Extension Service. *Food and nutrition.* Washington, D.C.: U.S. Government Printing Office, 1970.

U.S. Department of Agriculture, Food and Nutrition Service. *Good foods coloring book.* Washington, D.C.: U.S. Government Printing Office, 1970.

U.S. Department of Agriculture, Food and Nutrition Service. *Child nutrition programs.* Washington, D.C.: U.S. Government Printing Office, 1971.

U.S. Department of Agriculture, Food and Nutrition Service. *Nutrition.* Washington, D.C.: U.S. Government Printing Office, 1972.

U.S. Department of Health, Education, and Welfare (later U.S. Department of Education), Children's Bureau. *Food for groups of young children cared for during the day.* Washington, D.C.: U.S. Government Printing Office, 1960.

U.S. Department of Health, Education, and Welfare (now U.S. Department of Education), Children's Bureau. *Foods for the preschool child.* Washington, D.C.: U.S. Government Printing Office, 1969.

Werner, P., & Simmons, R. *Inexpensive physical education equipment for children.* Minneapolis: Burgess, 1976. (Practical suggestions for acquiring and constructing inexpensive equipment, plus many activity ideas for preschool and elementary children.)

Journals:

Health Bulletin for Teachers. (Metropolitan Life Insurance Co., School Health Bureau, Newark, N.J. Free.)

Health Education. (Official journal of the American Alliance for Health, Physical Education, Recreation, and Dance. 1201 16th St. NW, Washington, D.C. 20036.)

Journal of School Health. (American School Health Assn., 3335 Main St., Buffalo, N.Y. 14214.)

Todays' Health. (American Medical Assn. 535 N. Dearborn St., Chicago, Ill. 60610.)

Organizations which have publications available:

American Association for Health, Physical Education and Recreation, 1201 16th St., NW, Washington, D.C. 20036.

American Red Cross National Headquarters, 17th and D St., Washington, D.C. 20006.

National Safety Council, 429 N. Michigan Ave., Chicago, Ill. 60611.

Department of Health, Education, and Welfare (now Department of Health and Human Services), U.S. Public Health Service, Washington, D.C.

World Health Organization Publications, 1501 New Hampshire Ave., NW, Washington, D.C. 20036.

Bibliography for Children

Check your local library, school library, bookstore, or toy store for these titles and others:

Aetna Life and Casualty. *Tuffy talks about medicine.* Hartford, Conn.: Aetna Life and Casualty. (Coloring book. Order from Film Librarian, Public Relations and Advertising Dept., 151 Farmington Ave., 06115.)

Bendick, J. *Have a happy measle, a merry mumps, and a cheery chickenpox.* New York: McGraw-Hill. (1221 Avenue of the Americas, 10020.)

Children's Hospital of Philadelphia. *Danny's heart operation.* Philadelphia: Children's Hospital. (Public Relations Dept., 34th St., and Civic Center Blvd., 19104.)

Children's Hospital of Philadelphia. *Dee Dee's heart test.* Philadelphia: Children's Hospital. (Public Relations Dept., 34th St., and Civic Center Blvd., 19104.)

Clark, B., & Coleman, L. L. *Going to the hospital.* New York: Random House, 1971. (Ordering address: 457 Hahn Rd., Westminster, Md. 21157.)

Collier, J. L. *Danny goes to the hospital.* New York: Norton, 1970.

Froman, R. *Let's find out about the clinic.* New York: Grolier, F. Watts.

Guy, A. *Good-bye tonsils.* Racine, Wis.: Western, (1220 Mound Ave., 53404.)

Johnson and Johnson. *First aid for little people.* New Brunswick, N.J.: Johnson and Johnson. (Consumer Services Dept., 08903. Basic first aid for school-age children.)

McGovern, A. *The question and answer book about the human body.* New York: Random House, 1965. (Answers questions about cuts, fingerprints, wrinkles, itches.)

Poulet, V. *Blue bugs safety book.* Chicago: Children's Press, 1973. (1224 W. Van Buren St., 60607. Basic safety and signs. Good even for the youngest.)

Rey, H. A., & Rey, M. *Curious George goes to the hospital.* Boston: Houghton Mifflin, 1966. (2 Park St., 02107.)

Rey, H. A., & Rey, M. *Curious George takes a job.* Boston: Houghton Mifflin, 1974. (Paperbound; originally published, 1947.)

Rockwell, H. *My doctor.* New York: Macmillan, 1973. (Ordering address: Riverside, N.J. 08075.)

Scarry, R. *Richard Scarry's Nicky goes to the doctor.* Racine, Wis.: Western. (1220 Mound Ave., 53404.)

Tester, S. *My friend the doctor.* Elgin, Ill.: Cook, (60120.)

Weber, A. *Elizabeth gets well.* New York: Crowell, 1977. (10 E. 53d St., 10022.)

Wolde, G. *Betsy and the chicken pox.* New York: Random House, 1976. (Ordering address: 457 Halen Rd., Westminster, Md. 21157.)

Wolde, G. *Tommy goes to the doctor.* Boston: Houghton Mifflin. (2 Park St., 02107.)

Wolff, A. *Mom! I broke my arm!* New York: Lion Press, 1969. (Order from Sayre Publishing, Inc., 11 E. 39th St., New York, N.Y. 10016.)

And these books on dental care:

American Dental Association. *Cleaning your teeth and gums.* (211 E. Chicago Ave., Chicago, Ill. 60611. A small "how to" brochure with color photos.)

American Dental Association. *D is for dentist.* (211 E. Chicago Ave., Chicago, Ill. 60611. A comic book with questions and answers for school-age children.)

American Dental Association. *A visit to the doctor.* (211 E. Chicago Ave., Chicago, Ill. 60611.)

Garn, B. J. *A visit to the dentist.* New York: Grosset and Dunlap, 1959. (Dated but fun.)

Showers, P. *How many teeth?* New York: Crowell, 1962.

Books on food and nutrition:

Blossom, M., & Hertzler, A. *Food experiences for preschoolers: The food curriculum.* Columbia: University of Missouri–Columbia. (65201. A leaflet of food experiences.)

Craig, H. *Secrets to share.* Minneapolis: Denison, 1963. (Food groups and elements of foods. Grades K through 2.)

Croft, K. B. *The good for me cookbook.* San Francisco: Rand E. Research. (4843 Mission St., 94112. Multicultural foods. Healthful.)

Ferreira, N.J. *The mother-child cook book.* Menlo Park, Calif.: Pacific Coast, 1969.

Goodwin, M. T., & Pollen, G. *Creative food experiences for children.* Washington, D.C.: Center for Science in the Public Interest, 1977. (1779 Church St., 20036. Basics of nutrition; recipes.)

Lansky, V. *Feed me, I'm yours.* New York: Bantam, 1979. (Originally published, 1974.)

Lewin, E., & Lewin, B. *Growing food, growing up: A child's natural food book.* Pasadena, Calif.: Ward Ritchie. (474 S. Arroyo Pkwy., 91105.)

Marr, J. S. *The food you eat.* New York: Evans, 1973. (A doctor writes about nutrients.)

Martin, B. *Let's eat.* New York: Holt, 1967.

Overbeck, C. *The vegetable book* (S. Lerner, Illustrator). Minneapolis: Lerner, 1975. (Growing and eating vegetables.)

Parent's Nursery School. *Kids are natural cooks.* Boston: Houghton Mifflin, 1974. (2 Park St., 02107.)

Paul, A. *Kids cooking without a stove* (C. Inouye, Illustrator). New York: Doubleday, 1975.

Podendorf, I. *Food is for eating.* Chicago: Children's Press, 1970.

Stein S. B. *The kids' kitchen takeover.* New York: Workman, 1975. (Kitchen activities for ages 5 to 12.)

Books on health and safety:

Allison, L. *Blood and guts.* Boston: Little Brown, 1976. (Paper. A guide to the inner workings of the body for ages 8 and up.)

Bradenberg, F. *I wish I was sick too!* New York: Morrow, Greenwillow, 1976.

The hospital is where. (Poems and drawings by children. Space for readers to add their own pictures and poems.)

Kessler, E., & Kessler, L. *Our tooth story.* New York: Dodd, 1972.

Klein, A. *You and your body.* New York: Doubleday, 1977.

McLeod, E. W. *The bear's bicycle.* Boston: Little, Brown, 1975. (How to ride and how not to ride a bike, shown through illustrations of a boy and a bear.)

Rockwell, M. *My dentist.* New York: Morrow, Greenwillow, 1975. (What happens at the dentist's office.)

Rockwell, H. *My doctor.* New York: Macmillan, 1973.

Shay, A. *What happens when you go to the hospital.* Chicago: Reilly and Lee.

Winn, M. *The sick book.* New York: Scholastic, 1976. (Questions and answers.)

Movement books for children's use:

Carr, R. *Be a frog, a bird, or a tree.* New York: Doubleday, 1973. (Ordering address: 501 Franklin Ave., Garden City, N.Y. 11530. Illustrated. Simple wording.)

Doray, M. B. *See what I can do!* A book of creative movement. Englewood Cliffs, N.J.: Prentice-Hall, 1973. (07632.)

Udry, J. M. *The moon jumpers.* New York: Harper and Row, 1959. (A story to act out dealing with sensory awareness.)

Records. These are available from Children's Book and Music Center, 2500 Santa Monica Blvd., Santa Monica, Calif., 90404. Dealer number in parentheses.

Children's rhythms in symphony. (PE 133. Short orchestral pieces by Schumann, Prokofiev, and others for various movements.)

Coordinated classroom activities. (SG 218. Booklet containing suggested activities. Themes include colors, the circus, roundup, and safari.)

Creative moods. (PE 479. By S. Wienecke. Orchestral music in a wide variety of tempos and moods, for creative movement.)

Disco for kids. (PE 100. Narration and music on one side, music alone on the other.)

Learning Materials

Posters can illustrate many things to children about health and safety and about their own bodies:

Personal hygiene. (How to wash face, hands, and hair. How to brush and floss teeth.)

Health care. (Pictures of common doctors' and dentists' instruments.)

Nutrition. (Posters can show a variety of foods and the utensils used in preparing food.)

Traffic safety. (Children can learn the proper way to cross the street. They can become acquainted with the most important traffic signs and signals.)

Bicycle safety. (The right way to ride is important.)

Anatomy. (Pictures of body parts and pictures of children performing simple motor activities are instructive.)

Health hints. (Do the children know how to dress for the weather? Posters of clothing and outerwear will help.)

Different kinds of equipment may be useful for specific kinds of activities:

Equipment for locomotor activities. (Mats, tunnels, tables and chairs, barrels, boxes, handprint and footprint cutouts, ladders, steps, walkbeams, jump boards, ropes, hopscotch patterns, obstacle course, bedsprings, and trampolines.)

Equipment for nonlocomotor activities. (Mats, balance boards, walkbeams, rocking boards, push-pull toys, bounce boards, bedsprings, and trampolines.)

Equipment for gross-coordination activities. (Trampolines, jump ropes, scooters, bicycles, climbing towers, horizontal ladders, turning bars, chinning bars, and swings).

Other equipment for activities:

Balls. (All-purpose rubber or plastic.)

Soft-rubber ring sets.

Plastic hoops.

Bean bag kits.

Items for make-believe. (Toy doctor's kits, child-size doctor's smocks, police uniforms, sheriff's badges.)

Other resources on movement:

Barlin, A. L. *Teaching your wings to fly.* Santa Monica, Calif.: Goodyear, 1979. (Many illustrations of children moving.)

Barlin, A., & Barlin, P. *The art of learning through movement.* Los Angeles: Ward Ritchie, 1971. (Contains creative movement activities for exploring space, time, and force. Geared for grades K through 6. Simple, clear, and well illustrated.)

Collins, P. *Motion.* New York: McGraw-Hill, 1974.

Nelson, E. L. *Movement games for children of all ages.* New York: Sterling. 1975. (Descriptions of dozens of movement games.)

Winters, S. J. *Creative rhythmic movement for children of elementary school age.* Dubuque, Iowa: Brown, 1975.

For movement books and records:

Children's Book and Music Center, 2500 Santa Monica Blvd., Santa Monica, Calif. 90404.
Toys that teach catalog, Childcraft Education Corp., 20 Kilmer Rd., Edison, N.J. 08817.

Write to the following corporations for toys and equipment (for more vendors, see the next section, "Enrichment Materials"):

ABC School Supply, Inc., P.O. Box 13086, Atlanta, Ga. 30324.
American Gym Co., Inc., Box 131, Monroeville, Pa. 15146.
Atlas Athletic Equipment Co., 2339 Hampton, St. Louis, Mo. 63139.
Big Toys, 3113 South Pine, Tacoma, Wash. 98409.
Child Life Play Specialties, Inc., 55 Whitney St., Holliston, Mass. 01746.
Childcraft, 155 E. 23d St., New York, N.Y. 10010.
Community Playthings, Rifton, N.Y. 12471.
Conlin Bros., 7058 S. Greenleaf Ave., Whittier, Calif. 90602.
Creative Educational Distributor (CED), East Lancaster Ave., Wayne, Pa. 19087.
Creative Playthings, Inc., Princeton, N.J. 08540.
Game-Time, Inc., Litchfield, Mich. 49252.
Gym Master Co., 3200 S. Zuni, Englewood, Colo. 80110.
Gymnastics Supply Co., Box 1470, San Pedro, Calif. 90733.
Delmar F. Harris Co., P.O. Box 288, Dept. J, Concordia, Kans. 66901.
Austin C. Lent Playground Equipment Co., 2575 Minert Rds., Concord, Calif., 94518.
Lind Climber Co., 807 Reba Pl., Evanston, Ill. 60202.
Mexico-Forge Climbers, R.D. 1, Reedsville, Pa. 17084.
Elliot Morris, 678 Washington St., Lynn, Mass. 01901. (Bean bags.)
National Sports Company, 360 N. Marquette St., Fond du Lac, Wis. 54935.
Nissen Corp. 930 27th Ave., SW, Cedar Rapids, Iowa 52406.
Physical Education Supply Associates, Inc., P.O. Box 393, Trumbull, Conn. 06611.
Playtime Equipment Co., 808 Howard St., Omaha, Nebr. 68102.
Porter Athletic Equipment, Porter Levitt Co., 9555 Irving Park Rd., Schiller Park, Ill. 60176.
A. G. Spalding and Bros., Inc., Chicopee, Mass., 01014.
Toy Patio Village, 140 W. Sierra Madre Blvd., Sierra Madre, Calif. 91024. (213-355-6641.)
Toys That Care, P.O. Box 81, Briarcliff Manor, N.Y. 10510.
W. J. Voit Rubber Corp., 3801 South Harbour Blvd., Santa Ana. Calif. 92704.
Wham-O Corp., 835 E. El Monte Ave., San Gabriel, Calif. 91776.
Wilson Sporting Goods Co., 2233 West St., River Grove, Ill. 60171.

The following will supply information on health and nutrition or promotional materials:

American Association for Health, Physical Education and Recreation, 1201 16th St., NW, Washington, D.C. 60611.
American Dental Association 211 E. Chicago Ave., Chicago, Ill. 60611.
American Dietetic Association, 620 N. Michigan Ave., Chicago, Ill. 60611.
American Dry Milk Institute, Inc., 430 N. Franklin St., Chicago, Ill. 60606.
American Home Economics Association, 2010 Massachusetts Ave., NW, Washington, D.C. 20036.
American Institute of Baking, 400 E. Ontario St., Chicago, Ill. 60611.

American Medical Association 535 N. Dearborn St., Chicago, Ill. 60610.

American Public Health Association, Food and Nutrition Section, 1790 Broadway, New York, N.Y. 10019.

American School Food Service Association, Box 10095, Denver, Colo. 80210.

Borden, Inc., Columbus, Ohio 43215.

Campbell Soup Co., Camden, N.J. 08101.

Carnation Co. Home Service Dept., 5045 Wilshire Bld., Los Angeles, Calif. 90036.

Cereal Institute, Inc., 135 South LaSalle St., Chicago, Ill. 60603.

Checkerboard Kitchens Consumer Services, Public Relations, Ralston Purina Co., Checkerboard Sq., Dept. 209, St. Louis, Mo. 63188.

Chevron Chemical Co., Ortho Div., San Francisco, Calif. 94105.

Chicago Nutrition Association, Nutrition References, 200 S. William, Mt. Prospect, Ill. 60056.

Del Monte Corp., Market Plaza, San Francisco, Calif. 94105.

Duffy-Mott Co., Inc., 370 Lexington Ave., New York, N.Y. 10017.

Florida Citrus Commission, Youth and School Service Dept., Box 148, Lakeland, Fla. 33802.

Freemountain Toys, Inc., The Vegimill, David Dobson, Sales Manager, 23 Main St., Bristol, Vt. 05443.

General Foods Corp., White Plains, N.Y. 10625.

General Mills, General Offices, Minneapolis, Minn. 55440.

Green Giant Co., Consumer Services Dept., LeSueur, Minn. 56058.

H. J. Heinz Co., Box 57, Pittsburgh, Pa. 15230.

Hormel and Co., General Offices, Chicago, Ill. 60690.

Hunt-Wesson Foods, Inc., Fullerton, Calif. 92634.

ITT Continental Baking Co., Home Economics Dept., P.O. Box 731, Rye, N.Y. 10580.

Kellogg's Dept. of Home Economics Service, Battle Creek, Mich. 49016.

Kraft, Inc., Chicago, Ill. 60690.

Thomas J. Lipton, Inc., Englewood Cliffs, N.J. 07632.

McCormick and Co., Inc., Baltimore, Md. 21202.

McDonald's Action Packs, P.O. Box 2594, Chicago, Ill. 60690.

Metropolitan Life Insurance Co., 1 Madison Ave., New York, N.Y. 10010.

MJB Kitchens, San Francisco, Calif. 94107.

Nabisco, Inc., East Hanover, N.J. 07930.

National Dairy Council, 111 N. Canal St., Chicago, Ill. 60603.

National Livestock and Meat Board, 36 S. Wabash Ave., Chicago, Ill. 60603.

National Soft Drink Association, 1101 16th St., NW, Washington, D.C. 20036.

Nestle Company, Inc., White Plains, N.Y. 10605.

Nutrition Education Materials Catalogue, National Dairy Council, 111 North Canal St., Chicago, Ill. 60606.

Nutrition Foundation, Inc., 99 Park Ave., New York, N.Y. 10016.

Pillsbury Co., 840-B Pillsbury Bldg., Minneapolis, Minn. 55402.

Planters, Standard Brands Inc., New York, N.Y. 10022.

Quaker Oats Co., Chicago, Ill. 60651.

Rice Council, P.O. Box 22802, Houston, Tex. 77027.

Roman Meal Co., Tacoma, Wash. 98409.

Society for Nutrition Education, National Nutrition Education Clearinghouse, 2140 Shattuck Ave., Suite 110, Berkeley, Calif. 94704.

Standard Milling Co., 1909 Central St., Kansas City, Mo. 64105.

Sunkist Growers, Inc., Consumer Services, P.O. Box 7888, Van Nuys, Calif. 91409.

Superintendent of Documents, Government Printing Office, Washington, D.C. 20402.

U.S. Department of Agriculture, Consumer Information, Pueblo, Colo. 81009.

U.S. Department of Agriculture, Food and Nutrition Service, Appraisers Bldg., Rm. 734, 630 Sansome St., San Francisco, Calif. 04111.

U.S. Department of Health, Education, and Welfare (now U.S. Department of Health and Human Services), Public Health Service, Food and Drug Administration, 5600 Fishers Lane, Rockville, Md. 20852.

Washington and Idaho, Dry Pea and Lentil Commissions, State Line Office, P.O. Box 8566, Moscow, Idaho 83848.

Enrichment Materials

Unusual pieces of equipment and where to get them:

Ladder Exerciser. Creative Playthings. (Order from William G. Johnston Co., P.O. Box 6759, Pittsburgh, Pa. 15212. A safe, nontipping ladder.)

Vari-Balance Boards. Holbrook-Patterson, Inc. (170 S. Monroe St., Coldwater, Mich. 49036. A set of solid maple boards.)

Home Exercise Mat. Child Life-Play Specialties, Inc. (55 Whitney St., Holliston, Mass. 01746. An exercise mat for home use.)

Giant Balloons. Edmund Scientific Co., (300 Edscorp Bldg., Barrington, N.J. 08007. Heavy-duty: 3 feet in diameter.)

Resource books on movement:

Bentley, W. G. *Learning to move and moving to learn.* New York: Citation Press, 1970. (A good section on making simple equipment.)

Gilbert, A. G. *Teaching the three R's through movement experiences.* Minneapolis: Burgess, 1977. (Excellent ideas for integrating movement activities into all areas of the curriculum. Specific activities in language, mathematics, science, social studies, and art.)

Porter, L. *Movement education for children.* Washington, D.C.: NEA, Assn. of Elementary, Kindergarten, and Nursery Teachers, 1969. (Includes a good film list.)

Records for movement:

All purpose folk dances. Michael Herman's Folk Dance Orchestra. (RCA LPM 1623.)

Around the world in dance. Buzz Glass. (AR 542.)

Balance skills. (Children's Book and Music Center catalog no. PE 101. Exercises for floor or balance beam. Preliminary gymnastics and dance; also special education. With booklet. 2500 Santa Monica Blvd., Santa Monica, Calif. 90404.)

Come dance with me. (Two records with book. Children's Book and Music Center catalog no. D 325. Creative dance. By Virginia Tanner.)

Getting to know myself. (Hap Palmer.)

Goin' places. (Tijuana Brass, Alpert. A and M 4101.)

Homemade band. (Hap Palmer. AR 545.)

Learning basic skills through music. 2 vols. (Hap Palmer. AR 521 and 522.)

Movin.' (Hap Palmer. AR 546.)

Rhythmic activities (Vol. 1). Florence Bassett and Cora Mae Chesnut. (No. 5127.)

Films, loops, and filmstrips on movement:

Apparatus skills. (Film, color. Gabor Nagy, Filmfair Communications, 10946 Ventura Blvd., Studio City, Calif. 91604.)

Balance skills. (Film, color, Gabor Nagy, Filmfair Communications, 10946 Ventura Blvd., Studio City, Calif. 91604.)

Ball skills. (Film, color, Gabor Nagy, Filmfair Communications, 10946 Ventura Blvd., Studio City, Calif. 91604.)

Basic movements. (Film loop, 8 mm, color. Ealing Corp., 2225 Massachusetts Ave., Cambridge, Mass. 02140.)

Basic movement skills. (Film, color. Gabor Nagy, Filmfair Communications, 10946 Ventura Blvd., Studio City, Calif., 91604.)

Body awareness. (Film, color. Gabor Nagy, Filmfair Communications, 10946 Ventura Blvd., Studio City, Calif., 01604.)

Body movements. (Film, color, 11 min. General Learning Corp., 3 E. 54th St., New York, N.Y. 10022.)

Dance your way. (Film, color, 10 min. Bailey Films, 1961. Order from Kent State University, Audio Visual Aids Center, Kent, Ohio 44242.)

Functional fitness. (Film loop, 8 mm, color. Ealing Corp., 2225 Massachusetts Ave., Cambridge, Mass. 02140.)

Manipulative activities. (Film loop, 8 mm, color. Ealing Corp., 3 E. 54th St., New York, N.Y. 10022.)

Movement experiences for children. (Film, black-and-white, 8 min. Northern Illinois University, 1967. Northern Illinois University, Dept. of Instructional Media Distribution, Altgeld 114, De Kalb, 60115.)

Movement experiences for primary children. (Film, color, 15 min. Northern Illinois University, 1968. Northern Illinois University, Dept. of Instructional Media Distribution, Altgeld 114, De Kalb, 60115.)

Movement exploration: What am I? (Film, color, 11 min. Film Associates, 1968. Order from Kent State University, Audio Visual Aids Center, Kent, Ohio 44242.)

Movement kits:

Bean bag activities and coordination skills. (Songs for bean bag activities. Available from Children's Book and Music Center, 2500 Santa Monica Blvd., Santa Monica, Calif. 90404. Record: PE 830. Dozen square bean bags: PE 486. Six animal bean bags: PE 487.)

Lummi sticks. Rhythm games based on Maori stick games. With record and instruction sheets. Children's Book and Music Center catalog no. PE 699. 2500 Santa Monica Blvd., Santa Monica, Calif. 90404.

Books for health, safety, and nutrition:

Cooking and eating with children: A way to learn. Washington, D.C.: ACEI, 1974. (3615 Wisconsin Ave., 20016. 48 pp. on the importance of good nutrition. Recipes. Guide for children's participation.)

The thing the professor forgot. U.S. Government Consumer Information Center. (Pueblo, Colo. 81009. A coloring book with rhymes, on nutrition.)

Posters on health and safety are available from:

Bicycle Institute of America, Inc., 122 E. 42d St., New York, N.Y. 10017.

Constructive Playthings, 1040 E. 85th St., Kansas City, Mo. 64131.

Johnson and Johnson, Consumer Relations Div., New Brunswick, N.J. 08903.

Records on health, safety, and nutrition:

Do you know how you grow? Inside. (Children's Books and Music Center catalog no. SG 171. 10-inch record. Songs and narration on food and growth, with booklet. Elementary grades. 2500 Santa Monica Blvd., Santa Monica, Calif. 90404.)

Do you know how you grow? Outside. (Children's Book and Music Center Catalog no. SG 172. 10-inch record with booklet. Songs and narration on external development. 2500 Santa Monica Blvd., Santa Monica, Calif. 90404.)

Health can be fun and *Songs of safety.* (Children's Book and Music Center catalog no. SG 174. Songs by Frank Luther. Sports safety, nutrition, and personal care. 2500 Santa Monica Blvd., Santa Monica, Calif. 90404.)

Films on health, safety, and nutrition:

Alexander's breakfast secret. (Filmstrip, activity sheets, guide, and evaluations. Cereal Institute, Inc., Multimedia Kit, 135 S. La Salle St., Chicago, Ill. 60603.)

Learning to brush (Film, 10 min., color, Modern Talking Pictures. No. 7107. 2323 New Hyde Park, N.Y. 11040.)

Nutrition for little children. (Filmstrip, color, with record or cassette. Teaches importance of nutrition. Teacher's guide. Available in Spanish. Order from Children's Book and Music Center, 2500 Santa Monica Blvd., Santa Monica, Calif. 90404.)

Safety for children. (23 visuals. 3M Co., Visual Products Div., Box 3334, St. Paul, Minn. 55101.)

Books to foster mental health and cooperative play:

American Assn. for Health, Physical Education, and Recreation. *Homemade innovative play equipment.* (Order from Council for Exceptional children, 1920 Association Dr., Reston, Va. 22091.)

Freed, A. *T. A. for tots coloring book (Transactional analysis for everybody series).* Sacramento, Calif.: Jalmar, 1976. (Paper. Preschool to grade 3.)

Hewes, J. J. *Build your own playground!* Boston: Houghton Mifflin. (2 Park St., 02107.)

Idea exchange: Playgrounds. LINC Publications. (Idea Exchange, 800 Silver Ave., Greensboro, N.C. 27403.)

Orlick, T. *The cooperative sports and games book.* New York: Pantheon, 1978. (Games in which nobody loses.)

Playground equipment designs. (Learning Stuff, P.O. Box 4123, Modesto, Calif. 95352.)

For role playing:

Sparky membership kit. (National Fire Protection Assn., 470 Atlantic Ave., Boston, Mass. 02210. Firefighter's badge, inspector's handbook, and membership card in Sparky's fire department.)

Community Resources

Places to visit:

Dance studios.	Police stations
Sporting goods stores.	Exercise clinics.
Parks.	Gymnasiums.
Athletic events.	Roller rinks.
Hospitals.	Dance recitals.
Fire stations.	Gymnastic meets.

Speakers:

Dancers (folk, ballet, etc.).
Athletes (professional or amateur).
Doctors and dentists.
Nurses or medics.
Nutritionists or dieticians.
Cafeteria workers.

Counselors.
Firefighters.
Police officers.
Safety inspectors.
Lifeguards.

Where to find a speaker:

Department of motor vehicles.
Local health department.
American Red Cross.
Medical or dental society.
Highway department.
A marching band.
American Automobile Association.

Local dairy council.
A bicycle shop.
Insurance companies.
Mental health clinics.
Local branch of the National Safety
 Council.

Section 3

COGNITIVE DEVELOPMENT: ACTIVITIES AND RESOURCES

"Cognitive development" means the development of thought processes. From a very early age onward, children think. They become aware of similarities and differences, of quantity, of time, and of space. They learn to classify, so that they can handle information efficiently. They ask questions and seek answers. They observe; and they start to formulate and test ideas and solve problems. People who work with young children quickly become aware of the children's insatiable curiosity and their urge to explore. Children want to see everything, touch everything, taste everything, and learn about everything. There is no need to instill motivation in young children—motivation is probably stronger at this time than at any other. It is more appropriate for teachers and caretakers to be concerned lest they stifle motivation. Motivation must be nurtured; teachers and caretakers must capitalize on it by providing tools, skills, and materials so as to let children learn.

In this section, we deal with the child's cognitive development. As in the section on psycho-physical-motor development, we begin with objectives and activities for infants and toddlers and then go on to objectives, activities, and resources for older children. Here we have two major subdivisions: science and mathematics. We've confined our objectives, activities, and resources to these two areas because we consider them especially well suited to illustrate the development of cognitive processes such as classifying, seriating, predicting, observing, formulating and testing hypotheses, recording and interpreting data, and generalizing. We are not suggesting, of course, that cognitive development is confined to science and mathematics, or that science and mathematics do not have components other than the cognitive.

We want to emphasize that our primary concern in this section is with process—for once the tools of thinking are developed and children's curiosity and exploration are encouraged, the stage is set for a lifetime of learning.

Objectives and Activities for Infants and Toddlers

Beginning at birth, children engage in informal experiences and activities that foster cognitive development. For both infants and toddlers, such activities satisfy curiosity and the urge to explore, observe, manipulate and seek out problems. For 2- and 3-year olds especially, activities are needed which will continue to meet these objectives and in addition will provide practice in labeling and symbolizing. Experiences of this nature lead into later activities—activities characteristic of preschool and school: comparing and contrasting, classifying, seriating, and matching (which are the foundation of mathematics); and predicting, observing, generalizing, forming and testing hypotheses, and interpreting data (which are the foundation of science). Thus early cognitive experiences lead naturally and logically into later ones; and, in particular, the objectives and activities we offer here for infants and toddlers lead naturally and logically into the objectives and activities we offer next for older children.

Infants and toddlers—children in what Piaget called the "sensory-motor stage"—tend to explore the world with their senses. They are learning to use their eyes, ears, nose, hands, feet, mouth, and skin to take in and process information about the world. Activities that foster eye-hand coordination, stimulate response to sounds, and help the child develop the ability to distinguish similarities and differences are beneficial in several ways: they give immediate enjoyment, provide opportunities for interaction between child and caretaker, and lay a foundation for the later development of skills that will be needed in thinking, reading, and performing mathematical and scientific operations. Such activities also help the child develop a positive attitude toward learning. Enjoyment and reinforcement help the child to build confidence that make the child willing and eager to reach out.

The following table gives suggested objectives and activities for children from birth to 36 months.

Sequential Objectives and Activities for Cognitive Development:
Birth to 36 Months

LEVEL	OBJECTIVE	ACTIVITY
Birth to 1 month	1. To encourage the realization that some sounds heard come from outside oneself.	1. Shake a rattle first on one side of the child's head, then on the other.
	2. To stimulate early visual and auditory perception.	2. Hang a mobile over the crib; the parts should make a noise as they move.
	3. To develop the ability to distinguish shapes and colors.	3. Hang bright-colored plastic toys across the crib, or along its sides.
	4. To encourage visual tracking.	4. Move a flashlight or pen light, covered with colored cellophane, back and forth within the child's view.

(Continued)

**Sequential Objectives and Activities for Cognitive Development:
Birth to 36 Months (continued)**

LEVEL	OBJECTIVE	ACTIVITY
1 to 3 months	1. To develop the sense of touch.	1. Rub the child's arms and legs with materials of different textures (e.g., silk, cotton, velvet, flannel, terry-cloth).
	2. To develop the concept of the permanence of objects.	2. Move your face back and forth within and beyond the child's field of vision, so that the child can follow and anticipate the movement.
	3. To develop visual acuity.	3. Frequently change the objects that the child looks at (e.g., patterned sheets, mobiles).
	4. To stimulate curiosity and encourage experimentation.	4. Place a few bright-colored objects within the child's reach.
	5. To develop spatial awareness.	5. Show the child various objects from various angles and distances.
3 to 6 months	1. To expand the concept of the body and things outside the body.	1. Show the child his or her image in a mirror alone and then while holding a toy.
	2. To develop tactile acuity.	2. Give the child different types of household objects to feel—objects with different textures (sticky, fuzzy) and shapes (round, square).
	3. To strengthen the concept of object permanence.	3. Play peek-a-boo with the child.
	4. To develop visual awareness.	4. Bounce a ball so that the child can follow it visually.
6 to 9 months	1. To develop the ability to recognize wholes from parts.	1. Hide half a toy under a blanket, leaving the other half visible; encourage the child to pull the toy out or remove the blanket.
	2. To develop concepts of object permanence and conservation.	2. Encourage the child to drop objects which you will retrieve—make a game of this.
	3. To develop the concept of the body and the location of its parts.	3. Give the child hats to try on, encouraging the child to find the head.
	4. To lay a foundation for problem solving.	4. Turn the child's toys upside down and encourage the child to turn them right side up.
9 to 12 months	1. To develop the ability to categorize; and to expand the child's picture of the world.	1. Collect objects from outdoors for the child to handle and manipulate (e.g., pine cones, rocks, sticks, shells).
	2. To encourage experimentation.	2. Give the child measuring cups of graduated sizes and let the child play with them with water or sand.
	3. To reinforce the concept of object permanence and encourage problem solving.	3. Hide a loud-ticking clock or a playing radio and encourage the child to find it.
	4. To develop the ability to look for things.	4. Have the child watch as you wrap or hide objects; then have the child unwrap the object or remove it from its hiding place.
	5. To develop problem-solving skills.	5. When both the child's hands are full, hand him or her an "extra" toy or some other attractive object.

LEVEL	OBJECTIVE	ACTIVITY
12 to 18 months	1. To stimulate problem solving and inventive thinking.	1a. Put the child's favorite toy on a shelf, just barely within reach. b. Give the child a covered box and let the child figure out how to get the cover on and off. c. Drop a toy into a deep container or bag and let the child figure out how to remove it.
	2. To apply physical skills to problem solving.	2. Clamp clothespins around the edge of a coffee can or oatmeal box and let the child figure out how to remove them and put them on again.
	3. To apply physical skills to everyday experiences.	3. Wear an apron with various fastenings—a zipper, buttons, snaps, laces—and let the child help you get dressed.
	4. To encourage exploration and discovery.	4. Give the child a special shelf, low table, cupboard, or box, filled with "touchable" items.
	5. To develop the concepts of relative size and sequence.	5. Give the child nesting toys to play with and encourage the child to fit the small ones into the large ones. (Cans of different sizes will do.)
	6. To stimulate trial-and-error experimentation; and to lay a foundation for conservation.	6. Encourage water play with containers of various sizes.
	7. To lay a foundation for reversibility.	7. Fill and empty a container; or cover and uncover a toy.
18 to 24 months	1. To develop spatial thinking and the concept of causality. 2. To reinforce object permanence.	1. Use a piece of cardboard or wood as a ramp for toy cars and trucks. a. Play hide and seek with toys or people. b. Hide an object in your hand and have the child guess which hand, or what the object is.
	3. To develop the ability to recognize and classify objects by using the senses.	3a. Fill small jars with strong-smelling liquids and encourage the child to identify them by smell. b. Have the child sort objects by feel (facecloths versus handkerchiefs, say; or apples versus tennis balls). c. Encourage the child to identify sounds as, say, loud or soft; or familiar or unfamiliar; or music or not-music.
	4. To stimulate the child's awareness of ability to act as a cause; and to stimulate the ability to use means for an end. 5. To reinforce conservation and encourage problem solving.	4. Have the child wind up various things: e.g., music box, toy train, jack in the box. 5. Encourage sand and water play with a variety of containers and materials (e.g., measuring cups and spoons, sieve, colander, pail, shovel).
	6. To develop spatial awareness and improve problem solving skills.	6. Give the child two-piece puzzles (made by mounting or drawing a picture on stiff cardboard and cutting it in half), or cutouts (made by cutting a shape from the center of a piece of stiff cardboard), and have the child put the puzzle together or fit the cutout into its hole.

(Continued)

LEVEL	OBJECTIVE	ACTIVITY
24 to 36 months	1. To develop the concept of seriation and the ability to group logically and abstractly.	1. Encourage sorting of a large variety of objects (buttons, sponges, balls, beads, etc.) according to different criteria (big-little, hard-soft, heavy-light, etc.).
	2. To improve visual discrimination.	2. Have the child sort shades of the same color, using swatches of material or paint chips.
	3. To encourage thinking, reasoning, and decision making.	3. Allow the child to choose between two alternatives.
	4. To develop a sense of spatial relationships and to stimulate intuitive thinking and reasoning.	4. Provide puzzles and pegboards.
	5. To stimulate curiosity and observation.	5. Go on a nature walk and observe, collect, and discuss specimens. Give the child a pail or bag for collecting specimens.
	6. To stimulate thinking, reasoning, and participation.	6. Play a guessing game; e.g., "I am thinking of something green."

Objectives and Activities for Older Children: Science

Introduction: Objectives

It is our belief that a good teaching program does not "cover" science but rather creates situations in which children can "uncover" the concepts of science. In science, perhaps even more than in other areas, children learn best from the inside out—by construction rather than instruction.

The teacher's responsibility is (1) to capitalize on both the natural curiosity of children and the mass of observations, perceptions, and other experiences which children have had; (2) to establish an environment which allows children to construct generalizations based on concrete experiences; (3) to understand the breadth and depth of the discipline; (4) to help children undertake progressively more sophisticated inquiry within various conceptual areas; and (5) to present diverse content to match the diverse experiences, interests, and abilities of the children.

To accomplish this, the teacher needs to rely on the efforts of educators (who are familiar with children and their learning environments) and scientists (who are, of course, familiar with the various scientific disciplines). A number of programs have been designed to provide background material for teachers, books and worksheets for children, and audiovisual and laboratory materials (see "Resources for Science" following the activities). We believe that every teacher can feel comfortable teaching science to young children, who have a natural interest in the processes and content of science. What is needed is, first, an enriched environment, stocked with easily accessible materials that help children to use scientific processes and arrive at major generalizations and, second, a carefully thought-out and balanced series of objectives and activities which build systematically from the simple to the complex in major conceptual areas.

We present objectives and activities for science in six major conceptual areas:

1. Living things.
2. The earth
3. The solar system.
4. Air, water, and weather.
5. Growing bodies.
6. Matter and energy.

Within each area, we have developed a hierarchy of generalizations, progressing from simplicity to greater complexity, and it is these generalizations which are our objectives.

On the table of objectives for science, the six conceptual areas—or curriculum areas—are the horizontal axis; once again, the vertical axis is age levels. The objectives—stated, as we have just noted, as generalizations which the children are to arrive at—are classified by area and age level. We should stress that this table of objectives is not meant to be definitive: teachers may feel free to add to it or delete from it.

Activities need to be planned to provide experiences leading to the development of each generalization. Samples of such activities follow the table of objectives; as in Section One, they are keyed to the table. These activities are the foundation for later, more advanced experiences in the upper primary grades and in secondary school. The objective for each activity is one of the generalizations from the table; remember that the "key" to the table is read "area-level-objective," so that "1-A-1" means "area 1, level A, objective 1."

Try some of these objectives and activities, modify or expand them, group them into units of study (see the section on social studies for an explanation of developing units), and develop more of your own. Your goal should be a living, growing science program which supplies different activities for the different interests and needs of your children and provides many opportunities to use the basic processes of science and to arrive at major scientific generalizations.

Turn the page for the table of objectives. . . .

Major Objectives for Science

		CURRICULUM AREAS	
	(1) LIVING THINGS	(2) THE EARTH	(3) THE SOLAR SYSTEM
LEVEL A (AGES 3 TO 5)	1. In our world, everything is either living or nonliving.* 2. Living things in our world are either plants or animals. 3. There are many kinds of plants and animals in our world. 4. All our plants and animals need air and water to live. 5. Green plants need light to grow.* 6. Human animals need plants and other animals, and many of them need us.	1. The earth is made up of many non-living things. 2. Rocks are hard, nonliving things. 3. There are many kinds of rock; different kinds look and feel different.* 4. Gravel, pebbles, and sand are small pieces of rock.	1. We live on a planet called "earth." 2. The earth gets heat and light from the sun.* 3. Light from the moon sometimes helps us see at night. 4. People from earth have visited the moon.
LEVEL B (AGES 4 TO 6)	1. Most of our animals can move from place to place. 2. Animals live in many kinds of places and in many different ways, and they have many kinds of homes.* 3. Plants grow in many kinds of places. 4. Most plants do not move about as animals do. 5. All living things—humans, other animals, and plants—need certain conditions in order to live. 6. All living things reproduce their own kind.	1. The earth is made up of masses of of land and water. 2. Land masses on earth are made up of rock and soil. 3. Soil is made of broken-down rock and decayed plant and animal matter. 4. We can use rock in many ways.	1. Our planet, earth, is almost round. 2. There is air all around the earth, and space beyond that. 3. Earth is smaller than the sun and larger than our moon. 4. We have rockets and other equipment to explore space beyond earth.* 5. There are many stars, planets, and moons besides our sun, the earth, and its moon.
LEVEL C (AGES 5 TO 7)	1. In our world, some animals eat plants, some eat other animals, and some eat both. 2. Plants have different ways of getting and storing food.* 3. Some animals move from place to place as the seasons change. 4. All living things change as they grow. 5. All living things—humans, other animals, and plants—reproduce, so that their species continue.	1. Rocks on earth are constantly being worn and broken down by wind, water, changes in temperature, plants, and chemical action.* 2. Different kinds of soil are formed from different kinds of rock.* 3. Most of the earth is covered with water, and most of that is salt water. 4. The bodies of water on earth are important to different kinds of life. 5. Soil is important to life and should be conserved.	1. The earth revolves around the sun once a year; this makes our seasons. 2. The earth also rotates on its axis once every 24 hours; this makes day and night. 3. The sun helps us in many ways.* 4. The sun and stars are always shining, even when we cannot see them. 5. The stars vary in size, brightness, and distances from earth.* 6. Our nearest neighbor in space is the moon. 7. Scientists and astronauts study and explore space with rocket ships, other vehicles, and various instruments.
LEVEL D (AGES 7 TO 9)	1. Plants and animals need each other. 2. Many plants and animals are adapted to live in certain places, do certain things, or protect themselves from enemies.* 3. All living things have special parts to do specific things. 4. Humans should be good ecologists and conservationists, to keep the world running smoothly.	1. The earth's surface is constantly changing. 2. Rocks are formed in different ways and are made of different materials. 3. The earth is made up of layers of rock and soil.* 4. Fossils are remains of plants and animals preserved in sedimentary rock.* 5. The first living things on earth were in the sea; some later adapted to life on land. 6. We are learning to use and conserve the resources of the sea.	1. The sun is the center of our solar system. 2. The sun is a star; it consists of hot gasses. 3. There are nine planets in the solar system. 4. Earth and the eight other planets circle around the sun in fixed orbits.* 5. The same side of the moon always faces the earth. 6. We have learned much about the moon.* 7. We are learning more about the solar system by observing and exploring.

*Asterisk signifies that an activity has been provided for this objective.

70

	(4) AIR, WATER, AND WEATHER	(5) GROWING BODIES	(6) MATTER AND ENERGY
LEVEL A (AGES 3 TO 5)	1. Air is all around us.* 2. Although we cannot see air, we can feel it and see what it does.* 3. Moving air can do many things for us.* 4. Water has many uses. 5. There are many kinds of weather conditions.* 6. Weather conditions affect how we feel and help us decide how to dress and what to do.	1. The face is made up of many parts. 2. Certain parts of the body have special jobs that help us see, hear, smell, taste, and feel.* 3. Our hands, feet, arms, and legs allow us to move.* 4. The body contains many bones of different sizes and shapes.	1. Sounds are made by people, animals, and moving objects.* 2. Sound travels in all directions, and we pick it up with our ears. 3. Sounds can be pleasant or unpleasant and can help or harm us. 4. Light, which lets us see, can travel great distances. 5. Shadows are made when light is blocked. 6. We use many tools to do many different jobs.
LEVEL B (AGES 4 TO 6)	1. Wind can help us or harm us.* 2. Water can help us or harm us. 3. Weather conditions can help us or harm us. 4. We can observe weather conditions, and sometimes we can explain them. 5. The surface of the earth is warmed in the daytime and cools at night; this affects the air above it.	1. Skin forms a protective covering for the body. 2. Hair—thick or thin—covers most of the human body. 3. Baby teeth fall out, making room for the teeth that should last us the rest of our lives. 4. The heart beats all the time—whether we are awake or asleep, resting or exercising—but it beats at different rates.* 5. Our lungs expand and contract as we breathe. 6. Our bones form a frame for the body and protect its inner parts.	1. To get light or heat, we need the sun, fire, or electricity. 2. Heat and fire can help us or harm us. 3. We can learn how to make sounds and how to make them louder or softer. 4. We can use magnets to pick up certain things.* 5. It took many, many years for humans to develop simple machines. 6. Energy is the force that gets work done.
LEVEL C (AGES 5 TO 7)	1. We cannot have fire without air. 2. Water droplets or tiny ice crystals make up the clouds which bring us rain or snow.* 3. Water evaporates from earth and returns to the air. 4. We use different instruments to measure weather conditions.* 5. We can often predict the weather if we observe carefully and use our information. 6. We generally can predict what the weather will be like in different seasons and in different parts of the world.	1. Our eyes and ears consist of many parts. 2. Every movement we make uses some of our muscles. 3. The heart pumps blood to all parts of the body. 4. The lungs send air to all parts of the body.*	1. Sound waves are vibrations which travel in many ways. 2. We can often see things before we hear them, because light travels faster than sound. 3. We can control many kinds of sound, light, and heat to make them useful. 4. Our world is made up of different kinds of matter: solid, liquid, and gas. 5. Magnets can repel as well as attract. 6. Machines can change the amount, speed, and direction of a force. 7. There are six basic kinds of machines; these six make work easier for us.* 8. By using more energy, we can increase the speed or amount of work done.
LEVEL D (AGES 7 TO 9)	1. Air is real and takes up space. 2. We can use air effectively by heating or cooling it. 3. We can do many things with water by controlling its flow, direction, temperature, and chemical balance and by combining it with other things.* 4. We have many ways of responding to predicted changes in weather. 5. By protecting our ecology, we can make the world better.	1. The abdomen consists of the stomach and many other parts.* 2. All the food we eat passes through the stomach. 3. The stomach is a main part of the digestive system. 4. Muscles are used for movement, posture, and heat production. 5. The muscles work together in pairs or groups—never alone.	1. Solid matter can be grouped into categories (e.g., wood, metal, plastic).* 2. We can use magnetic force to act through some materials and determine direction.* 3. Energy overcomes friction to accomplish work. 4. Complex machines are made from combinations of the six simple machines. 5. We can get work done faster by using machines. 6. There are many types of energy, and many of them need to be conserved.

Activities for Science: Living Things

Description Sorting objects and pictures according to whether they are, or represent, living or nonliving things.
Title (for children) "Alive, Alive-Oh."
Curriculum area Science (living things).   **Age range** 3 to 5.

What is our objective? "In our world, everything is either living or nonliving" (table: 1-A-1).
What will we need? Objects, living and nonliving (e.g., rock, scissors, paper, book, potted plant, turtle, hamster, gold-fish in bowl); old magazines, scissors, paste, file cards; well-defined area to serve as a learning center.
How will we do it?
1. The teacher sets up a center for learning about living and nonliving things—with objects to be sorted, magazines to find pictures in, materials for mounting pictures, and room for groups of children to discuss what is observed.
2. The children sort the various objects—living things on one side, nonliving things on the other—and share their observations.
3. The children cut pictures of things out of the magazines and mount each picture on a file card.
4. Teacher and children play this game: The teacher holds up the file cards one by one—if the picture on it shows a living thing, the children call out "Alive, alive-oh!" They can sing the phrase if they know the song. (It's from "Molly Malone.")

What else can we do? Follow-up: Ask the children to draw one living thing and one nonliving thing, trying to think of things that weren't on the file cards or in the center. Each child explains what he or she has drawn.

Description   Observing the effect of light on green plants.
Title (for children)   "Green Light Means Grow."
Curriculum area   Science (living things).   **Age range**   3 to 5.

What is our objective?   "Green plants need light to grow" (table: 1-A-5).
What will we need?   For each child (or small group of children): a cardboard box and a potted bean seedling. The teacher will need a knife or a pair of scissors.
How will we do it?
1. Teacher and children discuss what green plants need in order to grow.
2. The teacher gives each child (or small group) a cardboard box and a bean seedling, and cuts a slot in one side of the box about ½ inch by 4 inches.
3. The children place the boxes over the seedlings.
4. For the next few days, the children remove the box just to water the plant and then quickly replace it.
5. After a few days, the children observe how the plant grows toward and then through the slot, reaching for the light. Children and teacher talk about what they have observed.

What else can we do?   Other activities: Tape black paper over one leaf of a plant and cellophane over another leaf. The children watch the two leaves over a ten-day period and discuss their observations. Another graphic demonstration is to raise two identical plants for ten days, one in light and one in darkness.

Description   Making a "woodland" terrarium.
Title (for children)   "There's No Place Like Home."
Curriculum area   Science (living things).   **Age range**   4 to 6.

What is our objective?   "Animals live in many kinds of places and in many different ways, and they have many kinds of homes" (table: 1-B-2).
What will we need?   Gallon jar (glass) with cover, soil, small branches, leaves, water, small animals (snails, salamanders, earthworms, lizards, etc.), cornmeal, cabbage, live insects, drawing materials, tape recorder.
How will we do it?
1. Using the gallon jar, soil, branches, leaves, and water, teacher and children make a terrarium.
2. The children put the small animals into it, cover it, and keep it in a cool place, making sure that it stays moist but not wet.
3. Each day, the children feed the animals in the terrarium with cornmeal, leaves, bits of cabbage, and live insects.
4. The children observe what goes on in the terrarium, noting what the animals do and how they live.
5. The children can record their observations by drawing; or the teacher can tape-record their observations; or both.

What else can we do?   Follow-up: The children's drawings of their observations can be displayed on mural paper.
Other activities: An ant farm can be bought, set up, and observed; and the class can make a mural of animals' homes (burrows, nests, etc.) and attach laminated pictures of animals to the appropriate homes.

Description   Experimenting with celery and colored water to see how food gets to and through plants.
Title (for children)   "Going Up?"
Curriculum area   Science (living things).   **Age range**   5 to 7.

What is our objective?   "Plants have different ways of getting and storing food" (table: 1-C-2).
What will we need?   One or more stalks of celery—enough so that there will be one rib for each child; two clear glasses for each child; knives; water; red and blue food coloring; drawing materials.
How will we do it?

1. Teacher and children discuss how plants get and store food, and the teacher gives each child a rib of celery, two glasses, and a knife.
2. Two batches of colored water are made—one red, one blue.
3. Each child cuts his or her rib of celery lengthwise, about halfway up. Holding the rib cut side down, the child puts one cut side into a class of red-colored water and the other side into a glass of blue-colored water.
4. The children observe what happens and record their observations by means of colored drawings.

What else can we do?   **Variation:** White carnations can be colored using the same procedure; they can be used as gifts or to decorate the room.   **Another activity:** Teacher and children can make a chart to show different ways in which plants store food (carrots in the root, corn in the seeds, etc.).

Description   Making three-dimensional pictures of camouflaged animals.
Title (for children)   "Where Am I?"
Curriculum area   Science (living things).   **Age range**   7 to 9.

What is our objective?   "Many plants and animals are adapted to live in certain places, do certain things, or protect themselves from enemies" (table: 1-D-2).
What will we need?   Research materials; magazines or old workbooks; construction paper (18- by 24-inch pieces); pencils, crayons, scissors, paste; collage materials—leaves, twigs, cotton (to represent snow), etc.
How will we do it?

1. Teacher and children discuss protective coloring, and the children do some research about specific instances. (A trip to the zoo is appropriate, if possible.)
2. The children go through old magazines and workbooks to find pictures of the animals they've learned about. It's a good idea for each child to choose one animal—rabbit, pheasant, snake, or whatever—and find several pictures of it.
3. The children paste their pictures on a sheet of construction paper and then hide the animals with the appropriate natural materials—cotton (for snow) hiding white rabbits, leaves and twigs hiding pheasants, etc.
4. The children take turns showing and explaining their pictures, using the results of their research.

What else can we do?   **Other activities:** A "committee meeting" of different kinds of animals to discuss how to protect themselves adaptively; a chart of animals that change color for protection; a chart of animals with other adaptive characteristics (porcupine quills, hibernating bears, etc.); research on specially adapted plants.

Description Setting up a rock exhibit and classification center.
Title (for children) "Rock, Rock. Who's There?"
Curriculum area Science (the earth).   **Age range** 3 to 5.

What is our objective? "There are many different kinds of rock; different kinds look and feel different" (table: 2-A-3).
What will we need? Rocks, rocks, and more rocks; nails, sandpaper, metal files; well-defined area to serve as a learning center.
How will we do it?
1. Teacher and children have a rock hunt, to find as many different kinds as possible.
2. The teacher sets up a good-sized display area with rocks that differ in size, shape, texture, color, and hardness.
3. Examining the rock exhibit, children observe that all the rocks have some things in common.
4. Then the children, taking turns at the center, sort the rocks by size, shape, etc., and do things to the rocks to see what happens—scratch with a nail, rub with a file, rub with sandpaper, wet the rocks.
What else can we do? **Follow-up:** A "group experience story" can be written, recording what the children have learned and observed.

Description Using a sand table to demonstrate changes which take place on and under the earth's surface.
Title (for children) "Changing Times."
Curriculum area Science (the earth).   **Age range** 5 to 7.

What is our objective? "Rocks on earth are constantly being worn and broken down by wind, water, changes in temperature, plants, and chemical action" (table: 2-C-1).
What will we need? Sand table, water, ice cubes, hair drier, sunlamp.
How will we do it?

1. On the sand table, each child or small group (in turn) digs and mounds to simulate hills and valleys.
2. Each child experiments to see what will happen to the sand formations when various things are done:
   a. Water the sand by sprinkling and pouring.
   b. Turn a sunlamp on the sand for 10 to 20 minutes.
   c. Drop crushed ice and whole ice cubes on the sand.
   d. With the teacher's help (for safety's sake), blow on the sand with a hair drier.
3. Children who can write list what they did and what happened each time; children who can't yet write dictate their results to the teacher.

What else can we do? **Follow-up:** Compare the children's results. What accounts for differences and similarities? The children share ideas on this.

Description Making "soil" from different kinds of rock.
Title (for children) "Stone Ground."
Curriculum area Science (the earth).   **Age range** 5 to 7.

What is our objective? "Different kinds of soil are formed from different kinds of rock" (table: 2-C-2).
What will we need? Sandstone, microscope, cloth bags (e.g., flour sacks), hammer, jars and labels, different kinds of rocks. For older children: pencils and notebooks for recording observations.
How will we do it?

1. For this experiment, children who can write record their own observations; younger children dictate theirs to the teacher.
2. The child rubs together two pieces of common sandstone and observes the rubbings under a microscope.
3. The child puts small pieces of different kinds of rock into small cloth sacks, and pounds with a hammer to smash the rock.
4. The smashed rock is placed into jars which are labeled appropriately by child or teacher.
5. The "soils" in the jars are observed carefully for similarities and differences.

What else can we do? **Variation:** This activity can begin with a walk to collect the rocks that will be used.
Follow-up: A "rock and earth" scrapbook can be kept throughout a unit on "the earth."

Description   Experimenting with water and soil to learn how soil forms layers.
Title (for children)   "The Big Shake."
Curriculum area   Science (the earth).   **Age range**   7 to 9.

What is our objective?   "The earth is made up of layers of rock and soil" (table: 2-D-3).
What will we need?   Plastic gallon jugs, water, samples of different kinds of soil, pencils, paper, crayons.
How will we do it?
1. The children fill 1-gallon plastic jugs with one kind of soil (about 1 quart) and water (about 3 quarts).
2. The children shake the jars and then let them stand, observing as the soil forms layers and noting especially the size of particles at each layer. Observations are recorded as colored sketches.
3. The same experiment is repeated with each type of soil. Results are compared to see if there is a consistent order to the layering of different kinds of particles.
What else can we do?   **Variations:** Include rock, pebbles, and sand with the samples of soil. Another variation is to put the soil samples into small jars with an equal volume of water, shake them up, set them aside for a few days, and observe the results.

Description   Casting a mold of a life form to simulate a fossil.
Title (for children)   "Docile Fossil."
Curriculum area   Science (the earth).   **Age range**   7 to 9.

What is our objective?   "Fossils are remains of plants and animals preserved in sedimentary rock" (table: 2-D-4).
What will we need?   To begin with: books with pictures of fossils, and some actual fossils. For the activity itself: Modeling clay, small cardboard boxes, small life forms (leaves, pods, bones, shells, etc.), plaster of paris, water.
How will we do it?
1. Teacher and children read about fossils and how they are formed, and discuss and examine pictures of fossils and real fossils.
2. Each child puts some damp clay in the bottom of a small cardboard box, and carefully presses one of the life forms into the clay, making a deep impression.
3. The object is removed from the clay, and the child pours a small amount of plaster of paris mixed with water into the mold.
4. When the plaster of paris has hardened, the child removes it from the clay.
5. The resulting "fossils" are displayed around the room.
What else can we do?   **Follow-up:** A museum-like display can be set up, with "fossil" molds, real fossils, and children's drawings and reports.   **Other activities:** Children can break up sedimentary rock with hammers, looking for fossils; a chart can be made on posterboard showing how a real fossil is formed.

Description Experimenting with thermometers and sunlight to observe that sunlight is changed to heat energy when it is absorbed by matter.

Title (for children) "Sunny Side Up."

Curriculum area Science (the solar system).　　　　**Age range** 3 to 5.

What is our objective? "The earth gets heat and light from the sun" (table: 3-A-2).

What will we need? For each child or each small group of children: two clear glasses, water, two thermometers.

How will we do it?

1. Each child (or each small group) puts water in two glasses and puts a thermometer in each glass.
2. One glass is placed in a cool shady spot, the other in direct sunlight.
3. The children observe what happens by watching and feeling:
   a. They watch the mercury climb in the sunlight but not in the shade.
   b. They feel the water in the two glasses.
4. Teacher and children discuss what happened and why. What makes the water warm? What does the climbing mercury mean? They compare this with their own experiences ("How do we feel when we're out in the sun? In the shade?").

What else can we do? **Another activity:** Soak paper towels in water. Put some in a cool shady spot and some in direct sunlight. Teacher and children discuss what happens and why.

Description Using balloons to show how rockets work.
Title (for children) "Away We Go."
Curriculum area Science (the solar system).   **Age range** 4 to 6.

What is our objective? "We have rockets and other equipment to explore space beyond earth" (table: 3-B-4).
What will we need? Balloons (one for each child).
How will we do it?
1. Teacher and children each blow up a balloon, and press against it to feel the pressure of the air inside.
2. Now teacher and children release the balloons so that the air can escape, and they observe what happens.
3. Teacher and children discuss how the air goes in one direction and the balloon in the opposite direction, and how a rocket works on the same principle.

What else can we do? **Variation:** Films or photographs of rockets can be used. **Another activity:** Visit a museum or planetarium to see space equipment exhibited; or invite a speaker from the aerospace industry.

Description Making a sundial.
Title (for children) "Dialing for Time."
Curriculum area Science (the solar system).   **Age range** 5 to 7.

What is our objective? "The sun helps us in many ways" (table: 3-C-3).
What will we need? Small shallow boxes, pencils, clay, large sheets of white construction paper.
How will we do it?
1. Each child fills a small box with clay and stands a pencil in it.
2. Each box is placed near a sunny window, on a large sheet of white paper.
3. At several specific times each day, the children look at the "sundials" and observe the position of the shadow cast by the pencil. The position of the shadow and the time are noted on the paper, along with the date. Each day, a fresh sheet of paper is used.
4. At the end of a week, the children compare their daily sheets. Teacher and children discuss the results and any special conditions (Was there a cloudy day? Was the sun behind a cloud at observation time?).

What else can we do? **Follow-up:** After a week, can the children tell the approximate time from the sundials, without looking at a clock? **Other activities:** The class can make a chart showing various ways the sun helps us; or the children can write or dictate individual or group reports on how the sun helps us.

Description Forming a "human model" of the solar system.
Title (for children) "Who's It? Orbit!"
Curriculum area Science (the solar system).   **Age range** 7 to 9.

What is our objective? "Earth and the eight other planets circle around the sun in fixed orbits" (table: 3-D-4).
What will we need? Ten children; books or articles about the planets and their orbits; poster paper, string, scissors, and paste.
How will we do it?
1. This is a group project for ten children, who will enact the sun and the nine planets. One child chooses to "be" the sun, and each of the others chooses one of the planets.
2. The children learn the relative positions of the planets with respect to the sun, and each child learns a few facts about his or her planet (the "sun" learns about it, of course).
3. The ten children then give a presentation to the class (in the schoolyard, if there is not room indoors). Each child wears a piece of poster paper with a picture he or she has drawn of the sun or a planet and a large label (SUN, MERCURY, etc.). The children begin by orbiting around the sun in their proper positions.
4. Then each child in turn tells the class a few interesting things about the body he or she is portraying (e.g., "I am MERCURY. I am the closest planet to the sun. Etc."). The children end the presentation by orbiting together again.
What else can we do? **Follow-up:** The class can make charts of the solar system, or a three-dimensional model using clay, styrofoam balls, or different-sized playing balls.

Description Making a clay model of a surface like the moon's.
Title (for children) "Crater Face."
Curriculum area Science (the solar system).   **Age range** 7 to 9.

What is our objective? "We have learned much about the moon" (table: 3-D-6).
What will we need? Books and articles about the moon, with good pictures of its surface; hardening clay; round cake pans; tools for working clay (e.g., tongue depressors, putty knives, palette knives); marbles.
How will we do it?
1. Teacher and children discuss the moon, and the children do some research to learn what its surface is like.
2. Each child fills a cake pan with mushy hardening clay. While the clay is still soft, the children use various tools to make formations like those on the moon's surface; "craters" are made by dropping marbles into the clay (the marbles are then removed).
3. When the clay dries, the children use their models to illustrate the features of the moon's surface—mountains, valleys, craters, "seas," etc.
What else can we do? **Follow-up:** If a good telescope is available, the children can observe the moon when it is visible by day, to see which of the formations they made can be identified. **Other activities:** The children can write a tourists' guidebook for the moon or plan a "field trip" to the moon (What would they need to take along? What training would they need?); or the class can visit a planetarium when a program on the moon is being presented.

Description Experimenting with "feeling" air.
Title (for children) "Air Blow."
Curriculum area Science (air, water, and weather).　　　**Age range** 3 to 5.

What is our objective? "Air is all around us; and although we cannot see air, we can feel it and see what it does" (table: 4-A-1 and 4-A-2).
What will we need? For each pair of children: basin, water, tin can, hammer, nail.
How will we do it?
1. For this activity, the children work in pairs. Each pair of children first checks the tin can to be sure it is "empty" and then, using the hammer and nail, punches a hole in the bottom of the can.
2. The children slowly push the can into the basin of water, bottom side up, with one child holding his or her hand over the hole. They then repeat this with the other child's hand over the hole.
3. Children and teacher discuss what happened. What did the children feel when they held a hand over the hole? What was coming out of the hole? Was the can really empty?
What else can we do? Follow-up: Each child gets an "empty," squeezable plastic bottle and squeezes it, holding it under the chin. What do the children feel? Was the bottle really empty?

Description Building a walnut-shell boat and exposing it to air currents.
Title (for children) "Smooth Sailing."
Curriculum area Science (air, water, and weather).   **Age range** 4 to 6.

What is our objective? "Wind can help us or harm us" (table: 4-B-1).
What will we need? For each child: half of a walnut shell, clay, toothpick, small triangle of paper (the "sail"), glue. For the class or each group: a basin of water and a paper fan, or a bellows if possible.
How will we do it?
1. The children make sailboats by putting some clay in the walnut shell and setting the sail—a triangle of paper glued to a toothpick—in it.
2. The boats are floated in a basin of water.
3. The children blow on the boats to see what happens—gently at first, then harder. What do the boats do? What must the children do to make the boats move in a given direction?
4. Then the children use the fan or the bellows to create a windstorm. What happens to the boats now?
5. The children share their observations.
What else can we do? Follow-up: The children blow gently on a dandelion that has gone to seed (a "blow-flower") to spread its seeds, and then "uproot" it from a sand table with a bellows or fan. **Another activity:** The children can cut out pictures from magazines or make their own drawings to illustrate helpful and harmful effects of wind.

Description Using water, ice, and glass jars to make "clouds."
Title (for children) "Clouding the Issue."
Curriculum area Science (air, water, and weather).   **Age range** 5 to 7.

What is our objective? "Water droplets or tiny ice crystals make up the clouds which bring us rain and snow" (table: 4-C-2).
What will we need? Pictures of clouds, glass jars with lids, ice cubes, hot water, poster board, marking pens or crayons.
How will we do it?
1. Teacher and children look at clouds and pictures of clouds and discuss what they consist of and how they might be formed.
2. The children separate into small groups, each of which gets a glass jar (clear), hot water, and ice cubes.
3. The teacher pours 2 to 3 inches of hot water into each jar, and the children cover each jar with its lid.
4. The children put three or four ice cubes on the lid and watch closely to see what happens.
5. The children share their observations and then make an illustrated poster showing the question they began with ("How are clouds formed?") and the answer they found.
What else can we do? Other activities: The children can make a chart showing the water cycle, using pictures cut from magazines or their own drawings; cotton can be used to make different kinds of clouds, which are then mounted on a chart.

Description Making a rain gauge and a simulated thermometer.
Title (for children) "Weather Watching."
Curriculum area Science (air, water, and weather).   **Age range** 5 to 7.

What is our objective? "We use different instruments to measure weather conditions" (table: 4-C-4).
What will we need? For the rain gauge: jars, rulers, felt-tipped pens. For the "thermometer": large metal zippers, heavy cardboard, felt-tipped pens, duct tape.
How will we do it?
The rain gauge:

1. Each child or group gets a straight-sided, clear glass jar with a flat bottom and measures off and marks ¼-inch vertical intervals with a felt-tipped permanent marker.
2. The gauges are put outdoors in a level open space to collect rain.
3. The children record the daily rainfall. Older children can write up the results; younger children can dictate them.

The "thermometer":

1. Each child or group gets a large metal zipper and attaches it (closed) to a piece of heavy cardboard (say, 12 inches square) with duct tape, and measures off degrees on the cardboard next to the zipper's teeth (using a felt-tipped marker).
2. Each day at the same time, the children check the temperature on an outdoor thermometer and move the zipper up or down to the appropriate position.
3. Older children write up their results; younger children dictate theirs.

What else can we do? **Follow-up:** Children and teacher listen to weather reports on radio or television and compare the results with their own. **Other activities:** Build and install a weather vane; set up a "weather station" in the classroom.

Description Setting up a display to show many ways in which water is used.
Title (for children) "Wonderful Wet Stuff."
Curriculum area Science (air, water, and weather).   **Age range** 7 to 9.

What is our objective? "We can do many things with water by controlling its flow, direction, temperature, and chemical balance and by combining it with other things" (table: 4-D-3).
What will we need? Depending on what kinds of things are included in the display: paper, construction paper, crayons, marking pens, scissors and paste, old magazines, basins, cups, glasses, tubing, rocks, plants, dolls, small plastic figures of people and animals, soap, dried or canned soup, gelatin mix, etc.; display area with tables.
How will we do it?

1. Teacher and children discuss various ways in which water is used and make a list under several headings (e.g., "For growing plants," "For drinking and in recipes," "For energy," "For traveling," and so on).
2. Teacher and children decide which of the uses they've listed can be illustrated in a display—by means of pictures, models, written descriptions, charts, etc.
3. Tables are arranged to form a display area, and a display is set up with the exhibits grouped in the categories listed in step 1. The children can make exhibits out of pictorial materials, or build their own models, or use objects.
4. When the exhibit is complete, another class is invited to view it, and the children take turns explaining the exhibits.

What else can we do? **Other activities:** The children can keep "water diaries" for a week, listing all the ways they use water; children and teacher can discuss and list ways in which water is wasted and how it can be conserved.

Activities for Science: Growing Bodies

Description Identifying and describing unseen objects by touch.
Title (for children) "Sensational'"
Curriculum area Science (growing bodies).   Age range 3 to 5.

What is our objective? "Certain parts of the body have special jobs that help us see, hear, taste, smell, and feel" (table: 5-A-2).
What will we need? Large cardboard box, paper to cover the box, a long sock, various small objects (e.g., pencil, sandpaper, cotton ball, key, toothbrush, golf ball).
How will we do it?
1. The teacher fills a large cardboard box with assorted small objects and covers it with heavy paper, having first made a hole in the paper and attached a long sock.
2. Each child in turn reaches into the box through the sock, feels the objects one by one, and tries to identify and describe each object.
3. Teacher and children discuss how the sense of touch helped them learn about the things in the box.
What else can we do? Other activities: Similar activities can be set up for the other senses. For instance, for smell there can be small bottles filled with liquids to be identified (vinegar, ammonia, peppermint oil, etc.); for hearing, opaque bottles or boxes with one object in each (penny, key, pin, jingle bell) to be identified by shaking the receptacle. "Concentration" is a good game for sight: Present a tray containing eight to ten small objects; remove one object; present the tray again. Can the children identify the missing object?

Description   Creating footprint designs with paint; and using the hands to mix paint.
Title (for children)   "Footprint Art."
Curriculum area   Science (growing bodies).   **Age range**   3 to 5.

What is our objective?   "Our hands, feet, arms, and legs allow us to move" (table: 5-A-3).
What will we need?   Powdered tempera paint, water, basins, large sheets of paper. For cleaning up afterwards: sponges, soapy water, basins, and towels.
How will we do it?
1. The children use their hands to mix powdered paint and water.
2. Teacher and children put the paint into basins, forming a thin layer on the bottom.
3. The children step barefoot into the basins to cover their soles with paint, then step out onto paper and move around slowly to make footprint designs.
4. Children and teacher discuss what kinds of movements of hands and feet were used to make the paint and create the designs, and about what other kinds of things hands and feet—and arms and legs—can do.
What else can we do?   **Variation:** "Handprint" designs.   **Other activities:** Make cardboard puppets with movable arms and legs; do exercises involving hands, feet, arms, and legs. Problem solving is also appropriate ("Show me a way to get across the room without using two feet").

Description   Listening to heartbeats with a stethoscope.
Title (for children)   "Thumping Hearts."
Curriculum area   Science (growing bodies).   **Age range**   4 to 6.

What is our objective?   "The heart beats all the time, but it beats at different rates" (table: 5-B-4).
What will we need?   Each pair of children needs a stethoscope. The teacher needs a clock or watch with a sweep second hand. Either the teacher or the children need paper and pencil for recording.
How will we do it?
1. The children work in pairs, taking turns listening to each other's heartbeat.
2. While the teacher measures a set period of time (e.g., 30 seconds), the children count heartbeats—first while resting and then after running in place.
3. Older children record the results themselves; younger children dictate their results.
4. Teacher and children talk about what happened. Why were the heart rates different?
What else can we do?   **Variations:** Heartbeats can be recorded with a tape recorder and stethoscope; and children can count their own or each other's heartbeats by feeling the pulse.

Description　Making a model of the lungs.
Title (for children)　"Ins and Outs of Air."
Curriculum area　Science (growing bodies).　　　**Age range**　5 to 7.

What is our objective?　"The lungs send air to all parts of the body" (table: 5-C-4).
What will we need?　Bellows, large balloon, pencils and paper.
How will we do it?
1. Each child puts a large balloon over the mouth of a bellows.
2. The child pumps the bellows to force air in and out.
3. Older children record their observations (verbally or with drawings); younger children dictate theirs.
4. Teacher and children discuss how this model is like the lungs.

What else can we do?　**Follow-up:** Working in pairs, the children take turns lying on the floor and breathing deeply. Each child observes the contraction and expansion of his or her partner's chest. Then the children vary their breathing deliberately; finally, they observe their breathing after strenuous exercise. They share their observations and relate them to the model. **Another follow-up activity:** Teacher and children examine and discuss diagrams and pictures of the lungs.

Description　A game involving labeling parts of the abdomen.
Title (for children)　"Digging Digestion."
Curriculum area　Science (growing bodies).　　　**Age range**　7 to 9.

What is our objective?　"The abdomen consists of the stomach and many other parts" (table: 5-D-1).
What will we need?　For each pair of children: medical chart of the abdomen (or one large chart for everyone to use), black construction paper and chalk, white construction paper and pencils, scissors.
How will we do it?
1. The children work in pairs; using the medical chart as a model, they draw life-size pictures of the major parts of the abdomen on black paper (with white chalk), and they make labels (on white construction paper) for the parts.
2. The children cut out the parts and labels.
3. Each pair of children scrambles its parts and labels and plays a game: Who can correctly label all the parts?
4. Teacher and children discuss the parts of the abdomen and what each does.

What else can we do?　**Other activities:** The children can assemble and examine "Visible Man" (a commercial educational toy), or study transparent overlays or x-rays of the abdomen.

Description Identifying tape-recorded sounds.
Title (for children) "Play It Again, Sam."
Curriculum area Science (matter and energy).   **Age range** 3 to 5.

What is our objective? "Sounds are made by people, animals, and moving objects" (table: 6-A-1).
What will we need? Tape recorder, blank tapes, and objects that make sounds (e.g., pencil sharpener, bell, rhythm instruments).
How will we do it?
1. Teacher and children go on a walk and tape some common sounds (e.g., schoolyard noises, traffic, a construction site).
2. Back in the classroom, the children listen to the tape and try to identify each sound: What is making the sound? Where is it happening?
3. The children are divided into teams. With the help of the teacher (to run the tape recorder), each team chooses and records some simple everyday sounds (a laugh, a pencil sharpener being operated, a cough, etc.).
4. Each team's tape is played in turn, and the other teams try to identify the sounds.

What else can we do? Variations: The teacher makes a brief recording of each child's voice and then plays the recordings for the class. Can the children identify each other's voices? Can each child identify his or her own voice? For another variation, use a commercial tape or record of sound effects. How many can the children identify?
Another activity: The children cut out pictures of things (or situations) that are identified with specific sounds (e.g., a bell—ringing; a ball game—cheers) and mount them on tagboard. The teacher holds up the mounted pictures in turn, and the children make or imitate the appropriate sounds.

Description Learning what substances can be picked up by a magnet, and making mobiles to record the results.
Title (for children) "Slim Pickings."
Curriculum area Science (matter and energy).　　　**Age range** 4 to 6.

What is our objective? "We can use magnets to pick up certain things" (table: 6-B-4).
What will we need? Magnets; various small objects (bottle caps, pins, paper clips, erasers, pencils, small toys, toothpicks, corks, pieces of cloth, string, or yarn, etc.); coat hangers; cut lengths of string; labels (MAGNETIC and NOT MAGNETIC).
How will we do it?
1. Teacher and children assemble a variety of small objects and test them with a magnet.
2. As the objects are tested, the children sort them into two piles—"magnetic" and "not magnetic."
3. Each child makes two mobiles, using two coat hangers. Magnetic objects are suspended from one coat hanger with lengths of string, nonmagnetic objects from the other. The child attaches a label to each mobile (MAGNETIC to one, NOT MAGNETIC to the other).
4. The mobiles are hung around the classroom.

What else can we do? Follow-up: The children can subdivide the objects that magnets won't pick up, to see what categories they can identify (glass, wood, plastic, etc.); objects not previously tested can be presented to the children, who predict whether or not they will be magnetic and then test their predictions.

Description Experimenting with the six basic machines.
Title (for children) "Back to Basics."
Curriculum area Science (matter and energy).　　　**Age range** 5 to 7.

What is our objective? "There are six basic kinds of machines; these six make work easier for us" (table: 6-C-7).
What will we need? Objects to illustrate the six machines: balance scales, seesaw, wheelbarrow, nutcracker, shovel, scissors, blocks and boards, wheeled toys (with axles), wedges, nails, knives, screws, screwdrivers, bicycle or tricycle, etc.
How will we do it?
1. Teacher and children discuss the six basic machines—lever, inclined plane, pulley, wedge, screw, and wheel and axle—and group the assembled objects according to which machine each represents. The children experiment with each group in turn.
2. Levers: The children experiment with a nutcracker, can opener, shovel, scissors, etc.
3. Inclined plane: The children use blocks and boards to build an inclined plane and then experiment with toy vehicles.
4. Pulley: The children can experiment with a Tinker Toy pulley or a bicycle.
5. Wedge: The children experiment with nails, knives, and chisels; older children can use wedges to split wood.
6. Screw: The children experiment with screws and screwdrivers in soft wood, or with nuts and bolts, or both.
7. Wheel and axle: The children experiment with wheeled toys, an eggbeater, a doorknob, etc.

What else can we do? Follow-up: The children cut pictures of machines out of magazines and paste them on a large chart in the six basic groups.

Description   Categorizing solid matter: a game.
Title (for children)   "What's the Matter?"
Curriculum area   Science (matter and energy).   **Age range**   7 to 9.

What is our objective?   "Solid matter can be grouped into categories (e.g., wood, metal, plastic), (table: 6-D-1).
What will we need?   Various objects; large, covered cardboard box; blindfold; timer.
How will we do it?
1. Teacher and children decide on several categories of matter (wood, metal, plastic, cloth, glass, etc.).
2. The children divide into teams of five or six members; each team collects objects falling into the categories chosen; and all the collected objects are placed in a large closed box.
3. The children take turns reaching into the box while blindfolded—each child pulls out an object and identifies the category it belongs in. Each time a child makes a correct identification, his or her team gets 1 point.
4. If two or more teams are tied at the end, have a playoff: all the objects are dumped out of the box, and the winning teams see who can categorize them all in the shortest time.

What else can we do?   Follow-up: Subdivide one of the categories (e.g., different kinds of cloth or wood).
Another activity: Play the "adjective game"—clues are given, consisting only of adjectives ("hard," "clear," etc.), and the children guess the material.

Description   Using a compass in a treasure hunt.
Title (for children)   "Way to Go!"
Curriculum area   Science (matter and energy).   **Age range**   7 to 9.

What is our objective?   "We can use magnetic force to act through some materials and determine direction" (table: 6-D-2).
What will we need?   Large tagboard poster of a compass; small compass for each child or group of children; a "treasure" (a popular snack, say); one sheet of directions for each child or group.
How will we do it?
1. Using the large poster, the teacher explains how the compass works.
2. Using their small compasses, the children show that they can find directions.
3. Each child or team gets a direction sheet—each set of directions starts at a different point, and all converge on the "treasure."
4. Using their compasses to follow the directions ("Start at the flagpole. Go 5 paces north. Now hop 6 times west. Etc."), the children search until one team finds the treasure.

What else can we do?   Follow-up: Finding directions can be refined by the use of "northeast," "southwest," etc. A more difficult hunt can be set up, with the direction sheets including these new concepts.

Resources for Science

Bibliography for Teachers

Abruscato, J., & Hassard, J. *The whole cosmos: Catalog of science activities.* Salt Lake City: Goodyear, n.d. (A collection of over 250 activities in the life sciences, the earth sciences, the physical sciences, the aerospace sciences, and speculative fiction. With over forty creative and esthetic activities: poems, stories, anagrams, crossword puzzles, and a one-act play. Includes twenty-three biographies of people in science. It's for kids of all ages!)

Althouse, R., & Main, C. *Science experiences for young children.* New York: Teacher's College, 1975. (Available in a boxed set. Ten booklets on the biological and physical sciences that provide a variety of activities arranged in sequential order. Each concept appears in a number of activities to broaden and reinforce its meaning.)

Carmichael, V. *Science experiences for young children.* Los Angeles: Southern California Association for the Education of Young Children, 1969. (Dealing with a variety of science subjects—e.g., plants, animals, machines, the human body. This book provides book lists, activities, and related crafts ideas.)

Carvajal, J., & Munzer, E. *Conservation education: A selected bibliography.* Danville, Ill.: Interstate, 1971. (A carefully selected, annotated bibliography covering plants, animals, interdependence of living things, earth science, and ecology. Reading levels kindergarten through adult. This volume lists books also on the role of human beings in the environment, books on teaching techniques, and picture books. Cross-referenced index permits matching books to specific purposes.)

Cobb, V. *Science experiments you can eat.* Philadelphia: Lippincott, 1972. (Using the kitchen as a laboratory, this delightful little book provides a series of experiments and explanations for the changes that take place in food processing and preparation.)

Games for the science classroom: An annotated bibliography. Washington, D.C.: National Science Teacher, 1977. (One hundred thirty instructional games and simulations for science teaching organized under the categories of biological science games, physical science games, earth and space science games, and general science games. An excellent introduction that describes the rationale, use, and evaluation of instructional games.)

Harlan, J. *Science experiences for the early childhood years.* Columbus, Ohio: Merrill, 1976. (Suggestions for designing small-group activities for preschool and elementary school children to reveal scientific concepts. Directions for easy experiments are supplemented with reinforcing experiences in math, reading, creative arts.)

Hillcourt, W. *The new field book of nature activities and hobbies.* New York: Putnam, 1970. (close to 1,000 activities designed to foster children's appreciation of nature are included in this valuable resource. Bibliographies, supply sources, and lists of organizations are also provided.)

King, J., & Schippers, J. *Preschool science activities.* Stockton, Calif.: Jerry D. King and John V. Schippers, c/o University of the Pacific, 1972. (An attempt to fill the void in published, meaningful experiences for very young children. This book is provided as a guide to assist the teacher in including a variety of activities and experiments dealing with such topics as air, water, rocks, tools, and sound.)

Nickelsburg, J. *Nature program for early childhood.* Reading, Mass.: Addison-Wesley, 1976. (This attractive book takes about thirty subjects in nature and suggests over a hundred activities young children can do to explore and understand their natural world. The subjects fall under the following headings: outdoor group projects, projects with small animals, indoor projects, watching things, looking for things in the ground, projects with plants. It is a rather straightforward, helpful collection of inductive learning activities with animals and plants.)

Schmidt, V., & Rockcastle, V. *Teaching science with everyday things.* New York: McGraw-Hill, 1968. (Directed at the teacher with no previous background in science, and emphasizing activities that do not require special or costly equipment. This small book includes both subject-matter and teaching suggestions. Coverage includes such areas as air and weather, sun, moon, and stars, powders and solutions, forces and motions.)

Skelsey, A., & Huckaby, G. *Growing up green.* New York: Workman, 1973. (Source of information about plants and gardening. Suggests appropriate activities for early childhood.)

Stone, A., Geis, F. & Kuslan, L. *Experiences for teaching children science.* Belmont, Calif: 1971. (A major contribution of this book is the chapters on tools for teaching science. Provides ideas and instructions for activities, experiences, and games for children. Discusses books, audiovisual materials, and criteria for evaluating their quality.)

Journals and periodicals:

American Biology Teacher. (National Association of Biology Teachers, 11250 Roger Bacon Dr., Reston, Va. 22090.)

American Journal of Physics. (American Association of Physics Teachers, 57 E. 55 St., New York, N.Y. 10022.)

Journal of Chemical Education. (Division of Chemical Education, American Chemical Society, College of Wooster, Wooster, Ohio 44691.)

Nature and Science. (Natural History Press, Garden City, N.Y. 11530.)

Physics Today. (American Institute of Physics, 57 E. 55 St., New York, N.Y. 10022.)

Science. (American Association for the Advancement of Science, 1515 Massachusetts Ave., NW, Washington, D.C. 20005.)

Science and Children. (National Science Teachers Assn., 1202 16th St., NW, Washington, D.C. 20036.)

Science Newsletter. (Science Service, Inc., 1719 N St., NW, Washington, D.C. 20036.)

Science Teacher. (National Science Teachers Assn., 1201 16th St., NW, Washington, D.C. 20036.)

Science World. (Scholastic Magazines, Inc., 904 Sylvan Ave., Englewood Cliffs, N.J. 07632.)

Bibliography for Children

Where to find books for children:

Libraries (school, college, public).
Bookstores.
Hobby shops.
Science magazines (reviews, listings, advertisements).
Bibliographies in adult science books.
Science catalogs.
Other teachers.
Garage sales. (As usual, a potentially abundant source.)

Bibliographies of elementary science books for children:

American Association for the Advancement of Science. *The science book list for children*. (1515 Massachusetts Ave., Washington, D.C. 20005.)

Board of Education of the City of New York, Bureau of Curriculum Research. *A selected bibliography in Elementary Science*. (Curriculum Center, 130 W. 55th St., 10019.)

Busch, P. *The urban environment*. Chicago: Ferguson, 1975. (An excellent bibliography of books for children and adults, as well as films and multimedia kits.)

Mallinson, G. C., & Mallinson, L. M. *A bibliography of reference books for elementary science*. Washington, D.C.: National Science Teachers Assn. (1201 16th St., NW, 20036.)

U.S. Office of Education. *Science books for boys and girls: A bibliography*. Washington, D.C.

For evaluations of children's science books:

Science books: A quarterly review. (J. Deason, Ed. Association for the Advancement of Science, 1515 Massachusetts Ave., Washington, D.C., 20005.)

Children's science series from various publishers:

Basic science education series. New York: Harper and Row. (Primary level.)
Encyclopaedia Britannica *True-to-life* books. Chicago: Encyclopaedia Britannica, Inc.
Gans, R., & Branley, F. M. (Eds.). *Let's-read-and-find-out* science books. New York: Crowell.
Golden library of knowledge series. New York: Golden Press.
Golden nature guide series. New York: Simon and Schuster.
How and why wonder books. New York: Grosset and Dunlap.
Learn about series. Racine, Wis.: Whitman.
Lowery, L. F., & Moore, E. *I wonder why readers*. New York: Holt.
My easy-to-read true book series. New York: Grosset and Dunlap.
Question and answer series. New York: Golden Press.
True book series. Chicago: Children's Press.
Webster beginner science series. New York: McGraw-Hill.

Science and nature magazines:

Curious Naturalist. (Audubon Society, Lincoln, Mass. 01773.)
International Wildlife. (National Wildlife Federation, Washington, D.C.)
National Geographic. (National Geographic Society, Washington, D.C.)

National Wildlife. (National Wildlife Federation, Washington, D.C.)
Ranger Rick. (National Wildlife Federation, Washington, D.C.)

Books children can use:

Brandwein, P. F., & Cooper, E. K. *Concepts in science.* New York: Harcourt, Brace and World, 1967. (Illustrated text; vocabulary at end of book; many science areas covered.)

Case, M. T. *Look what I found: The young conservationist's guide to the care and feeding of small wildlife.* Riverside, Conn.: Chatham Press, 1971.

Goldstein-Jackson, K., et al. *Experiments with everyday objects.* Englewood Cliffs, N.J.: Prentice-Hall, 1978. (Over seventy easy experiments for kids. Fun.)

Mallinson, G. G., et al. *Science 1.* Morristown, N.J.: Silver Burdett, 1965.

Piltz, A., et al. *Discovering science: A readiness book.* Columbus, Ohio: Merrill. (Large pictures; few words.)

Learning Materials

Suggested Basic Materials

First, some laboratory instruments and apparatus:

Magnifiers and microscopes.
Scales.
Measuring sets. (Spoon and cup types.)
Magnets.
Weather instruments. (Thermometer, barometer, rain gauge, weather vane.)
Batteries and bulbs.
Stethoscope.

Models and specimens:

Anatomical models (for instance, skeletons).
Dinosaur models.
Rocks.
Sand.
Fossils.
Bones.

For the life sciences:

Gardening tools.
Seeds.
Water.
Live plants.
Terrariums.
Animals.
Cages.
Aquariums.
Butterfly nets.

For reference:

Maps and globes.

For ideas:

Catalogs, science and general. (Look for packaged kits, sets of materials grouped together with a theme.)

Fleming, B., Hamilton, D., & Hicks, J. *Resources for creative teaching in early childhood education.* New York: Harcourt Brace Jovanovich, 1972. (Lists suggested science materials and how to store them.)

Harlan, J. D. *Science experiences for the early childhood years.* Columbus, Ohio: Merrill, 1976. (An appendix of salvage sources, consumable materials, and things to borrow.)

Sources and Suppliers

To evaluate free or inexpensive materials, ask:

Do they contain an objectionable amount of advertising, sales promotion, or propaganda?
Is the information accurate and free of distortion?
Is the material available in quantities for your group?
Is the material suitable for the age level?

General types of sources:

State agencies.
Discarded textbooks.
Objects, including discards, you find around the house.
Publications and materials from universities.
General supply catalogs.

Some publications:

Beruschlein, M., & Saunders, J. *Free and inexpensive teaching materials for science education. Chicago Schools Journal Supplement,* 1953, *34,* (5, 6). (Available as reprint from Chicago Teachers College.)

Educator's guide to free science materials. (Educator's Progress Service, Randolph, Wis. 53956.)

Environmental and outdoor education materials catalog. (Environmental and Education Materials Co., Box 585, Lander, Wyo, 82520.)

Phillips, B. *Index to free teaching aids.* Harrisburg, Ill. Free Teaching Aids Co. (62946.)

Write to:

American Assn. for Health, Physical Education, and Recreation, 1202 16th St., NW, Washington, D.C. 20036.
American Fisheries Society, 1040 Washington Bldg., Washington, D.C. 20005.
American Forest Products Industries, Inc., 1835 K St., NW, Washington, D.C. 20006.
American Forestry Assn., 919 17th St., NW, Washington, D.C. 20006.
Animal Welfare Institute, P.O. Box 3492, Grand Central Sta., New York, N.Y. 10017.
Arizona Game and Fish Dept., 1688 W. Adams St., Phoenix, Ariz. 85007.
California Department of Conservation Education, 1516 9th Street, Sacramento, Calif. 95815.
Carolina Biological Supply Co., Gladstone, Ore. 97027, or Burlington, N.C. 27215.
Cenco, 2600 S. Kostner Ave., Chicago, Ill. 60623.
Conservation Foundation, 1250 Connecticut Ave., NW, Washington, D.C. 20036.
Edmund Scientific Co., Barrington, N.J. 08007.

Environmental Defense Fund, P.O. Drawer 740, Stony Brook, N.Y. 11790.

Friends of the Earth, 30 East 42d St., New York, N.Y. 10017.

Georgia Game and Fish Commission, Education and Information Div., 401 State Capital Bldg., Atlanta, Ga. 30334.

Lab-Aids, Inc., Cold Spring Harbor, N.Y. 11100.

La Pine Scientific Co., 6001 S. Knox Ave., Chicago, Ill. 60629.

MacAlaster Scientific Co., 60 Arsenal St., Watertown, Mass. 02172.

National Audubon Society, 950 Third Ave., New York, N.Y. 10022.

National Geographic Society, 17th and M Sts., NW, Washington, D.C. 20036.

National Parks Assn., Washington, D.C. 20005.

National Wildlife Federation, 1412 16th St., NW, Washington, D.C. 20036.

Division of Surveys and Field Services, Peabody College, Nashville, Tenn. 37203.

Sargeant, E. H., and Co., 4647 W. Foster Ave., Chicago, Ill. 60630.

Science Kit, Inc., 2299 Military Rd., Tonawanda, N.Y. 14140.

Selective Educational Equipment (SEE), Inc., 3 Bridge St., Newton, Mass. 02195.

Sierra Club, 1050 Mills Tower, San Francisco, Calif. 94104.

Stansi Scientific Co., 1231 N. Honore St., Chicago, Ill. 60622.

Tuberculosis and Respiratory Disease Assn., National Headquarters, 1740 Broadway, New York, N.Y. 10019.

Turtox/Cambosco, 8200 S. Hoyne Ave., Chicago, Ill., or 342 Western Ave., Boston, Mass. 02135.

U.S. Army, Washington, D.C. 20250. (For certain training materials only.)

U.S. Bureau of Mines, Washington, D.C. 20250.

U.S. Chamber of Commerce, National Resources Dept., 161 H St., NW, Washington, D.C. 20036.

U.S. Department of Agriculture, Washington, D.C. 20250.

U.S. Environmental Protection Agency, Consumer Information Center, Pueblo, Colo.

U.S. Fish and Wildlife Service, Washington, D.C. 20250.

U.S. Forest Service, Washington, D.C. 20250.

U.S. Geological Survey, Washington, D.C. 20250.

U.S. Indian Service, Washington, D.C. 20250.

U.S. Navy, Washington, D.C. 20250. (For certain training materials only.)

U.S. Naval Observatory, Washington, D.C. 20250.

U.S. Office of Education, Washington, D.C. 20250.

U.S. Soil Conservation Service, Washington, D.C. 20250.

U.S. Weather Bureau, Washington, D.C. 20250.

Ward's, P.O. Box 1712, Rochester, New York 14603, or P.O. Box 1749, Monterey, Calif. 93940.

Welch Scientific Co., 7300 North Linder Avenue, Skokie, Ill. 60076.

Wilderness Society, 729 Fifteenth Street, NW, Washington, D.C. 20005.

Enrichment Materials

Types of materials:

Audiovisual aids. (Maps, charts, posters, displays, film loops, filmstrips, slides, records, tapes, discarded texts, kits.)

Observation accessories. (Ant farm, bird feeder, beehive, magnifier, butterfly garden, bug keeper, egg incubator, anatomical models.)

Kits and projects.

Kits and projects, listed by manufacturer or publisher:

AAAS Commission on Science Education. (1515 Massachusetts Ave., NW, Washington, D.C. 20005. Spiraling, flexible curriculum using a laboratory approach. A varied curriculum. Kits and objectives for each unit.)

Education Development Center. *Elementary school science project (ESS).* (55 Chapel St., Newton, Mass. 02160. Process-oriented and loosely Piagetian. No set curriculum, but a wide variety of topics and a fully stocked kit. Excellent newsletter.)

Howard University. *Elementary science project (ESP).* (Washington, D.C. Kits for the culturally different.)

McGraw-Hill. *Elementary science study units.* (Manchester, Mo. 63011. Grades 1 through 6. Many units to choose from. For the teacher who is not an authority on science.)

New York University. *Conceptually oriented program in elementary science (COPES).* (4 Washington Pl., Rm. 261, New York, N.Y. 10003. An experience approach, highly structured. Uses materials collected by the teacher rather than kits. Activities prepare children for later concepts. K through 2.)

University of California. *School curriculum improvement study (SCIS).* (Lawrence Hall of Science, Berkeley, Calif. 94720. A laboratory problem-solving approach with an emphasis on process rather than content. K through 6.)

Send for catalogs from these vendors of scientific audiovisual materials:

Cenco Educational Films, 1700 Irving Pk. Rd., Chicago, Ill. 60613.

Encyclopaedia Britannica Films, Inc., Filmstrip Div., 1150 Wilmette Ave., Wilmette, Ill. 60091.

Jim Handy Organization, 2821 E. Grand Blvd., Detroit, Mich. 48211.

Society for Visual Education, Inc., 1345 Diversey Pkwy., Chicago, Ill. 60614.

Walt Disney Productions, 477 Madison Ave., New York, N.Y. 10022.

Mapmakers:

Geo. F. Cram Co., Inc., 730 E. Washington St., Indianapolis, Ind. 46202.

Rand McNally and Co., P.O. Box 7600, Chicago, Ill. 60680.

Publications, including indexes and ideas for trips and projects:

Abruscato, J., & Hassard, J. *Loving and beyond: Science teaching for the humanistic classroom.* Santa Monica, Calif.: Goodyear, 1976. (Includes an excellent list of curriculums, fully annotated.)

Bathurst, E. G. & Hill, W. *Conservation experiences for children.* U.S. Dept. of Health, Education, and Welfare (later U.S. Department of Education) Bulletin No. 16. Washington, D.C.: U.S. Government Printing Office. (N. Capitol St., NW, 20402.)

Busch, P. S. *People and their environment: The urban environment.* Chicago: Ferguson, 1973. (6 N. Michigan Ave., 60602. Stresses the interdependence of living things. Each lesson includes an outdoor *urban* activity. Grades K through 3.)

Busch, P. S. *The urban environment.* Chicago: Ferguson, 1975. Bibliography includes a list of multimedia kits and study guides.)

Conservation Education Assn. *Conservation quickies.* Danville, Ill.: Interstate. (19 N. Jackson St., 61832.)

Conservation Education Assn. *Critical index of films* (H. Williams, Ed.). Danville, Ill.: Interstate, 1971.

Educator's guide to free filmstrips. (Educator's Progress Service, Randolph, Wis. 53956.)

Itse, E. (Ed.). *Hey bug! and other poems about little things.* New York: American Heritage, 1972. (One of many enrichment books about science.)

Ring, R. M., et al. *Outdoor activities in conservation study.* Springfield, Ill.: Office of the Superintendent of Public Instruction.

Russell, H. R. *Ten-minute field trips: Using the school grounds for environmental studies.* Chicago: Ferguson, 1973. (Practical and comprehensive nature-study approach for elementry grades.)

Ward's Natural Science Establishment. *How to lead a field trip.* Rochester, N.Y.: Ward's Natural Science Establishment.

Other organizations providing enrichment materials:

American Nature Study Society, John Gustafson, R.D. 1, Homer, N.Y. 13077. (Suggestions for forty different science topics.)

Be Kind to Animals Club, American Humane Education Society, 350 S. Huntington Ave., Boston, Mass. 02130. (Membership card, badge, newsletter, and more.)

Cornell University, Laboratory of Ornithology, Ithaca, N.Y. 14850. (Recordings of nature sounds.)

Educational Design Assocs., Box 712, Waldorf, Md. 20601. (Wildlife photo puzzles with a short narrative on each.)

Educational Modules, Inc., 266 Lyell Ave., Rochester, N.Y. 14608. (In one module, on noise pollution, a tape simulates hearing loss.)

Nasco, 901 Janesville Ave., Fort Atkinson, Wis. 53538. (Issues catalog of enrichment materials, such as the observation beehive.)

National Audubon Society, 950 Third Ave., New York, N.Y. 10022. (Books, charts, bulletins, and even a camp in Connecticut.)

Community Resources

For salvage materials:

Shoe stores (for boxes).
Ice cream parlors (for storage containers).
Photography studios (canisters, empty film spools, chemical bottles).
Telephone company (colored wire).
Electric and automotive repair shops (old magnets and motor parts).
Pharmacy or medical lab (eyedroppers, old vials, bottles).
Nurseries, plant stores, arboretums (seeds, plants, planters, old pots).
Chemical laboratories.
Factories and machine shops.
Persons trimming trees (for specimens).

For field trips, speakers, or information:

Government conservation sites.
Dams or reclamation projects.
The telephone company.
Museums of natural history.
Museums of science or industry.
Hatcheries.
Nurseries.
Taxidermists.
Game wardens.
Forest rangers.
Pollution control officers.
Sierra Club, or a local conservation group.
Botanical gardens.
Zoos.

Planetariums.
Local parks department.
Fire department.
Utility companies.
Doctors and dentists.
Sailors and navigators.
Scientists.
Geologists or rock hounds.
Weather forecasters.
Aquariums.
Hospital x-ray rooms.
Various outdoor sites (arboretums, parks, forests, farms, lakes, ponds, tide pools).

Objectives and Activities for Older Children: Mathematics

Introduction: Definitions and Objectives

In approaching mathematics, we have found it useful to draw an analogy with reading. In learning to read, children go through three stages: (1) "pre-reading," in which language is oral but children do form the idea that it can be symbolized in writing; (2) "connecting," in which children develop the tools for decoding symbols; (3) "symbolic," in which children actually become adept at decoding.

The same three stages exist in mathematics: (1) the premathematics stage, (2) the connecting stage, and (3) the symbolic stage. We like to call stage 1 "ready," stage 2 "set," and stage 3 "go." In this section, we provide objectives and activities for each of the three stages. Let us explain the stages further by use of examples.

Stage 1: "Ready." A boy in a *four*-member family sets the table with only *three* plates. When the family is seated the boy is asked, "Does everyone have a plate?" If the boy can solve the problem, he will probably use the principal of one-to-one correspondence; he does not need numbers or equations.

Stage 2: "Set." This stage is subdivided into (a) learning the language of mathematics and (b) the introduction of mathematical symbols. Let's return to the example we just used. Suppose that, to reinforce the idea of one-to-one correspondence, we asked the boy, "Draw us a picture of yourself, Mother, Dad, and Sis. Now draw a circle for each plate you put out," and then had the child match circles and figures. If we then labeled the circles "3" and the figures "4," we would be introducing mathematical language—subdivision a. If we asked the child, "How many more plates do we need to make four?" we would be presenting a simple equation, which we might then write for the child as:

$$0\ 0\ 0\ +\ \square\ =\ 0\ 0\ 0\ 0$$
$$3\ +\ \square\ =\ 4$$

or "Three plates plus how many plates equals four plates?" In so doing, we are introducing mathematical symbols—subdivision b.

Stage 3: "Go." At this stage the child can record mathematical experiences using abstract symbols and thus handle more complex operations.

Consider once more the example of the dinner plates. At this stage, we could give the child the following equation to solve:

$$3 + \square = 4$$

Or:

$$4 - 3 = \square$$

In setting objectives for mathematics, we identify nine major concepts or curriculum areas; (1) patterning; (2) comparing and ordering; (3) story problems; (4) geometry; (5) measurement; (6) numeral literacy; (7) mathematical tools and recording; (8) arithmetic processes; (9) fractions. These warrant attention from preschool through the primary grades; but we do not mean to suggest that they are exhaustive—teachers may certainly add to them or modify them. In the following list, we define and explain the nature of each of these areas by means of generalizations: the teacher will of course recognize these at once; the children will arrive at them only gradually.

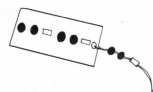

1. **Patterning.** A "pattern" is a design that recurs in a predictable way. Many things in the world have a pattern; once we understand the pattern, we can extrapolate it. In patterning, we use (a) objects, (b) pictorial representations of objects, and (c) numerical abstractions.

2. **Comparing and ordering.** "Comparing" is noting similarities and differences. We can compare such things as shape, number, time, volume, and length. "Ordering" is arranging in sequence. In comparing and ordering, we do several kinds of things:

   a. **Classifying.** "Classifying" is sorting according to attributes. Things in the world can be classified by properties which they have in common.

   b. **One-to-one correspondence.** "One-to-one correspondence" involves matching items in one group with items in another. By using one-to-one correspondence, we can learn whether two or more groups have the same number of items or different numbers of items.

   c. **Seriating.** "Seriating" means arranging in order. When we compare things, we can seriate them to indicate, e.g., increasing or decreasing values of some attribute; we can also indicate time sequences.

   d. **Conserving.** "Conservation" denotes "invariance." When we compare different states of the same thing, we realize that certain attributes remain the same despite changes in appearance—unless something has been added or taken away.

3. **Story problems.** "Story problems" are practical situations in which something is to be solved. In solving such problems, we apply mathematical principles and skills in three ways:

   a. **Intuition.** "Intuitive" operations involve perceptual clues and reasoning. Some simple problems can be solved by intuition before any specific instruction in mathematical skills has been received.

   b. **Estimation.** "Estimation" is the formation of an approximate judgment. In many problems, exact calculation is not necessary: an estimation can be made on the basis of, e.g., perceptual clues. Estimation is also useful as a first step in mathematical calculation and as a check on the reasonableness of a solution.

   c. **Formal mathematical operations.** Problems may have to be solved by means of written mathematical calculations.

4. **Geometry.** "Geometry" is a branch of mathematics that deals with the properties of space. It allows us to understand the world by identifying and classifying shapes, creating models, and solving spatial problems. In

geometry, we (a) identify; (b) compare; (c) construct; (d) define; (e) state relationships.

5. **Measurement.** "Measurement" is the process of ascertaining extent, quantity, etc.—usually by comparison with a standard. Measurement enables us to assign a quantifiable value to a property. By means of measurement, we (a) judge size, weight, and volume; (b) use money; (c) tell time; (d) determine temperature; (e) interpret calendars.

6. **Numeral literacy.** We define "numeral literacy" as the ability to say, read, and write numerals and understand their value. It is a prerequisite for communication about and performance of mathematical operations. Numeral literacy involves operating knowledge of several things:

   a. **Cardinal numbers.** A "cardinal" number is a universal term to express quality, degree, or position ("which one").

   b. **Ordinal numbers.** An "ordinal" number is a universal term to exposition ("which one").

   c. **Counting.** "Counting" is enumerating the units of a total. Counting allows us to name and eventually to order cardinal and ordinal numbers.

   d. **Number sense.** "Number sense" is assignment of a number to a group of elements. It allows us to use an abstract term to describe quantity.

   e. **Number-numeral association.** "Number-numeral association" is matching numerals and "number words" (spelled-out numbers) with the corresponding amount.

   f. **Place value.** "Place value" is a positional system of numeration. It defines the value of each digit in a number.

7. **Mathematical tools and recording.** "Mathematical tools and recording" involve symbols, vocabulary, tallying, and graphing. We need such tools and processes to perform, record, and communicate about mathematical operations.

   a. **Mathematical symbols and vocabulary.** The symbols and vocabulary of mathematics include signs (e.g., +, −, =) and words (e.g., "how much," "what part," "sum," "difference") indicating mathematical operations and results. We use them in performing formal mathematical operations.

   b. **Tallying.** In "tallying," we represent each item with a mark and group the marks in sets of 5. Tallying is a form of graphing.

   c. **Graphing.** "Graphing" is recording data in pictorial form so as to show trends or relationships. It is used to present information in a form that can be easily read and interpreted.

8. **Arithmetic operations.** The operations of arithmetic are addition, subtraction, multiplication, and division. These operations are ways of identifying, combining, and separating numbers; they are basic to mathematical computation.

   a. **Addition.** "Addition" is the uniting of disjoint sets or counting to a total to determine, e.g., "how many," "how much," "how long."

   b. **Subtraction.** "Subtraction" is the undoing of addition, or counting backwards.

   c. **Multiplication.** "Multiplication" is the repeated addition of groups which are equal in size.

   d. **Division.** "Division" is the undoing of multiplication, or the repeated subtraction of groups which are equal in size.

9. **Fractions.** A "fraction" is a part of a whole. Fractions can be combined or separated through mathematical operations. In dealing with fractions, we (a) use symbols and (b) perform informal and formal mathematical operations.

We believe that many and varied objectives and activities are needed to develop and reinforce these ideas. In the following table of objectives, we list the skills necessary for each generalization. As before, the curriculum areas—in this case, the nine major areas we have just listed—form the horizontal axis, and age levels form the vertical axis, so that the objectives are classified by area and level.

Following the table of objectives are sample activities, grouped by curriculum area. Once again, each activity is aimed at a specific objective, and the key ("area, level, objective") will enable you to find the objective on the table ("1-A-1" means "area 1, level A, objective 1"). We invite you to try the sample activities, modify them as necessary, and develop other activities of your own. It is our hope that you will collect a file of activities which will enable children to arrive at the generalizations we have noted, and others which you consider appropriate.

Finally, we would like to urge you to pay particular attention to the environment you create in your classroom. We recommend that you stress problem solving rather than memorization; and that you use concrete materials and "hands-on" activities that will allow the children to direct and correct themselves.

Turn the page for the table of objectives. . . .

	(1) PATTERNING	(2) COMPARING AND ORDERING	(3) STORY PROBLEMS	(4) GEOMETRY
	CURRICULUM AREAS			
LEVEL A (AGES 3 TO 5)	1. Create and copy patterns, using concrete objects. (R)*	1. Compare concrete objects to determine relative quantity, size, area, weight, and length. (R) 2. Match concrete objects one to one. (R) 3. Arrange concrete objects in sequence. (R) 4. Classify concrete objects on the basis of one common attribute. (R)	1. Determine whether simple mathematical statements are possible or impossible.* 2. Use concrete materials to solve simple problems (based on real-life situations) perceptually or intuitively. (R)	1. Identify, compare, and classify geometric shapes, using concrete objects. (R)*
LEVEL B (AGES 4 TO 6)	1. Copy a picture of a pattern, using concrete objects. (R) 2. Recognize, copy, and extend pictures of patterns. (R)	1. Compare objects, pictures or symbols to determine relative quantity, size, weight, and length. (R) 2. Match concrete objects and pictures or symbols, one to one. (R) 3. Arrange pictures or symbols in increasing order, decreasing order, and time sequence. (R)* 4. Classify pictures of objects by one common attribute; or classify concrete objects by more than one attribute. (R)	1. Use informal mathematical calculations to solve simple problems (based on real-life situations) intuitively. (R) 2. Make up simple problems. (R) 3. Estimate outcomes perceptually or intuitively. (S)*	1. Identify, compare and classify pictures of geometric shapes. (R)* 2. Identify, compare, and classify two-dimensional geometric shapes. (R) 3. Identify and compare lines, line segments, open curves, and closed curves. (R)

Key: R = "ready"; S = "set"; G = "go."

*Asterisk signifies that an activity has been provided for this objective.

	CURRICULUM AREAS				
	(5) MEASUREMENT	**(6) NUMERAL LITERACY**	**(7) MATHEMATICAL TOOLS AND RECORDING**	**(8) ARITHMETIC OPERATIONS**	**(9) FRACTIONS**
LEVEL A (AGES 3 TO 5)	1. Compare and classify objects as to size, weight, etc. (R)*	1. Recite the numbers one to ten. (R) 2. Use concrete objects to identify appropriate quantities for one to five items. (R)	1. Understand and use simple comparative mathematical vocabulary (e.g., "big, bigger"; "same as, more, less"). (R)*	1. Order quantities so that each has just one more or one less than the one before it. (R)	1. Recognize parts of a whole, using concrete objects. (R)*
LEVEL B (AGES 4 TO 6)	1. Use informal standard units for measuring objects. (S)*	1. Recite and recognize ordinal numbers one to six. (S) 2. Count from one to twenty; count from ten to one backwards. (S) 3. Use concrete objects to identify appropriate quantities for one to ten items. (S)* 4. Recognize cardinal numerals and their sequence. (S) 5. Match cardinal number sets. (S)	1. Record quantities by tallying. (S)* 2. Make "graphs," using concrete objects to record two variables. (S)	1. Using concrete objects, demonstrate the concept of addition as a process of joining sets or counting to a total. (S)* 2. Using concrete objects, demonstrate the concept of subtraction as undoing of addition or as counting backwards. (S)	1. Using pictures and diagrams, recognize parts of a whole. (S)* 2. Use fractional terms (e.g., "one half," "one quarter," "whole," "part"). (S)

(Continued)

	CURRICULUM AREAS			
	(1) PATTERNING	**(2) COMPARING AND ORDERING**	**(3) STORY PROBLEMS**	**(4) GEOMETRY**
LEVEL C (AGES 5 TO 7)	1. Reverse a pattern. (S)* 2. Recognize a number pattern based on the principle "one more." (S)	1. Compare and match sets of numbers. (S) 2. Compare and match numerals. (S) 3. Arrange sets of numbers in order of values. (S) 4. Identify numerals before, after, and between given numerals. (S) 5. Classify objects and pictures on the basis of two common attributes. (S) 6. Compare times or distances. (S) 7. Explain that simply rearranging does not change value or amount. (S)*	1. Give examples of cause and effect. (S) 2. Estimate answers to simple mathematical problems. (S) 3. Make "number sentences" from oral story problems. (S)* 4. Using formal mathematical calculations, solve one-step story problems. (S)	1. Construct geometric shapes or models. (R)* 2. Identify lines of symmetry. (R)
LEVEL D (AGES 7 TO 9)	1. Extend complex number patterns. (G)*	1. Classify objects by more than two common attributes. (S) 2. Compare and match sets of numeral combinations. (S) 3. Compare cost or volume. (S)* 4. Arrange numerals in a sequence from a given point in increasing or decreasing order. (S)	1. Identify steps in solving story problems. (S)* 2. Solve two-step story problems. (G) 3. Evaluate answers for reasonableness. (G)	1. Identify, define, and state relationships between points, lines, angles, curves, etc. (S)

Key: R = "ready"; S = "set"; G = "go."

*Asterisk signifies that an activity has been provided for this objective.

	CURRICULUM AREAS				
	(5) MEASUREMENT	(6) NUMERAL LITERACY	(7) MATHEMATICAL TOOLS AND RECORDING	(8) ARITHMETIC OPERATIONS	(9) FRACTIONS
LEVEL C (AGES 5 TO 7)	1. Use formal standard units for measuring objects. (G) 2. Know and exchange monetary units. (G) 3. Tell time to the hour and half hour. (G)* 4. Using actual measurements, estimate, measure, and compare. (G)	1. Recite and recognize ordinal numbers zero to 100. (S) 2. Count, read, and write cardinal numbers (numerals) zero to 100. (S) 3. Count to 100 by tens. (S)* 4. Read spelled numbers and match with numerals and number sets. (S) 5. Demonstrate and explain place value systems for ones and tens. (S)	1. Use the symbols $<$, $>$, =, +, and − and appropriate vocabulary to compare sets of numbers. (S) 2. Read and solve simple equations involving +, −, and =. (S) 3. Read and make a variety of simple graphs, showing two variables. (S)*	1. Know additions through a sum of 18. (G)* 2. Subtract simple-digit numbers from minuends through 18. (G)* 3. Perform one-digit column addition. (G) 4. Add two-digit numbers without regrouping. (G)	1. Using fractions, do mathematical calculations. (S) 2. Use fractional symbols (1/4, 1/3, 1/2). (S)*
LEVEL D (AGES 7 TO 9)	1. Identify relationships between different units of measurement. (G) 2. Make change. (G) 3. Tell time. 4. Determine length, weight, and quantity with standard units. (G) 5. Read thermometers. (G) 6. Interpret and use calendars. (G)	1. Convert cardinal numbers to ordinals. (S) 2. Count, read, and write cardinal numbers 0 to 1,000. (S)* 3. Count by groups (e.g., twos, fives) to 100. (S) 4. Read and write roman numerals 1 to 10, 50, and 100. (S) 5. Demonstrate and explain place value systems of hundreds and beyond. (S)	1. Construct graphs with more than two variables. (S) 2. Understand and use the vocabulary of the arithmetic processes ("addend," "subtrahend," etc.). (S) 3. Plot and interpret points on a graph. (S) 4. Identify and use the symbols and vocabulary of multiplication (X) and division (÷). (S) 5. Identify symbols and vocabulary for fractions. (S) 6. Identify and use symbols and vocabulary for money and measurement. (S)	1. Add two- and three-digit numbers without regrouping. (G) 2. Subtract two- and three-digit numbers without regrouping. (G) 3. Know multiplications through a product of 81. (G)* 4. Multiply any number by a one-digit number. (G) 5. Multiply any number by 10 or 100. (G) 6. Divide single-digit numbers into dividends through 81 with no remainder. (G) 7. Divide a two-digit by a one-digit number. (G)	1. Identify numbers of equal parts in a whole. (S) 2. Read and write fractions. (S)

Activities for Mathematics: Patterning

Description Making and copying patterns with colored straws.
Title (for children) "Pattern Play."
Curriculum area Mathematics (patterning).   Age range 3 to 5.

What is our objective? To create and copy patterns, using concrete objects (table: 1-A-1).
What will we need? Colored straws. (Optional: poster paper, glue.)
How will we do it?
1. The teacher sets out colored straws in a repeating pattern. (These can simply be placed in front of each participating child; or, if a group is participating, they can be glued on a piece of poster paper which is hung or propped up where the children can all see it.)
2. The children use their straws to copy the pattern, matching both color and position of the straws.
3. Next, each child creates his or her own pattern and then recreates it exactly.
What else can we do? Variations: This activity can be done with the children working in pairs: one child lays out a pattern and his or her partner reproduces it; then the children reverse roles. Another variation is to use objects other than straws—colored blocks, large wooden beads, or buttons, for example. Follow-up: Use a combination of objects to make the pattern to be copied (e.g., red bead, two blue straws, yellow block . . .); the children match object, color, and position.

Description Team game involving pattern reversal.
Title (for children) "Reverse-a-Thon."
Curriculum area Mathematics (patterning).   **Age range** 5 to 7.

What is our objective? To reverse a pattern (table: 1-C-1).
What will we need? Large pieces of tagboard (about 12 by 18 inches) with a geometric shape drawn on each.
How will we do it?
1. The children form two teams of four to six players each.
2. The children on team 1 stand in a row facing the class, each child holding a poster so that the row "reads," say, "triangle, circle, square . . . etc."
3. Using another set of posters, the children on team 2 arrange themselves to match the pattern created by team 1. (The class can judge whether the match is exact.)
4. On a signal, the children on team 2 rearrange themselves so that the pattern is reversed.
5. A point is scored for each correct match and each correct reversal. Then the teams exchange roles; and after that new teams are formed.

What else can we do? Variations: Instead of geometric shapes, numbers can be written on the posters. Or the teacher can write a numeral pattern on the chalkboard which the children are to duplicate and then reverse. For another variation, the teacher can write words or phrases backwards on the chalkboard; the children reverse them to discover their meaning.

Description A game involving placing numbered cards in sequences.
Title (for children) "Far-Out Fill-In."
Curriculum area Mathematics (patterning).   **Age range** 7 to 9.

What is our objective? To extend complex number patterns (table: 1-D-1).
What will we need? Index cards (3- by 5-inch), 26 for the teacher and 26 for each child; red felt-tipped pen for the teacher and blue felt-tipped pens for the children; a pocket chart.
How will we do it?
1. The teacher numbers one set of index cards from 0 to 25; each child numbers his or her set the same way (the teacher uses red; the children use blue).
2. The teacher places, say, four or five cards in the pocket chart so as to form a sequence in which one or two numbers are missing. (For example, a simple sequence would be: 3, 6, _, 12, _, 18.)
3. The first child uses his or her cards to fill in the empty pockets, and then explains the principle of the sequence and shows how to extend it.
4. The teacher sets up a new sequence for the second child, and so on.

What else can we do? Follow-up: A "pattern of the day" can be written on the chalkboard by the teacher; the children try to solve it at odd moments and during their free time.

child fills in with: 6 10
and extends with   14

Activities for Mathematics: Comparing

Description Arranging picture cards to show a sequence of steps.
Title (for children) "What's Your Order, Please?"
Curriculum area Mathematics (comparing and ordering).   Age range 4 to 6.

What is our objective? To arrange pictures or symbols in increasing order, decreasing order, and time sequence (table: 2-B-3).
What will we need? Sets of cards with pictures that show sequences (each set should consist of four or five pictures; if the cards are numbered or marked with tally marks on the reverse side, the children can check their own work).
How will we do it?
1. The teacher gives each child a set of picture cards showing a sequence of steps.
2. The child examines the pictures and arranges the cards in the appropriate sequences.
3. Each child tells the "story" of his or her sequence to the group.
What else can we do? Variation: The children can arrange the cards on a flannelboard or in a pocket chart.
Follow-ups: For fun, have the children arrange a story backwards (i.e., give the sequence in reverse order); the children can also arrange pictures of the seasons or holidays in order.

Description A chanting game with blocks—to distinguish adding or subtracting from simply rearranging.
Title (for children) "Flocks of Blocks."
Curriculum area Mathematics (comparing and ordering).   **Age range** 5 to 7.

What is our objective? To explain that simply rearranging does not change value or amount (table: 2-C-7).
What will we need? About twenty blocks (all the same size); open area.
How will we do it?
1. The children sit on the floor in a circle, with fifteen blocks in the center, in a pattern.
2. One child at a time looks at the blocks and then covers his or her eyes.
3. A second child either removes one or more blocks, adds one or more blocks, or simply rearranges the pattern, while the other children chant "Flocks of blocks/ On the floor./ Are there less,/ Or are there more?"
4. The first child then opens his or her eyes, examines the blocks in the center, and announces whether there are fewer, more, or the same number. The other children confirm or correct the answer.

What else can we do? Other activities: To demonstrate conservation, the children can put water from one container into another of a different shape, form and reform the same lump of clay, or cut a piece of paper into jigsaw shapes and put it back together again.

Description Making a catalog of toys and "shopping" for bargains.
Title (for children) "Buying the Bargain."
Curriculum area Mathematics (comparing and ordering).   **Age range** 7 to 9.

What is our objective? To compare cost (table: 2-D-3).
What will we need? Newspapers, magazines, catalogs, fliers from stores; scissors, glue; large scrapbook or looseleaf binder. Each child will need a pad or paper and pencil to record "purchases."
How will we do it?
1. Using the newspapers, magazines, etc., the children cut out pictures of toys or advertisements for toys, being sure to include the price. These cutouts are mounted in a scrapbook or looseleaf book, arranged by categories (dolls, wheeled toys, sporting goods, computerized toys, etc.).
2. As a group, the children discuss what kinds of toys they want to buy and how much money they will have to spend.
3. Over the course of a week, the children take turns going through the class "catalog" and choosing items to "buy." Each child makes notes of items chosen and how much each costs.
4. At the end of the week, the children compare "purchases" and total costs to see who has found the best bargains.

What else can we do? Another activity: In pairs, the children can play this variation of the card game "War": index cards are marked with items and prices, and the *lower* price wins each turn. (You can call this game "Price War.")

Activities for Mathematics: Story Problems

Description   Judging whether statements are possible.
Title (for children)   "Is It Possible?"
Curriculum area   Mathematics (story problems).   Age range   3 to 5.

What is our objective?   To determine whether simple mathematical statements are possible or impossible (table: 3-A-1).
What will we need?   Open space for the participating children; some objects to illustrate the statements.
How will we do it?
1. The children sit in a circle or semicircle around the teacher. The teacher explains what it means for something to be "possible" or "not possible," and teacher and children discuss these concepts.
2. Then the teacher makes simple mathematics-related statements and asks the children to say whether each is possible or not. The nature of these statements depends, of course, on the children's experience and level of sophistication; but these are reasonable examples (the names should be those of the participating children; "I" is the teacher).
   a. "I can touch the ceiling without standing on anything."
   b. "If Tom and Cathy each give me a cooky, I'll have 100 cookies."
   c. "Annie can run faster than a car."
   d. "It takes Bobby half a second to walk to school."
   e. "Brian is the oldest one in his family."
   f. "A tennis ball weighs more than a soccer ball."
   g. "This toy dog is as big as an elephant."
   h. "Laurie is as tall as a tree."
   i. "Millie can walk to school in 15 minutes."
   j. "An apple is about the same size as an orange."
   k. "Jamie weights 40 pounds."
What else can we do?   Follow-up: Have the children make up similar statements for each other to evaluate.

Description Deciding which of several presented items will fit into given bags.
Title (for children) "Bag It."
Curriculum area Mathematics (story problems).   **Age range** 4 to 6.

What is our objective? To estimate outcomes perceptually or intuitively (table: 3-B-3).
What will we need? Objects and bags of different sizes and shapes—say, five or six objects and five or six bags—and a table large enough to hold all of them; paper and pencils or crayons for drawing; numbered labels for the bags.
How will we do it?
1. The teacher arranges on a table the objects and bags—objects at one end, bags at the other.
2. For older children, the bags can be numbered from 1 to 5 or 6, and the children print these numbers on a piece of paper and draw next to each number a picture of the object that will fit into that bag.
3. Younger children can simply take turns matching the objects at the table—but by sight only (they should not try to put the objects in the bags).
4. When all the objects and bags have been matched up, the children test their predictions by putting the objects into the bags.
What else can we do? **Other activities:** Assorted lidded containers are separated from their lids, and the children match them up by sight; assorted children's clothing, doll's clothing, and adults' clothing are presented to the children, who decide (by sight) who the clothing will fit, and test their predictions by trying the clothes on themselves or a doll or having the teacher try them on.

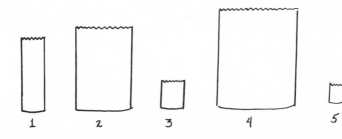

Description Formulating and using a "step chart" to solve story problems.
Title (for children) "Watch Your Steps."
Curriculum area Mathematics (story problems).   **Age range** 7 to 9.

What is our objective? To identify steps in solving story problems (table: 3-D-1).
What will we need? Chalkboard and chalk for the teacher; paper and pencils for the children.
How will we do it?
1. Teacher and children discuss what steps to take in solving story problems, and the teacher lists the steps in sequence on the chalkboard. Naturally, each class will arrive at a somewhat different list; but the teacher should direct the discussion so that these essential steps are noted:
   a. What is the situation at the beginning? Express it as a number. (E.g., "Jane has *20* marbles.")
   b. What happens? Express it as an arithmetic operation. (E.g., "She loses 7 to Scott. 'Loses' means 'take away,' and that means *subtraction*.")
   c. Perform the arithmetic operation. (E.g., "20 *minus* 7 equals 13.")
   d. Check the answer by intuition (e.g., "Yes, 13 is *less* than 20") and then by reversing the operation (e.g., "The reverse of subtraction is addition; 13 *plus* 7 equals 20").
2. The children discuss each step and then write it down, so that each child ends up with his or her own copy of the complete list.
3. The children solve several problems, going step by step through the list. If they get stuck or make mistakes, they evaluate their skill at handling each step and concentrate on the places where they are weak.
What else can we do? **Follow-up:** The teacher writes an incomplete "Number sentence" on the chalkboard (e.g., "20 − 7 = ?"); the children turn it into a story problem which they then solve using their charts.

Activities for Mathematics: Geometry

Description Making collages from precut geometric shapes.
Title (for children) "Shape Up."
Curriculum area Mathematics (geometry).   **Age range** 3 to 5.

What is our objective? To identify, compare, and classify geometric shapes using concrete objects (table: 4-A-1).
What will we need? For each child: 20 or so precut geometric shapes (made of construction paper), a large piece of construction paper, paste or glue, felt-tipped pen. The shapes should include circles, triangles, squares, and rectangles.
How will we do it?
1. Teacher and children talk about how things in the world are often shaped like geometric figures (e.g., fir trees = triangle; orange = circle; sailboat = triangle; building = rectangle). The teacher can use objects to demonstrate.
2. Each child gets about 20 precut geometric shapes and a large piece of construction paper and pastes some of the shapes onto the paper to make a picture of something in the "real world," adding details with a felt-tipped pen. The teacher can suggest ideas (boats on the water, a row of houses).
3. Each child's picture is labeled by the teacher to indicate what shapes were used (TRIANGLES; SQUARES), and the pictures are hung in the classroom.

What else can we do? **Follow-up:** On a walk through the school or neighborhood, the children identify geometric shapes they see. **Other activities:** "Shape lotto" and "shape dominoes."

Description A game involving identifying geometric shapes in pictures.
Title (for children) "Shuffled Shapes."
Curriculum area Mathematics (geometry).   **Age range** 4 to 6.

What is our objective? To identify, compare, and classify pictures of geometric shapes (table: 4-B-1).
What will we need? For each pair of children: 10 to 15 picture cards representing geometric shapes (these can be drawings of objects or pictures of objects cut out and mounted on 3- by 5-inch index cards); and a "game board" consisting of, say, 4 or 5 library pockets mounted on poster paper, each card marked with a geometric shape (square, circle, triangle, half circle, rectangle). For older children, the library pockets can also be labeled ("SQUARE," etc.).
How will we do it?
1. The children work in pairs. They shuffle the cards and then turn them up one by one.
2. As the cards are turned up, the partners take turns identifying the shape represented by the picture and putting the card in the appropriate pocket on the game board.
3. For younger children, the teacher can check the pocketed cards to see how many are correctly sorted—the team gets a point for each correct identification.
4. Older children can swap game boards so that each team adds up the points for another team.
What else can we do? Other activities: The children can mount large magazine pictures on heavy paper and outline geometric shapes with felt-tipped pens; the teacher can give each child a piece of drawing paper with a simple geometric shape drawn on it, and the child draws a picture around the shape.

Description Making a "geoboard" with wood and nails.
Title (for children) "Geometric Carpentry."
Curriculum area Mathematics (geometry).   **Age range** 5 to 7.

What is our objective? To construct geometric shapes and models (table: 4-C-1).
What will we need? For each child: scrap lumber (1 x 12's, for preference), sandpaper, 25 nails plus a few spares, hammer, colored rubber bands. For the teacher: ruler or straightedge, felt-tipped marker.

How will we do it?
1. Each child gets a piece of wood and smooths the edges and sides with sandpaper.
2. The teacher draws five straight vertical rows and five straight horizontal rows of X's on each child's piece of wood (25 X's in all).
3. Each child hammers a nail halfway into the center of each X on his or her board. The result is a "geoboard."
4. The children experiment with rubber bands, stretching them around the nails to make various shapes.
5. After the experimentation, the teacher asks the children to construct specific shapes and combinations of shapes (e.g., a circle within a triangle, two rectangles end to end).
What else can we do? Other activities: Children can draw geometric shapes on graph paper; models of three-dimensional shapes can be made out of boxes and balloons covered with papier-maché; and boxes can be made by cutting, folding, and gluing or taping paper.

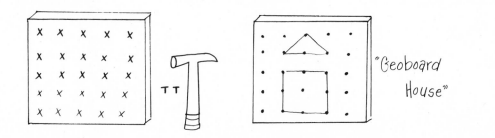

Activities for Mathematics: Measurement

```
┌ ─ ─ ─ ─ ─ ─ ─ ─ ─ ─ ─ ─ ─ ─ ─ ─ ─ ─ ─ ─ ─ ─ ─ ─ ┐
```

Description   Building block towers and comparing their heights.
Title (for children)   "Blockbuster."
Curriculum area   Mathematics (measurement).   **Age range**   3 to 5.

What is our objective?   To compare and classify objects as to size, weight, etc. (table: 5-A-1).
What will we need?   Blocks, for the teacher and each child.
How will we do it?
1. Teacher and, say, five or six children sit in a close circle on the floor, each with a pile of blocks (or there can be a communal pile in the middle). The teacher builds a block tower.
2. Starting with the first child on the left, the teacher says, "Build a tower taller than mine." On to the next child: "Build one shorter than Ronny's." And the next: "Build one shorter than Lena's." And so on, around the circle.
3. After each child has built his or her tower, the group decides: Is it the height the teacher asked for? They do this before the next child gets his or her "assignment."
4. When all the towers are built, the children get to knock them down.
5. As a finale, the teacher gives all the children 1 minute, in which each is to build the tallest tower possible. The children work simultaneously, and when the minute is up they decide which tower is tallest.

What else can we do?   Other activities: Play a "guessing game" with the children. Go around a circle of children with questions like "Name something taller than you are" and "What can you name that's smaller than this book?" Each child answers as quickly as possible. To give children a "feel" for weights, have them hold two objects of very different weights, one in each hand.

Description Measuring things in "feet"—one's own feet.
Title (for children) "Footsies."
Curriculum area Mathematics (measurement).   **Age range** 4 to 6.

What is our objective? To use informal standard units for measuring objects (table: 5-B-1).
What will we need? For each child: piece of cardboard (say, 8½ by 11 inches). For the teacher: pencil for tracing; scissors.
How will we do it?
1. The teacher makes an outline of each child's foot on the cardboard, and cuts it out. (Older children can cut out their own "feet.")
2. Each with the cutout of his or her own foot, the children measure objects in the room.
    a. They begin by estimating (by sight) which objects are about the same size as their "foot" rulers, and check by measuring (holding the ruler against the object).
    b. They go on to measure longer objects—first guessing how long (how many "feet") each object will be and then checking their predictions, either by moving one "foot" ruler along the object to be measured or by using several "foot" rulers.
What else can we do? **Variation:** The hand can be used as the unit of measure (this makes a good cutout).
Follow-ups: Use more abstract, but still personal, units: distance from elbow to tip of index finger; distance from tip of nose to tips of fingers with arm extended; pace. **Another activity:** Estimate the size of familiar objects in units of other familiar objects (toothpick, drumstick, etc.) and check by measuring.

Description Making an hourly diary of one day, from getting up to bedtime.
Title (for children) "Round the Clock."
Curriculum area Mathematics (measurement).   **Age range** 5 to 7.

What is our objective? To tell time to the hour and half hour (table: 5-C-3).
What will we need? For each child: 15 sheets of paper (8½ x 11 inches), two sheets of construction paper for the front and back cover, pencils and crayons, stapler. On each of the fifteen sheets of paper, the teacher has reproduced the face of a clock (no hands) about one-third to one-half page in size—leaving room for a drawing and label to be added by the child.
How will we do it?
1. On the piece of construction paper that will be the front cover, children who can write print "ROUND THE CLOCK WITH (NAME)." For younger children, the teacher does this.
2. The children staple the book together—front cover, pages, back cover.
3. The children go through their books, crayoning in the hands on each clock face. They start with the hour when they get up and end with the hour when they go to bed.
4. For each hour of the day, the children make a drawing to show what they are doing at that time. Older children can add labels (e.g., "I am eating lunch"). If necessary, the teacher reminds them of the time the clock shows and suggests what they might be doing then.
What else can we do? **Another activity:** The children can make cardboard clock faces, with the long hand drawn at 12 and the short hand (a cardboard cutout) fastened on with a brad. For children who have moved on to telling time to the half hour, both hands can be movable.

Sample
page →

booklet

I feed my dog at
6:00.

Description   Using jars as "banks" and washers as "money" to identify quantities from 1 to 10.
Title (for children)   "Mini Banks."
Curriculum area   Mathematics (numeral literacy).   **Age range**   4 to 6.

What is our objective?   To use concrete objects to identify appropriate quantities for one to ten items (table: 6-B-3).
What will we need?   Ten baby-food jars for each participating child; stickers numbered from 1 to 10; container and small metal washers (at least 45) for each child.
How will we do it?

1. The teacher cuts a slot in the lid of each jar and puts a numbered sticker on each jar; these jars are the "banks." The washers are the "money."
2. Each child gets a set of ten jars labeled "1" to "10," and a container full of washers.
3. The teacher helps each child to recognize the numbers on the stickers.
4. Each child counts out the appropriate number of washers for each jar (the right amount of money for each bank) and puts them into the jar through the slot in the lid.

What else can we do?   **Variation:** Here is another, similar setup—Each child gets an egg carton (bottom half or top half) with ten of the cups labeled "1" to "10" by the teacher and the remaining two cups filled with beads, beans, chips, or any other small objects. The children transfer appropriate quantities of these objects to the numbered cups.
Another variation: Use spelled-out numbers ("ONE," "TWO," etc.) to label the "banks" or egg cups.

Description   A card game involving ordering to 100 by tens.
Title (for children)   "Sad Sack."
Curriculum area   Mathematics (numeral literacy).   **Age range**   5 to 7.

What is our objective?   To count to 100 by tens (table: 6-C-3).
What will we need?   For each pair of children: a deck of "Sad Sack" cards (consisting of two 0's, two 10's, two 20's, two 30's, two 40's, two 50's, two 60's, two 70's, two 80's, two 90's, two 100's, and two "sad sacks").
How will we do it?
1. "Sad Sack" is a card game for two players. First player shuffles, second cuts, and first places the entire deck face down on the table.
2. Players take turns drawing cards. Each card drawn is placed face up in front of the player who drew it. If a player draws a duplicate of a card he or she has already drawn, it is returned to the bottom of the deck. A player who draws the "sad sack" must return it to the bottom of the deck, along with one of the cards he or she has already drawn.
3. The object is to complete a sequence from 0 to 100 by tens. First player to do so wins, if the player displays them in correct sequence. If there is at least one card out of sequence, the player must return a card to the bottom of the deck, and play continues.
What else can we do?   **Follow-up:** In scoring classroom and schoolyard games, have the children count by tens for a change.

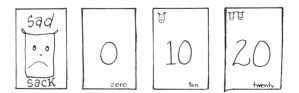

Description   Using maps and mileage charts to practice reading and writing cardinal numbers.
Title (for children)   "On a Trip."
Curriculum area   Mathematics (numeral literacy).   **Age range**   7 to 9.

What is our objective?   To count, read, and write the cardinal numbers 0 to 1,000 (table: 6-D-2).
What will we need?   Road maps, atlases, mileage charts; paper and pencil for each child. For the class: one large map showing the town or city where the school is located and at least 2,000 miles of the surrounding regions.
How will we do it?
1. On a large map, teacher and children locate their own town, measure off 1,000 miles from it in several directions, and draw a circle around it with a 1,000-mile radius.
2. Using road maps (with mileage charts) and atlases, each child plans ten trips he or she would like to take within the circle and makes a list of the ten destinations and how many miles away each is.
3. The children take turns reading their lists. As each child reads, the others add new destinations and mileages to their lists.
4. When all the lists are complete, the class decides who planned the longest trip and who planned the shortest trip.
What else can we do?   **Other activities:** The children can take turns calling out four-digit numbers for the class to write down; the children can collect advertisements for appliances, reading and recording the prices.

Description Some simple exercises for practicing comparative terms.
Title (for children) "It's the Most!"
Curriculum area Mathematics (mathematical tools and recording).   **Age range** 3 to 5.

What is our objective? To understand and use simple comparative mathematical vocabulary (table: 7-A-1).
What will we need? Objects to be compared—e.g., blocks, beads, beans. Objects and materials for working with quantities—e.g., sand and pails, water and cups.
How will we do it? The teacher guides the children in using comparative terms as they work with concrete objects and discuss their own experiences. Examples:
1. Block towers—Children and teacher make three towers. "Which is tall? Taller? Tallest?"
2. Sand table—"Show me how we can have more sand in the pail. Show me how we can have less sand."
3. Piles of objects—"Let's make a big pile. Now a bigger pile. Now the biggest pile."
4. Discussing school activities—"Which takes longest, collecting papers or eating lunch or eating a snack?"
5. Counter boxes—"Which box has most beans?" "Here's a box filled with beans and buttons. Let's divide them up. Are there more beans or more buttons?"
6. Making choices—"Do you want more time to finish that drawing? Do you need more paper? Would you like more juice?"
7. Balance scale—"Which is heavier, the Ping-Pong ball or the orange?"
8. Simple observations—"Look at Eric, Molly, Josie, and Fred. Whose hair is longest? Whose is shortest?"
What else can we do? **Follow-up:** Present three blocks on a tray. Cover it while removing or adding blocks. Ask: "Do we have less? More? The same?"

Description Some simple exercises for practicing tallying.
Title (for children) "Tally Ho!"
Curriculum area Mathematics (mathematical tools and recording). **Age range** 4 to 6.

What is our objective? To record quantities by tallying (table: 7-B-1).
What will we need? Pencils and paper for tallying; objects to count.
How will we do it? The teacher looks for opportunities to have the children tally in various situations. Examples:

1. The class votes on something and the children record the votes by tallying.
2. As the children sit down for lunch each day, "count noses" and tally them.
3. When the whole class is playing a game where the score is kept, the children tally the score on the chalkboard.
4. Use tallying to record ordinary classroom events and activities—"How many children have returned their library books? Brought in their homework?"
5. The class can take an opinion poll and tally the results. "How many for? How many against? How many undecided?"
6. Record statistics by tallying. "How many hours do we use the playground each week? The lunchroom? The auditorium?" "How many children are wearing running shoes today?" "How many blonds in the class?"
7. Play games in which individuals record their scores by tallying.
8. Count objects and tally the results. "How many pencils are there in the classroom?" "How many books?"

What else can we do? **Variation:** In any exercise where the children keep individual tallies, have them exchange tally sheets and "interpret" each other's records. **Follow-up:** Teacher and children discuss how people counted before they "invented" numbers; the children might like to dramatize this.

Description Some simple exercises for practicing graphing.
Title (for children) "Portraits of Numbers."
Curriculum area Mathematics (mathematical tools and recording). **Age range** 5 to 7.

What is our objective? To read and make a variety of simple graphs, showing two variables (table: 7-C-3).
What will we need? Lots of graph paper; pencils, crayons, felt-tipped pens.
How will we do it? The teacher looks for and creates opportunities for the children to make graphs having to do with their school experiences. Examples:

1. Record attendance (for one week, say) on a line graph. Horizontal axis: Date or day of the week. Vertical axis: Number of children present.
2. Take a simple survey (e.g., "Do you like baseball?") and record the results on a bar graph. Vertical axis: Number of respondents. Bar 1: "Yes." Bar 2: "No." Bar 3: "Don't care."
3. Record weather on a bar graph for, say, one month. Vertical axis: Number of days. Bar 1: Sunny. Bar 2: Cloudy Bar 3: Rain. Bar 4: Mixed.
4. Record individual scores on tests on a bar graph. Vertical axis: Number of children. Bar 1: 100% to 90%. Bar 2: 89% to 80%. Etc.
5. Record class scores on tests on a line graph to see whether the class is improving over time. Vertical axis: Score. Horizontal axis: Test dates.
6. Answer some questions about the school. "How many children eat in the cafeteria and how many bring lunch?" (Vertical axis: Number of children. Bar 1: Cafeteria. Bar 2: Box lunches.) "How many children are there in each class?" (Vertical axis: Number of children. Bar 1: Room A. Bar 2: Room B. Etc.)

What else can we do? **Follow-up:** The teacher can make graphs of various situations and present them to the class for interpretation. ("This graph shows how many children take the bus to school and how many walk. Can you tell me the answer?")

Description Demonstrating addition as joining sets, using cups of beans.
Title (for children) "Beans Plus."
Curriculum area Mathematics (arithmetic operations).   **Age range** 4 to 6.

What is our objective? Using concrete objects, to demonstrate the concept of addition as a process of joining sets or counting to a total (table: 8-B-1).
What will we need? For each pair of children: 3 small paper cups holding a total of 10 beans. (Optional: a tray.)
How will we do it?
1. The children work in pairs. Each pair gets three paper cups containing ten beans in all. (Cups and beans can be presented to each pair on a tray.)
2. The children take turns counting the beans in each cup and totalling the three sets.
3. Then each pair of children changes the number of beans in each cup and repeats the process of counting and totalling.
What else can we do? **Follow-up:** Increase or decrease the total number of beans. **Another follow-up:** The teacher prepares cards, each card showing a set of beans. Three cards at a time are hung from hooks on a pegboard. The children add up the sets shown.

Description Solving addition and subtraction problems (combinations up to 18) by hanging paper oranges from a tree poster.
Title (for children) "Orange Add-Ups."
Curriculum area Mathematics (arithmetic operations). **Age range** 5 to 7.

What is our objective? To know additions through a sum of 18, and to subtract single-digit numbers from minuends through 18 (table: 8-C-1 and 8-C-2).
What will we need? Poster with a large drawing of an orange tree in whose branches are 18 circles (about the size of oranges) numbered 1 through 18; in each circle is a hook. Cardboard box, crate, or basket containing orange-size circles cut out of orange poster paper or construction paper, each with a hole punched near the top edge; on each "orange" is an addition or a subtraction (e.g., 7 + 3; 12 − 11).
How will we do it?
1. Each child in turn, with eyes shut, reaches into the "fruit basket" or "orange crate" (or whatever the class wants to call it) and pulls out an "orange."
2. The child examines the problem on the orange and then hangs the orange in the circle on the tree that gives the "answer."
3. The class says whether the answer chosen is correct or not.
What else can we do? **Variation:** If the "answer" is written (very small, so that the children won't catch sight of it before they should) on the back of each orange, the children can check their own work. **Another activity:** The children can play "War" with a special set of cards (made by the teacher or themselves) with additions or subtractions on the face (6 + 9; 18 − 2). As the cards are turned up, the largest sum or difference wins.

Description A racing-car game for practicing multiplication facts.
Title (for children) "Multi 500."
Curriculum area Mathematics (arithmetic operations). **Age range** 7 to 9.

What is our objective? To know multiplications through a product of 81 (table: 8-D-3).
What will we need? Playing board (a circular or oval track drawn on poster paper or cardboard, consisting of a "start" and, say, twenty to twenty-five spaces leading to a "finish"; in each space is written a multiplication, e.g., 3 x 3, 10 x 2), one small toy car for each player, dice or number cubes, answer sheet (a multiplication table, preferably laminated).
How will we do it?
1. This game can be played by two to four children.
2. The players begin by lining their cars up at the "start." Each child in turn rolls a die or number cube and moves his or her car the number of spaces indicated.
3. The child must "solve" the multiplication written in the space where he or she has landed. The other players then check the answer against the answer sheet (which is of course kept face down beforehand).
4. If the answer is correct, the car stays on that space—if it is incorrect, the car goes back to "start" or to the last space it was on.
5. First player to reach "finish" is the winner.
What else can we do? **Another activity:** The preceding activity, "Orange Add-Ups," can be adapted for multiplication.

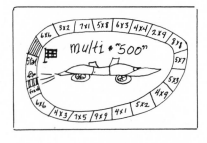

Activities for Mathematics: Fractions

Description   Some simple exercises for practicing identifying parts of a whole.
Title (for children)   "Partly Wholly."
Curriculum area   Mathematics (fractions).   **Age range**   3 to 5.

What is our objective?   To recognize parts of a whole, using concrete objects (table: 9-A-1).
What will we need?   Lots of objects that illustrate parts of a whole: paper to fold or cut, measuring cups and spoons, apples or oranges to section, a pie or cake to cut into wedges, brownies to be cut into squares, etc.
How will we do it?
1. The teacher finds and makes opportunities for the children to recognize parts and wholes in everyday classroom activities; e.g.:
    a. Cut or fold paper into parts; put cut parts back together again.
    b. Cut up foods—fruits, pies or cakes, cookies, etc.
    c. Experiment with measuring spoons and cups.
    d. Use liquid containers of different sizes—cups, pints, quarts, gallons.
    e. Divide the class in half for a game.
2. The teacher can also set some simple exercises; e.g.:
    a. Fold one arm in half.
    b. Fold a leg in half.
    c. Fold your body in half.
    d. Run halfway across the room.
What else can we do?   **Another activity:** Jigsaw puzzles.

Description Matching halves of construction-paper shapes and figures to form wholes.
Title (for children) "Half and Half."
Curriculum area Mathematics (fractions).   **Age range** 4 to 6.

What is our objective? Using pictures and diagrams to recognize parts of a whole (table: 9-B-1).
What will we need? Two shoeboxes labeled, say, "Fraction Box 1" and "Fraction Box 2" or "Half 1" and "Half 2."
In box 1: halves of various shapes cut out of construction paper (e.g., circles, triangles, rectangles) and halves of various representations (e.g., dog, elephant, house, car). In box 2: the other half of each figure in box 1. For the children: construction paper; glue or paste.
How will we do it?
1. Teacher and children discuss halves and wholes.
2. Taking turns, the children reach into box 1 and pull out one cutout at a time.
3. Then each child glues the piece onto construction paper, and goes to box 2 to find the other half—the piece that will complete the figure.
4. Each child gets five or six turns, so that there are at least five or six complete figures pasted on the construction paper.
What else can we do? **Variation:** This activity can be done with magazine pictures that have been mounted on construction paper and cut into halves. **Another activity:** A flannelboard can be used for displaying parts and wholes.

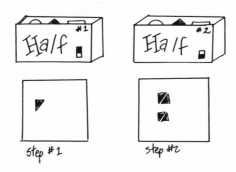

Description Dividing figures into parts by following directions expressed as fractional symbols.
Title (for children) "A Shady Deal."
Curriculum area Mathematics (fractions).   **Age range** 5 to 7.

What is our objective? To use fractional symbols (1/4, 1/3, 1/2) (table: 9-C-2).
What will we need? Geometric shapes cut out of construction paper or cardboard (circles, squares, rectangles; possibly triangles, but children might find these a bit tricky), paper and pencils, crayons for shading.
How will we do it?
1. Each child gets a set of the cutout shapes (one of each), blank paper, crayon, and pencil.
2. Using the cutout to make an outline, the child chooses one shape and draws it on a blank piece of paper. Underneath, the child writes "1/4, "1/3," or "1/2."
3. Each child passes his or her paper to the child on the left, who must separate the figure into the number of parts indicated by the denominator (this is done by drawing a line or lines with the pencil) and then shading one part (with the crayon) to indicate the numerator.
4. The children hand the papers back to each other and judge whether the directions have been followed—i.e., whether the fraction has been represented.
5. This is repeated with several different shapes. The resulting drawings are hung around the room.
What else can we do? **Other activities:** "Lotto" and "Bingo" can be adapted to give practice with fractions (for "Lotto," match spelled-out fractions to numerical fractions; for "Bingo," use fractions instead of whole numbers on the cards); paper can be folded into halves, thirds, and quarters and each part labeled.

Resources for Mathematics

Bibliography for Teachers

Baratta-Lorton, M. *Mathematics their way.* Menlo Park, Calif.: Addison-Wesley, 1976. (Excellent book that develops understanding of and insight into the patterns of mathematics through the use of concrete materials. Book includes activities, worksheets, observation sheets, assessment of skills, Ditto masters, and sample letters to parents to explain how children learn mathematics and to involve parents in the process.)

Barron, L. *Mathematics experiences for the early childhood years.* Columbus, Ohio: Merrill, 1979. (Combining theory and practical classroom ideas, this book deals with each of the basic mathematical areas. Mainstreaming, diagnosis, methods, and materials for math in early childhood are also covered.)

Biggs, E., & MacLean, J. *An active learning approach to mathematics.* Ont., Canada: Addison-Wesley (Canada), 1969. (The emphasis in this book is on helping children to *learn* mathematics, rather than helping teachers to *teach* mathematics. Active, creative learning is fostered by the methods and materials suggested. Attention is also given to assessing, and reporting on children's progress.)

Burns, M. *The I hate mathematics! book.* Boston: Little, Brown, 1975. (For ages four to eight, this unusual book contains a potpourri of activities that make mathematics fun. Some organizational headings for the different activities are: counting, seeing symmetry, math and magic, curiosity, and rainy-day and "sick" math games.)

Copeland, R. *Math activities for children.* Columbus, Ohio: Merrill, 1979. (The activities in this book are grouped in seven basic mathematical areas. Format is easy to follow and ideas are based on theories of Piaget. Activities are sequenced and keyed to appropriate age levels.)

Forte, I. *Creative math experiences for the young child.* Nashville: Incentive, 1973. (This is an attractively presented collection of activities and worksheets utilizing a child-centered approach to basic number concepts. It focuses on numerals, sets, sizes, shapes, time, money, measurement, fractions, and math vocabulary. The activities can be used for class or individual instruction at the preschool or primary-grade level.)

Holt, M., & Dienes, Z. *Let's play math.* New York: Walker, 1973. (A collection of games to teach concepts such as sets, shapes, ordering, time and simple geometry. This book suggests activities for preschool and primary children. All games utilize common children's toys or do-it-yourself materials.)

Kaplan, S., Madsen, S., & Gould, B. *The big book of collections: Math games and activities.* Salt Lake City: Goodyear, 1975. (A collection of various activities, charts, learning centers, activity cards, tables, and hands-on materials for primary and early elementary math.)

Kennedy, L., & Michon, R. *Games for individualizing mathematics learning.* Columbus, Ohio: Merrill, 1973. (This book is designed for teachers who want to use games as one way of individualizing learning in mathematics. All games included are related to performance objectives in six different mathematical areas. Games can be made by teachers or parents and can be used by children with a minimum amount of adult supervision.)

Journals:

Arithmetic Teacher. (Official publication of the National Council of Teachers of Mathematics, 1201 16th St., NW, Washington, D.C. 20036.)
School Science and Mathematics. (535 Kendall Ave., Kalamazoo, Mich. 49007.)

Mathematics newsletter:

Mathematics: A Way of Thinking. (19225 Vineyard Lane, Saratoga, Calif. 95070.)

Bibliography for Children

Numbers and counting:

Anno, M. *Anno's counting book.* New York: Crowell, 1977. (Great beginning number book for little ones. Focuses on numbers in nature.)
Carle, E. *1, 2, 3, to the zoo.* New York: Collins, 1968. (Collins and World Publishing Co., Inc., 2080 W. 117th St., Cleveland, Ohio 44111.)
Elkin, B. *Six foolish fishermen.* New York: Scholastic, 1957.
Friskey, M. *Chicken little, count-to-ten.* New York: Children's Press, 1964.
Gretz, S. *Teddy bears 1 to 10.* Chicago: Follett. (1010 W. Washington Blvd., 60607.)
McLeod, E. *One snail and me.* Boston: Little, Brown, 1961.
Oxenbury, H. *Numbers of things.* New York: F. Watts, 1968.
Peppe, R. *Circus numbers.* New York: Delacorte, 1969. (Dial Press, 1 Dag Hammarskjold Plaza, 245 E. 47th St., 10017.)
Seignobose, F. *Jeanne-Marie counts her sheep.* New York: Scribner's, 1957.
Sendak, M. *One was Johnny.* New York: Harper and Row, 1962.
Slobodkin, L. *Millions and millions and millions!* New York: Vanguard, 1955.
Steiner, C. *Ten in a family.* New York: Knopf, 1960.
Tudor, T. *1 is one.* New York: Random House. (457 Hahn Rd., Westminster, Md. 21157.)
Ungerer, T. *One, two, where's my shoe?* New York: Harper and Row, 1964.

Understanding mathematical comparison:

Berenstain, S., & Berenstain, J. *Bears on wheels.* New York: Random House, 1969.
Berkley, E. *Big and little, up and down.* New York: Scott, 1960.
Branley, F. *Big tracks, little tracks.* London: Crowell-Collier, 1960.
Brenner, B., & Ungerer, T. *Mr. Tall and Mr. Small.* New York: Scott, 1966.
Schapp, C., & Schapp, M. *Let's find out what's big and what's small.* New York: Franklin Watts, 1959.
Schlein, M. *Heavy is a hippopotamus.* New York: Scott, 1954.

Shapes:

Atwood, A. *The little circle.* New York: Scribner's, 1967.
Budney, B. *A kiss is round.* New York: Lothrop, 1954.
Craig, M. J. *Boxes.* New York: Norton, 1964.
Emberley, E. *The wing on a flea: A book about shapes.* Boston: Little Brown. (200 West St., Waltham, Mass. 02154.)
Felster, E. *The Sesame Street book of shapes.* New York: Time-Life, 1970.
Hoban, T. *Circles, triangles and squares.* New York: Macmillan, 1974.
Kessler, E., & Kessler, L. *Are you square?* New York: Doubleday. (501 Franklin Ave., Garden City, N.Y. 11530.)
Lerner, S. *Square is a shape.* Minneapolis: Lerner, 1970.
Reiss, J. J. *Shapes.* Scarsdale, N.Y.: Bradbury Press. (2 Overhill Rd., 10583.)
Schlein, M. *Shapes.* New York: Scott, 1952.
Shapur, F. *Round and round and square.* London: Abelard-Schuman, 1965.

Other mathematical subjects:

Hoban, T. *Over, under and through.* New York: Macmillan, 1973. (Spatial concepts come alive in black and white.)
Hoban, T. *Push, pull, empty, full.* New York: Macmillan, 1972. (An open-ended book of photographs dealing with opposites.)
Podendorf, I. *Things are alike and different.* Chicago, Ill.: Children's Press. (1224 W. Van Buren St., 60607.)
Sitomer, M., & Sitomer, H. *How did numbers begin?* New York: Crowell, 1976. (An interesting version of how numbers may have come into use. Lively illustrations.)
Trivett, J. *Building tables on tables.* New York: Crowell, 1975. (A book about the relationships of $+$, $-$, and $\times$. Explains multiplication so that children will understand.)

Learning Materials

Suggested Basic Materials

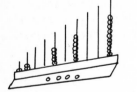

Dominoes.
An abacus.
Jigsaw puzzles. (Construct numerals. Match numerals and number patterns.)
Matching tiles (Match numerals with patterns.)
Beaded cards (number patterns).
Cutouts (numerals, geometric shapes).
Plastic scale and weight sets.
Calendars (blank, to be filled in).
Fraction circles and squares.
Toy clocks.
Measures (dry and liquid).
Plastic counters.
Tangrams.
Number blocks.
Pegboard games.
Montessori shapes and stencils.
Rulers and yardsticks.
Play money and cash register.
Chips and numbered tops for games of chance.
Play store; play post office.

Sources and Suppliers

Commercial sources:

Activity Records, Educational Activities, Inc., Freeport, N.Y. 11520.

Milton Bradley Co., Springfield, Mass. 01101.

Creative Publications, 3977 E. Bayshore Rd., P.O. Box 10328, Palo Alto, Calif., 94303.

Cuisenair Co. of America, Inc., 12 Church St., New Rochelle, N.Y. 10805.

Developmental Learning Materials, 3505 N. Ashland Ave., Chicago, Ill. 60657.

Didax Inc., 3 Dearborn Rd., P.O. Box 2258, Peabody, Mass. 01960.

Edmund Scientific Co., 300 Edscorp Bldg., Barrington, N.J. 08007.

Instructo Corp., Paoli, Pa. 19301.

Invicta International Educators Innovative Educational Services, Inc., P.O. Box 29096, New Orleans, La. 70189.

Judy-Ed Aids, The Judy Company, Minneapolis, Minn. 55401.

Kaplan School Supply, 600 Jonestown Rd., Winston-Salem, N.C. 27103.

LaPine Scientific Co., Dept. D4, 6009 S. Knox Ave., Chicago, Ill. 60629.

Learning Games, Inc., 34 S. Broadway, White Plains, N.Y. 10601.

Novo Educational Toy and Equipment Corp., 11 Park Pl., New York, N.Y. 10007.

Playskool (a Milton Bradley Company), Chicago, Ill. 60618.

School Days Equipment Co., 973 N. Main St., Los Angeles, Calif., 90012.

Scott Resources, Inc., Box 2121, Fort Collins, Colo. 80521.

Selective Educational Equipment, Inc., 3 Bridge St., Newton, Mass. 02150.

Skillbuilder Playthings, Ltd., 1725 De Sales St., NW, Suite 312, Washington, D.C., 20036.

Teaching Resources, 100 Boylston St., Boston, Mass. 02116.

Teech-Um Co., Box 4232, Overland Park, Kans. 66204.

Texas Instruments, Education and Communications Center, P.O. Box 3640, M/584, Dallas, Tex. 75285.

Webster Div., McGraw-Hill Book Co., Manchester Rd., Manchester, Mo. 63011.

Noncommercial sources:

Your house (anything you have several of that kids can count and sort).

Discards (calendars, stamps, clocks, scales, telephones, thermometers).

Your immediate environment. (What can you count? What can you measure? Count children, disks, swings, crayons. Measure children, furniture, the playground, the temperature. Look for shapes.)

The kids' homes (egg cartons for sorting, objects for counting, math-type games, items to weigh and measure).

Garage sales.

For inexpensive materials, go to:

Grocery stores.

Fabric stores.

Toy stores.

Paint stores or lumber outlets (for yardsticks).

Some do-it-yourself ideas:

Children can make their own "geoboards."

Have a piece of pegboard cut to size. (Use golf tees instead of pegs.)

Use commonplace items as counters (blocks, beads, seed pods, beans, sticks, buttons, macaroni, bottle caps, stones, poker chips, paper clips, pennies, toothpicks).

Enrichment Materials

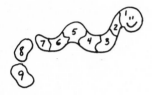

General sources of enrichment materials:

School supply houses.
Educational catalogs.
Curriculum laboratories.
Libraries.

Programs, projects, and kits.:

Hodgins, A., & Kernes, M. *Development of number readiness; Early childhood enrichment* series. Milton Bradley, 1970. (Number readiness skills for preschool and kindergarten. Designed for small group learning centers. Includes teacher's guide. Can be used by paraprofessionals. Dominoes, number cards, counters, pegboards, match-ups.)

Karnes, M. *GOAL mathematical concepts.* Milton Bradley, 1973. (For use in small groups. A sequential program. Can be used by a paraprofessional. Diagnostic and basal. "GOAL" means "game-oriented activities for learning." Lesson plans fall into the following categories: shapes, sets, counting, numerals, addition and subtraction, measurement, and patterning and progressions.)

Lakeshore. *Unifix.* (A kit for preschool to grade 2. Uses Unifix cubes and supplementary materials. Matching, patterning, number values, number sequence, and simple addition and subtraction. Materials for up to ten students. Teacher's guide.)

Lavatelli, C. *Early childhood curriculum: A Piaget program.* Boston: American Science and Engineering. (20 Overland St., 02215.)

Milton Bradley. *Experiences in number readiness* kit. (A large set of manipulative materials and activities. Matching, patterning, grouping by number, counting, recognition of the numerals.)

Nuffield Mathematics Project. *I do, and I understand.* New York: Wiley, 1967. (Used in British infant schools. Project consists of resource booklets and task cards and deals with spiraling concepts. Contains suggestions for the teacher rather than lesson plans. A "hands-on" approach using concrete experiences.)

Stanford University. *School mathematics study group (SMSG).* (SMSG, Cedar Hall, Stanford University, Stanford, Calif. 94305. Manuals, films, newsletters.)

Unversity of Minnesota. *Minnesota mathematics and science teaching project (Minnemast).* (TSCE, University of Minnesota, Minneapolis, Minn. 55455. Coordinated units focusing on the relationships between science and mathematics. Grades K through 3.)

Toys and games:

Invicta Attribute block set. (Sixty durable poly blocks in five geometric shapes and several colors and sizes.)
Milton Bradley Mathfacts Games.

Records and kits that include records (available from Children's Books and Music Center, 2500 Santa Monica Blvd., Santa Monica, Calif. 90404):

Basic mathematics
Counting. (Narrator, Ruby Dee. Teacher's guide.)
Dancing numerals. (With Henry "Buzz" Glass. Learning counting, etc., through music, games, and charts.)
Let's learn to add.
Let's learn to subtract.
Listen, sing and learn. (Six-record set. Mathematics and other primary subjects set to music. Bright, entertaining.)

130

Math readiness: addition and subtraction. (Songs.)
Math readiness: Vocabulary and concepts. (Songs.)
Math zingo. (A bingo-type game. Multiple grooving allows several sets of calls to be put on one side of record: each time arm is set at start of record, one call begins by chance. Complete playing kit with each long-playing record.)
Numbers and time. (Songs.)

Records available elsewhere:

Counting songs. (The Judy Co., Barclay School Supplies, 26 Warren St., New York, N.Y. 10007. Three 7-inch, 33-rpm records. Six old favorites. Booklet.)

Sources of films:

Children's Book and Music Center, 2500 Santa Monica Blvd., Santa Monica, Calif. 90404. (Young Math Filmstrips: *Bigger and smaller, Odds and evens*, more.)
National Film Board of Canada, 1251 Avenue of the Americas, New York, N.Y. 10019.
New York University Film Library, 26 Washington Pl., New York, N.Y. 10003.
Newenhouse/Nova, 1825 Willow Rd., Northfield, Ill. 60093.
Time-Life Films, 43 W. 16th St., New York, N.Y. 10011.

Community Resources

Most valuable may be parents of students, who may be able to demonstrate:

Following a recipe.
Sewing from a pattern.
Balancing a checkbook.
Telling time, as it's done in other lands.
Coin collecting.
Stamp collecting.
Using an adding machine, calculator, etc.

For understanding measurement and making things from specifications:

Lumberyard. (Order lumber to build something.)
Fabric or yard goods shop.

To show how numbers are used, take field trips to:

Bank or savings and loan association.
Grocery store.
Post office.
Stamp and coin shop.
Museums.
Clock shop.

Go to the following for materials:

Telephone company. (Directories.)
Thrift shop or repair shop. (Old clocks, radios, scales.)
Insurance companies. (Free calendars.)
Clothing store. (Collect clothes to sort by size.)

Section 4

LANGUAGE DEVELOPMENT: ACTIVITIES AND RESOURCES

"Language development" is in essence the development of the ability to communicate by means of words—that is, to send and receive verbal messages.

In this section, as in Sections 2 and 3, we begin by presenting objectives and activities for infants and toddlers. Here, our objectives and activities focus on laying a foundation for language development and encouraging the early stages of such development. We then go on to objectives, activities, and resources for older children—here, we are in the realm of the "language arts." The term "language arts" usually refers to three processes: (1) oral communication, which comprises listening and speaking; (2) reading; (3) writing. These processes are, of course, related, and they develop progressively.

Is language development confined to these three specific areas? Obviously not. As human beings, we learn almost everything—it would be possible to argue that we in fact learn everything—through language. Every classroom subject involves language, not only because teaching and learning involve speaking, listening, reading, and writing but also because each subject has its own terminology.

Do oral communications, reading, and writing have components other than the linguistic? Obviously, they do. Each of these curriculum areas involves not only language development but also psycho-physical-motor, cognitive, and affective development. It's easy to find examples that illustrate this: listening involves aural acuity (psycho-physical-motor); we cannot form sentences, written or spoken, until our thought processes reach a certain level of maturity (cognitive); and we will not want to learn to read unless we value reading (affective).

In working with young children, we need to remember how pervasive language is; everything that takes place in the classroom involves it somehow.

Objectives and Activities for Infants and Toddlers

It can be argued that language is the major tool we use to function in our environment; if this is true, our attention to the earliest years—that is, to infancy and toddlerhood—becomes especially significant.

The following table, which lists objectives and activities for infants and toddlers, stresses (1) mutual and interactive communication, (2) the affective aspects of language (such as association with a loving caretaker), (3) the use of language for descriptive purposes, and (4) respect for the child (which can be shown by offering even the youngest reassurance and explanations associated with experiences).

The outgrowth of these experiences should be an appreciation of the power of language, its varied purposes, all the different opportunities for its use, and—most important—joy and pleasure in language: listening, speaking, and moving beyond oral communication into reading and writing.

Sequential Objectives and Activities for Language Development: Birth to 36 Months

LEVEL	OBJECTIVE	ACTIVITY
Birth to 1 month	1. To develop intimacy and awareness of communication based on personal contact.	1. Whisper into the child's ear.
	2. To introduce the concept of oral communication.	2. Coo at the child.
	3. To introduce verbal communication.	3. Talk to the child.
	4. To stimulate interest in the process of talking.	4. Let the child explore your mouth with his or her hands as you talk.
1 to 3 months	1. To develop oral communication.	1. Imitate the sounds the child makes.
	2. To develop auditory acuity.	2. Talk to the child in different tones.
	3. To develop the concept that different people sound different.	3. Encourage others to talk and coo to the child.
	4. To develop the concept of oral and musical communication of feelings.	4. Sing songs of different moods, rhythms, and tempos.
3 to 6 months	1. To develop the concept of positive use of verbal communication.	1. Reward the child with words.
	2. To stimulate excitement about words.	2. Talk expressively to the child.
	3. To develop the concept that words and music can be linked.	3. Sing or chant to the child.
	4. To develop the ability to name things and events.	4. Describe daily rituals to the child as you carry them out.

(Continued)

Sequential Objectives and Activities for Language Development: Birth to 36 Months (continued)

"Bear"

duck
Dd

bird

"Carrots"

LEVEL	OBJECTIVE	ACTIVITY
6 to 9 months	1. To develop use of words and reinforce intimacy.	1. Talk constantly to the child and explain processes such as feeding, bathing, and changing clothes.
	2. To develop the concept that things have names.	2. Name toys for the child as the child plays, foods and utensils as the child eats, and so on.
	3. To develop the concept that there is joy in the written word.	3. Read aloud to the child, enthusiastically.
	4. To develop the concept that language is used to describe.	4. Describe sounds to the child as they are heard.
9 to 12 months	1. To develop the concept that body parts have names.	1. Name parts of the body and encourage the child to point to them.
	2. To reinforce the concept that things have names.	2. Describe and name things seen on a walk or an automobile trip.
	3. To stimulate rhythm and interest in words.	3. Repeat simple songs, rhymes, and finger plays.
	4. To stimulate experimentation with sounds and words.	4. Respond to sounds the child makes, and encourage the child to imitate sounds.
12 to 18 months	1. To develop the ability to label things and follow directions.	1. Line up various objects and, naming one, ask the child to get it.
	2. To expand vocabulary and lay the foundation for later production of sentences.	2. Act out verbs ("sit," "jump," "run," "smile," etc.).
	3. To reinforce the concept of names and the ability to recognize names and sounds.	3. Use animal picture books and posters of animals.
	4. To encourage verbal communication.	4. Let the child talk on a real telephone.
	5. To reinforce the concept of labels and increase vocabulary.	5. Describe things at home or outside, on a walk or an automobile trip.
18 to 24 months	1. To stimulate imitation and verbalization.	1. Tape-record the child and others familiar to the child, and play the tapes back for the child.
	2. To improve the ability to name objects.	2. On a walk around the home or neighborhood with the child, point out and name familiar objects.
	3. To encourage repetition, sequencing, and rhythm.	3. Play counting games, sing songs, and tell and retell familiar stories.
	4. To develop auditory acuity, passive vocabulary, and the concept of language constancy.	4. With the child, listen to the same recording of a story or song over and over.
	5. To stimulate verbalization, selectivity and—eventually—descriptive language.	5. Cut out of magazines and mount on stiff cardboard: pictures of foods, clothing, appliances, etc. Have the child identify them as you show them. Use memorable descriptions: "orange, buttery carrots"; "the shiny blue car."
	6. To stimulate conversation.	6. With the child, prepare and eat a make-believe meal.

LEVEL	OBJECTIVE	ACTIVITY
24 to 36 months	1. To practice descriptive language and build vocabulary.	1. Keep a box of scraps of materials and small objects. Have the child select objects, using words to describe them ("fuzzy," "big," "red," etc.).
	2. To encourage verbalization, repetition, comprehension, and speaking in sentences.	2. Ask the child: "Show me the floor," ". . . the door," etc. When the child points, say "Here's the floor," etc., and encourage the child to imitate you.
	3. To develop the concept of written symbols.	3. Label the child's possessions. Use the child's name repeatedly: "Mike's bed," "Mike's toychest."
	4. To encourage specific and descriptive language.	4. Ask "Which one?" when the child gives a single-word description; and expand on the child's language. (E.g., child: "Cooky." You: "Yes; this is a ginger cooky.")
	5. To increase understanding of the relation between spoken and written language, and to stimulate the use of both.	5. Call to the child's attention familiar brand names or identifying symbols on products, buildings, and so on.

Objectives and Activities for Older Children

Introduction: Objectives

On our table of objectives for language development, the curriculum areas—the categories forming the horizontal axis—are the major process in language arts. We identify three major processes:

1. Oral communication—that is, listening and speaking.
2. Writing.
3. Reading.

We should point out, however, that this classification is an artificial invention applied to a global process; in other words, it is not so easy to separate oral communication from writing from reading as our tabular arrangement suggests. The language arts intermesh, in fact: each is related to the others. Obviously, you will want to stress different aspects at different times—if you are working with 3-year-olds, you will stress oral communication more than if you are working with third-graders. But the more your objectives and activities integrate the language arts, the more natural, meaningful, and productive they are likely to be for children.

As previously, the vertical axis of our table of objectives is age levels; objectives are categorized, then, by area—or process—and by level. Each of the activities following the table is keyed to an objective in the table: the objective is stated, and as before the "area, level, objective" key will enable you to find it on the table ("1-A-1" means "area 1, level A, objective 1").

Try our objectives and sample activities with individual children or groups of children; and feel free to expand on them, modify them, and invent others or let the children invent others. Remember that the overall goal is to help develop a generation of spirited, communicative, literate youngsters.

CURRICULUM AREAS		
(1) ORAL COMMUNICATION	**(2) WRITING**	**(3) READING**
1. Convey messages orally. 2. Expand speaking and hearing vocabulary on the basis of experiences and interactions with others.* 3. Develop acceptable oral language usages (e.g., use full, understandable sentences). 4. Share feelings, experiences, observations, and information. 5. Express "different" viewpoints (e.g., request a change). 6. Demonstrate comprehension (e.g., follow simple directions).* 7. Listen appreciatively (e.g., respond to tone, gestures, and body language). 8. Listen critically (e.g., follow a story line; identify new ideas). 9. Participate in small informal groups (e.g., converse with classmates and teachers; ask and answer questions). 10. Participate in dramatic arts (e.g., make up spontaneous fantasies; engage in imaginative play).	1. Effectively use the tools (e.g., paper, pencil, crayon) and the mechanics (scribbling, tracing, etc.) of writing. 2. Discover that writing can fill social needs (e.g., recognize one's own name).* 3. "Write" effectively to convey information (e.g., dictate experiences, observations, labels for pictures, and sentences).* 4. Compose creatively (e.g., dictate feelings and ideas).*	1. Expand problem-solving skills (e.g., use pictures to verify statements; answer questions; draw conclusions).* 2. Expand comprehension vocabulary on the basis of oral communications by others. 3. Use "word-attack" skills to identify written words (e.g., use picture clues, sight vocabulary).* 4. Listen to reading materials to gather information (e.g., listen to find specific answers). 5. Use reference sources to gather information (e.g., experts, field trips, observation, and experimentation). 6. Develop appreciation of literature (e.g., select from a bookshelf that includes picture books, stories written by the class, and other materials).

LEVEL A (AGES 3 TO 5)

*Asterisk signifies that an activity has been provided for this objective.

(Continued)

CURRICULUM AREAS		
(1) ORAL COMMUNICATION	**(2) WRITING**	**(3) READING**
1. Convey or relay messages orally. 2. Expand speaking and listening vocabulary on the basis of experiences and interactions with others. 3. Develop acceptable oral language usage (e.g., correct one's own grammatical errors; develop a vocabulary for talking about language; identify and use the noun-verb pattern).* 4. Share experiences and information for specific purposes. 5. Express "different" viewpoints (e.g., recognize divergent opinions, including one's own). 6. Demonstrate comprehension (e.g., follow a series of simple directions; respond appropriately to others' speech). 7. Listen appreciatively (e.g., show interest in sounds and descriptive language; identify with literary characters). 8. Listen critically (e.g., distinguish the real from the imaginary; identify described events as possible or impossible). 9. Participate in small informal groups (e.g., share at appropriate times; use greetings and farewells).* 10. Participate in dramatic arts (e.g., engage in spontaneous dramatic play; act out familiar stories).	1. Use the tools and mechanics of writing (e.g., use pencil and paper to copy words—such as names—and letters).* 2. Write effectively to meet social needs (e.g., use one's own name for labeling). 3. Write effectively to convey information (e.g., use one's own name and simple words as labels; contribute to group writing). 4. Compose creatively (e.g., dictate stories, using imagination, ideas, and feelings). 5. Recognize appropriate language conventions (e.g., capitalization of proper nouns; correct spelling of key words).*	1. Expand problem-solving skills (e.g., use pictures to verify statements; answer questions; draw conclusions; identify cause and effect).* 2. Expand comprehension vocabulary on the basis of oral communication by others.* 3. Use word-attack skills to identify written words (e.g., use picture clues, sight vocabulary, association of symbols and words, and simple, familiar labels; and anticipate redundant words, rhymes, repeated structural elements, enumerations, and patterns). 4. Use reading materials to gather information (e.g., find key ideas from picture clues). 5. Use reference materials (e.g., gather information from charts; picture books; word, color, or number books; and posters). 6. Develop an appreciation of literature (e.g., use the class library, including published books, books written by the class, and other materials).

LEVEL B (AGES 4 TO 6)

*Asterisk signifies that an activity has been provided for this objective.

	CURRICULUM AREAS		
	(1) ORAL COMMUNICATION	(2) WRITING	(3) READING
LEVEL C (AGES 5 TO 7)	1. Relay and change a message, using voice and body effectively (e.g., vary tone of voice, quality of voice, eye contact, and body language). 2. Expand speaking and listening vocabulary on the basis of experiences and interactions with others. 3. Develop acceptable oral language usage (e.g., choose correct forms or vocabulary when presented with alternatives). 4. Report experiences and present ideas, explanations, and directions clearly and succinctly.* 5. Express "different" viewpoints (e.g., state one's own position or tell one's own side of a story) clearly and succinctly. 6. Demonstrate comprehension (e.g., ask appropriate questions; restate ideas). 7. Listen appreciatively (e.g., respond to a speaker's mood or purpose).* 8. Listen critically (e.g., recognize a speaker's authority or expertise; distinguish between fact and fancy). 9. Participate in small or large informal groups (e.g., make introductions; share ideas in a group; participate in games). 10. Participate in dramatic arts (e.g., do improvisations and creative dramatizations; play roles, with appropriate language and facial expressions).	1. Use the mechanics of writing (e.g., print with correct size and spacing). 2. Write effectively to meet social needs (e.g., use names and salutations).* 3. Write effectively to convey information (e.g., use labels, phrases, and sentences). 4. Write creatively (e.g., write original sentences and simple stories). 5. Use appropriate language conventions (e.g., follow the rules for capitalization, spelling, and punctuation).*	1. Expand problem-solving skills (e.g., verify statements; draw logical conclusions from facts; answer questions; predict outcomes). 2. Expand comprehension vocabulary on the basis of reading and oral communications of others. 3. Use word-attack skills to identify written words (e.g., use contextual, picture, and configuration clues; sight vocabulary; classroom labels; and phonics).* 4. Read effectively to gather information (e.g., extract and relate main ideas of paragraphs; read silently or aloud to select supporting facts; distinguish between fact and fancy).* 5. Use reference materials (e.g., read and use graphs, tables of contents, and headings). 6. Develop appreciation of literature (e.g., use the school library; read a variety of materials for enjoyment including published books and books written by the class).*

(Continued)

	CURRICULUM AREAS		
	(1) ORAL COMMUNICATION	(2) WRITING	(3) READING
LEVEL D (AGES 7 TO 9)	1. Convey precise or subtle meanings and moods by using voice and body effectively.* 2. Expand speaking and listening vocabulary on the basis of experiences and interactions with others. 3. Develop acceptable oral language usage (e.g., vary sentence patterns and structure; use correct tense, number, gender, etc.). 4. Report experiences and present ideas, opinions, explanations, and directions accurately and logically, using one's own words and language patterns and those of others. 5. Express "different" viewpoints effectively (e.g., disagree courteously; persuade; convince).* 6. Demonstrate comprehension (e.g., identify a main idea; grasp a point; restate points made in a discussion; use and explain contextual clues; apply information). 7. Listen appreciatively (e.g., respond to literal and figurative meanings in prose and poetry). 8. Listen critically (e.g., distinguish between fact and opinion; determine relevance; identify a speaker's purpose).* 9. Participate in large and small formal and informal groups (discussions, study groups, research teams, presentations, social groups, etc.). 10. Participate in dramatic arts (e.g., follow a script; understand characterization).	1. Use the mechanics of writing (e.g., write legibly in print or script). 2. Write effectively to meet social needs (e.g., write different forms of letters, such as invitations). 3. Write effectively to convey information (e.g., write paragraphs, reports, and nonfiction accounts). 4. Write creatively (e.g., write poems, stories, and plays; make words say exactly what is intended; experiment with new words, forms, phrases, and figures of speech).* 5. Use appropriate language conventions (e.g., follow the rules for spelling, grammar, and punctuation).*	1. Expand problem-solving skills (e.g., answer questions; determine cause and effect; draw logical conclusions from implications; predict outcomes; generalize). 2. Expand comprehension vocabulary on the basis of extensive independent reading and oral communications of others. 3. Use word-analysis skills and structural analysis to identify new words (e.g., use roots, prefixes, suffixes, inflected endings, contractions, possessives, and hyphenated and compound words). 4. Read effectively to gather information (e.g., skim; read for main ideas; use various resources; and distinguish between fact and opinion and relevant and irrelevant information).* 5. Use reference materials (e.g., simple dictionaries, charts, maps, and encyclopedias).* 6. Develop appreciation of literature (e.g., visit the local library; read freely, selectively, and consistently; share reading experiences).

*Asterisk signifies that an activity has been provided for this objective.

Description   Using descriptive words to describe a hidden object.
Title (for children)   "FBI—Famous Bag Investigations."
Curriculum area   Language arts (oral communication).   **Age range**   3 to 5.

What is our objective?   To expand speaking and hearing vocabulary on the basis of experiences and interactions with others (table: 1-A-2).
What will we need?   Large paper bag or burlap sack; objects to identify (e.g., book, ball, small wheeled toy, cooky, pencil).
How will we do it?
1. Teacher and children discuss how words are used to identify things, and how this activity works. The participants form an "investigation circle."
2. The teacher puts an object into the bag or sack (not letting the children see what it is), and gives the bag to the first child.
3. The first child looks into the bag and then gives the others clues to the identity of the object inside (e.g., "It's round"; "It's red"; "You throw it"). The clues are given one at a time, with a pause after each for guesses. If no one guesses the object on the first clue, the child gives another, and so on.
4. Guesses, like clues, are to be given as complete sentences ("Is it a ball?" or, "It's a ball").
5. Whoever guesses correctly becomes the next clue giver. The teacher puts a different object into the bag and gives it to this child, and the game goes on.
What else can we do?   **Other activities:** Listening to stories and poems; enacting everyday situations (store, kitchen, etc.).

Description   Finding a hidden object by following directions.
Title (for children)   "Keeper of the Magic Box."
Curriculum area   Language arts (oral communication).   **Age range**   3 to 5.

What is our objective?   To demonstrate comprehension (table: 1-A-6).
What will we need?   A small box, which should look rather "special" (e.g., a velvet jewel case, a small brass box, a leather stamp box).
How will we do it?
1. Teacher and children discuss how we can tell people where to find things by using only words.
2. Two children at a time are chosen—one covers his or her eyes and the other hides the box.
3. When the "magic box" has "disappeared," the first child uncovers his or her eyes and the second gives directions (in complete sentences) for finding it: e.g., "Walk to the window"; "Turn around"; "Walk past the dress-up area"; "Look under the table."
4. When the first child finds the box, he or she becomes the next "keeper," and another child is chosen to search— and so on until all the children have had a turn at both roles.

What else can we do;   Other activities: "Mother, May I?" "Simon Says," and "Red Light, Green Light" are all good practice for giving and following directions; the teacher can also create opportunities for practice by asking children to enact specific things ("Show me how a kangaroo hops"; "Show me how a bird flies").

Description   Looking at pictures of persons, places, and things and thinking of appropriate verbs for them.
Title (for children)   "Fish Gotta Swim, Birds Gotta Fly."
Curriculum area   Language arts (oral communication).   **Age range**   4 to 6.

What is our objective?   To develop acceptable oral language usage (table: 1-B-3).
What will we need?   Magazines, scissors, paste, file cards (5- by 8-inch) or tagboard squares.
How will we do it?
1. Teacher and children discuss nouns and verbs—a noun is a word for a person, place, or thing; a verb is a word for something a person, place, or thing does. (Roughly—refinements and qualifications can come later.) Examples are given.
2. The children cut out of magazines pictures of persons, things, and places and mount them on index cards or tagboard.
3. When all the pictures are mounted, the teacher holds them up one by one, states the noun represented, and supplies an appropriate verb ("A dog barks"; "Ships float"). The teacher then asks, for each card, "What else?"
4. The children supply other appropriate verbs for each card ("A dog runs"; "Ships sink"). The children should use complete sentences.

What else can we do?   Follow-up: When the children have gotten the idea, reverse the activity, omitting the pictures— the teacher calls out a verb ("Swims") and the children respond with an appropriate noun. ("A fish").   **Another follow-up:**   Teacher and children discuss the fact that names are nouns. Each child gets a piece of drawing paper with his or her name written on it (older children can write their own names) and makes a drawing illustrating something he or she does. The children make sentences from this noun-verb combination ("Linda hops"; "Richard runs").
Another activity: "Noun-verb" lotto.

Description Learning (and using) greetings in other languages.
Title (for children) "Groovy Greetings."
Curriculum area Language arts (oral communication).   **Age range** 4 to 6.

What is our objective? To participate in small informal groups (table: 1-B-9).
What will we need? Chalkboard and chalk, or poster paper and marking pen. For older children: pencil and paper for keeping a list of greetings. The teacher will probably need some reference materials, to find new greetings.
How will we do it?
1. Teacher and children discuss how people speak different languages.
2. Each day for, say, two weeks or so, the teacher writes a "greeting of the day" on the chalkboard or a poster, using as many different languages as possible. E.g., "Hola" (Spanish), "Bonjour" (French), "Dag" (Dutch).
3. The teacher demonstrates how to pronounce the "greeting of the day" and explains what language it is.
4. Throughout the day, the children greet each other using the day's greeting.
5. Older children keep a list of all the greetings they've learned.
What else can we do? **Variation:** Include farewells ("Hasta Luego," "À bientôt," "Auf wiedersehen"). **Follow-up:** Keep a chart or list of all the variations of "Hello" and "Good-bye" in English ("Hi," "So long," "Be seeing you," "Howdy") and see how many the children can use in the course of a day. **An accompanying activity:** "It's a Small World" is an appropriate song for this objective.

Description A class project—a book of recipes contributed, dictated, and illustrated by the children.
Title (for children) "Creative Cookery."
Curriculum area Language arts (oral communication).   **Age range** 5 to 7.

What is our objective? To report experiences and present ideas, explanations, and directions clearly and succinctly (table: 1-C-4).
What will we need? 8½- by 11-inch paper (sturdy); pen or marking pens for the teacher; crayons or pencils for the children; colored construction paper for the covers; stapler or hole puncher and yarn or string; duplicating machine.
How will we do it?
1. Each child decides on a favorite recipe to include in the class cookbook, and brings it from home—in whatever form will aid memory (notes? pictures?).
2. Each child in turn dictates his or her recipe to the teacher. The teacher guides the children so that they learn to present the recipes logically: ingredients, amounts, processes (in order), cooking time, servings produced, serving instructions (e.g., "serve well chilled").
3. The teacher copies each dictated recipe on a sheet of 8½- by 11-inch paper, leaving at least half the sheet empty.
4. On the empty half of the sheet, each child makes a drawing to illustrate his or her recipe.
5. The recipe sheets are duplicated—one copy of each sheet for each child in the class.
6. The children put the recipes together between construction-paper covers, and "bind" their cookbooks by stapling or drawing string or yarn through punched holes. The cookbooks are taken home to share.
What else can we do? **Another activity:** Children can use a tape recorder to practice giving directions from their homes to school or vice versa; and they can take turns acting as teacher—assigning work and explaining directions.

Description Telling stories in a "good news, bad news" format, using stick puppets.
Title (for children) "Good and Bad News Bears."
Curriculum area Language arts (oral communication).　　　**Age range** 5 to 7.

What is our objective? To listen appreciatively (table: 1-C-7).
What will we need? For each child: two popsicle sticks (or tongue depressors, dowel sticks, or long pencils); two small paper plates; crayons; glue.
How will we do it?
1. Each child makes two stick puppets, as follows. On one paper plate, the child draws a smiling bear face; on the other, a frowning one. Each plate is glued to a stick, so that the child has a "good news bear" and a "bad news bear."
2. When the puppets are finished, the children form a circle. (Six to eight children per circle is about right.)
3. One child begins a story, *briefly* describing a situation and identifying it as good news or bad news (e.g., "Good news—I was invited to a birthday party") and holding up the appropriate puppet.
4. The next child *briefly* continues the story, alternating the type of "news" (if the opening was "good news," the next installment is "bad news") and again holding up the appropriate puppet (e.g., "Bad news—It was in China").
5. The story continues through as many installments as there are children in the circle, always alternating good news and bad news. (Or it may continue until the children decide that their story is finished.)
What else can we do? **Follow-up:** The children can use their "good news" and "bad news" puppets as they listen to stories, holding up the appropriate puppet at each development.

Description Reading sentences aloud and changing their meaning by changing stress and intonation.
Title (for children) "Changeable Chatter."
Curriculum area Language arts (oral communication).　　　**Age range** 7 to 9.

What is our objective? To convey precise or subtle meanings and moods by using voice and body effectively (table: 1-D-1).
What will we need? The teacher makes a number of "sentence strips"—sentences written on long strips of paper. (If the paper is flexible, these can be rolled up.) The nature of the sentences should be such that different accents and tones of voice will alter their meaning. (E.g., "Boy, would I like to jump in that water.")
How will we do it?
1. Teacher and children discuss how the *way* something is said can often change the meaning of the words—e.g., "I love spinach! (enthusiasm); "I loooove spinach" (heavy sarcasm).
2. The teacher gives each child (in the class or a group) a rolled-up sentence strip. The child unrolls it, reads it to himself or herself, and thinks about ways to change its meaning by tone of voice and accent.
3. In turn, the children read their sentences—first "straight" and then with an altered meaning, or with several different meanings.
4. After each strip is read, teacher and children discuss how its meaning was changed.
What else can we do? **Variation:** On the strips, have sentences which will sound true if read one way ("I always go to bed on time," with forthright look) and false if read another way ("I always go to bed on time," with giggles). Have the children read them both ways; the class or group decides if they're true or false. **Another activity:** Have the children pantomine stories, concentrating on changes in mood.

146

Description   Sharing viewpoints by "orating."
Title (for children)   "Soapbox Orators."
Curriculum area   Language arts (oral communication).   **Age range**   7 to 9.

What is our objective?   To express "different" viewpoints effectively (table: 1-D-5).
What will we need?   A "soapbox" (actually, a wooden fruit crate is best) or podium.
How will we do it?
1.   Teacher and children discuss the concept of "soapbox speakers"—people who are so enthusiastic about an idea that they just stand out in the street and talk about it. (Pictures of Hyde Park Corner in London would be appropriate.)
2.   The children draw up a list of several issues which they feel strongly about, but on which there's some disagreement among the children (e.g., "Should we be allowed to play outdoors when it's raining?").
3.   The children take turns as speakers—each gets up on the "soapbox" and tries to convince the others of his views on one of the issues.
What else can we do?   **Follow-up:** Members of the class can interview each other on the views they expressed as soapbox orators ("Now, sir, would you feel the same way about playing outdoors in a hurricane?").   **Other activities:** A class debate on some issue of importance or general interest; a mock presidential election, with speeches.

Description   Classifying statements as facts or opinions.
Title (for children)   "Facts and Feelings."
Curriculum area   Language arts (oral communication).   **Age range**   7 to 9.

What is our objective?   To listen critically (table: 1-D-8).
What will we need?   Two pocket charts. The teacher labels one chart "FACTS" and the other "FEELINGS" and makes a number of short sentence strips that will fit into the pockets. Each of the sentences should express a fact ("Alaska is the largest state in the United States") or an opinion ("Alaska is the best state in the United States").
How will we do it?
1.   Teacher and class discuss the difference between a fact and an opinion, giving some examples of each.
2.   The teacher distributes the sentence strips, one to each child.
3.   The children take turns reading their sentences to the class, and the class decides whether each sentence is a fact or an opinion. Each sentence strip is then placed in the appropriate pocket chart ("FACTS" or "FEELINGS").
4.   The children discuss what kinds of clues they can use to decide whether something is an opinion or a fact (e.g., value terms like "best" are usually clues to an opinion). (The teacher should include various kinds of clues on the sentence strips—not only value terms but also phrases like "I think . . ." and "I believe . . .")
What else can we do?   **Variation:** The children can make up their own strips for this activity.   **Another activity:** The teacher can state a brief problem, and then state several facts, one by one. As each is stated, the children decide whether it is relevant or irrelevant to the problem.

Activities for Writing

Description Dictating brief accounts of experiences and identifying the emotions involved.
Title (for children) "Mad? Sad? Glad?"
Curriculum area Language arts (writing).   **Age range** 3 to 5.

What is our objective? To "write" effectively to convey information (table: 2-A-3).
What will we need? The teacher prepares three looseleaf books: on the cover of one is a smiling face and the title "GLAD," on the second a sorrowful face and the title "SAD," on the third a scowling face and the title "MAD"; each book is filled with blank pages. The books are set out on a special table. The children may need drawing materials.
How will we do it?
1. Teacher and children discuss what kinds of things make us feel glad, sad, and mad; and the teacher sets out the three looseleaf books.
2. The teacher shows the blank pages in the books, and tells the children that they are to "write" the books by dictating their own experiences that made them happy, unhappy, or angry.
3. When moved to do so by an event, a child can dictate a brief account of it to the teacher, specifying which book it's to go in—"MAD," "SAD," or "GLAD."
4. The teacher prints each account on a separate sheet, which the child can remove and illustrate.
5. The books of illustrated accounts are kept on a table where all can share them. From time to time, the teacher may choose a page to read aloud and discuss with the children, or ask the children to choose a page.
What else can we do? **Another activity:** The teacher can mount pictures from magazines and ask the children to dictate labels for them, which are then printed and displayed with the pictures.

Description Dictating a description of an object on the basis of a fragmentary picture.
Title (for children) "Oh, Say, Can You Say?"
Curriculum area Language arts (writing).   **Age range** 3 to 5.

What is our objective? To compose creatively (table: 2-A-4).
What will we need? The teacher makes up several fragmentary pictures by drawing part of something on tagboard (e.g., a nose without a face, the front end of a car, a dog's tail, half of an ice cream cone) or cutting part of a picture of something from a magazine and mounting it on tagboard. For the activity, the teacher will also need more tagboard, or construction paper, and a marking pen.
How will we do it?
1. The teacher shows one of the fragmentary pictures and then glues it to the top of a large piece of tagboard or construction paper.
2. The children are asked to say what they think the picture might be. Each child in turn dictates his or her guess to the teacher, in the form "I say it's . . ."
3. The children's guesses are written under the picture by the teacher, who then reads them aloud to the class.
4. The activity continues with the next picture, and so on. The children are encouraged to guess freely and describe fully.
5. The pictures and the dictated comments are displayed around the room.
What else can we do? **Other activities:** The children can dictate labels for pictures supplied by the teacher or drawn by their classmates, or for photographs taken by the teacher of the class in action; they can also look at clouds and dictate what they see.

Description A special learning center for printing letters, numerals, and words.
Title (for children) "Print Shop."
Curriculum area Language arts (writing). **Age range** 4 to 6.

What is our objective? To use the tools and mechanics of writing (table: 2-B-1).
What will we need? A clearly defined area for the learning center; displays of printed material, etc.; materials for writing and copying; tables, chairs, etc.
How will we do it?
1. The teacher establishes a special learning center for printing. It is interesting to make this center reflect a real printing establishment in some simple ways—you might, for example, display a small hand-operated printing press, hang samples of printed matter (newspapers, say) and large-scale models of letters and numbers, have a type box and old pieces of type, and give each child who's working in the center a shop-type apron to wear. The press operators at a local newspaper may even show you how to make paper caps for the children to wear.
2. The center also has practical materials for the children to work with—models of letters and numbers, kinesthetic alphabet and numerals, letter templates, etc.; and plenty of writing paper, assorted pencils, colored crayons and marking pens, chalkboard and chalk, "magic" slates, and the like.
3. Using the models, the children copy letters, numerals, and words, trying for as close a match as possible—like a real print shop or typesetting room, this is a mechanical operation (and there is no reason why this analogy can't be drawn explicitly for the children).
4. The children's best work becomes part of the displayed material in the center.

What else can we do? **Follow-up:** As the children become more adept, they can copy whole sentences; later, they can do "real" work—make labels for the classroom, etc. Another (obvious) follow-up is a trip to the local newspaper or a small printing establishment.

Description Learning how to spell names and "key words" by using egg-shaped puzzles.
Title (for children) "Scrambled Eggs."
Curriculum area Language arts (writing). **Age range** 4 to 6.

What is our objective? To recognize appropriate language conventions (table: 2-B-5).
What will we need? The teacher makes a number of egg-shaped puzzles out of cardboard, tagboard, or construction paper—each with a child's name or "key word" that is shown correctly spelled when the puzzle is put together. Each puzzle is kept in a separate envelope (or a small bag).
How will we do it?
1. Each child gets a puzzle with his or her own name, and several puzzles with individual "key words."
2. The children practice arranging the pieces—a child knows that a word is spelled correctly when the puzzle fits together.
3. As they become better at recognizing words, this sequence may be reversed—the child knows how to put the puzzle together by recognizing how the word is spelled.

What else can we do? **Variation:** Commercial word puzzles are also available. **Other activities:** The children can use "Try-Task" letters (a commercial product); they can also fill in missing letters in their names or "key words" (M _ R G I E).

Description   Writing and recognizing classmates' names.
Title (for children)   "What's Your Name? Pudding Tame. (Ask Me Again and I'll Tell You the Same.)"
Curriculum area   Language arts (writing).   **Age range**   5 to 7.

What is our objective?   To write effectively to meet social needs; and to use appropriate language conventions (table: 2-C-2 and 2-C-5).

What will we need?   Chalkboard and chalk or poster paper and marking pen for the teacher; 5- by 8-inch file cards and marking pens for the children.

How will we do it?

1. The teacher makes a "master list" of the names of all the children in the class on the chalkboard or poster paper, using capital and lowercase letters as appropriate.

2. Each day for a week or so, the children practice writing the names of, say, five or six of the students—being sure to use capital letters and lowercase letters correctly. Keep this up until the names of all the children have been practiced.

3. When the children have had enough practice, each child copies each name on the list onto a file card. These file cards may be decorated.

4. Then each child passes out his or her cards to their namesakes. (Any mistakes? Try again.)

5. The cards can be used as bookmarks, seat savers, passes for leaving the room, etc.

What else can we do?   Other activities: Each child can make a graphic design based on his or her own name (e.g., by writing it in different styles or different directions); and the children can write short letters beginning "Dear _____."

Description   Putting final punctuation marks on unpunctuated sentence strips.
Title (for children)   "Sentence Stoppers."
Curriculum area   Language arts (writing).   **Age range**   5 to 7.

What is our objective?   To use appropriate language conventions (table: 2-C-5).

What will we need?   A number of sentence strips prepared by the teacher—each with a sentence lacking end punctuation—and a boxful of small cards, each containing a period, a question mark, or an exclamation point, sized so that they will fit in place on the sentence strips (these are the "stoppers"); also, a bulletin board or poster for displaying the finished sentences; cellophane tape.

How will we do it?

1. The teacher explains the use of the three end punctuation marks—period (.), question mark (?), and exclamation point (!)—giving examples and then asking the children for examples.

2. One by one, the teacher hands each child a sentence strip. The child examines the sentence, pulls the correct end punctuation mark out of the box of "stoppers," and—holding the mark in place while displaying the sentence—reads the sentence to the class with the correct inflection.

3. If the class decides that the punctuation mark chosen is correct, it is affixed in place with tape and the sentence is hung on the display board. If there's controversy or uncertainty about the proper mark, children and teacher discuss it.

What else can we do?   Variation: The children themselves can make up sentences for the strips.   **Other activities:** Individual letter cards are good for spelling practice; and poster-sized run-on sentences (in, say, blue ink) can be punctuated by the children (in, say, red).

Description   Illustrating plays on words and figures of speech.
Title (for children)   "Playing with Words."
Curriculum area   Language arts (writing).   **Age range**   7 to 9.

What is our objective?   To write creatively (table: 2-D-4).
What will we need?   Construction paper, drawing paper, crayons, pencils, markers.
How will we do it?
1. Teacher and children discuss how we can make plays on words—puns, double meanings, figure of speech, etc.   The teacher should be prepared to start things off with some good examples: e.g., "ice cream = "I scream" (pun); "shoehorn" (double meaning); "crying your heart out" (figure of speech).
2. When the children have the idea and can give some examples of their own, teacher and children discuss how such plays on words might be illustrated pictorially.
3. Each child thinks of a play on words and illustrates it.
4. The results are displayed around the room (or on a bulletin board).
What else can we do?   **Follow-up:** The children can look for plays on words in the books they read.   **Other activities:** Poetry is good practice for writing creatively—e.g., children can be asked to give the last line of a limerick or other verse.

shoehorn

Description   Writing sentences, complete with final punctuation marks, to describe pictured events.
Title (for children)   "Oh! May I ask a question?" he exclaimed.
Curriculum area   Language arts (writing).   **Age range**   7 to 9.

What is our objective?   To use appropriate language conventions (table: 2-D-5).
What will we need?   The teacher prepares mounted pictures of scenes showing action.   The children will need pencils and paper to begin with; later, they'll need paper for sentence strips.
How will we do it?
1. The teacher and the children discuss, or review, the three end punctuation marks—period, exclamation point, and question mark.
2. The teacher shows the class a picture and asks the children to write three sentences about it: one statement, one question, and one exclamation.
3. Each child writes three sentences, being sure to use the correct end punctuation.
4. When several pictures have been shown, and sentences have been written about them, the sentences are read aloud, corrected, and then mounted or written on sentence strips and displayed with the pictures.
What else can we do?   **Variation:** Instead of using pictures, the children can take turns enacting brief scenes (say, in twos or threes) for the rest of the class to write sentences about.   **Another activity:** Have the children correct improperly punctuated sentences.

Activities for Reading

Description   Working with sequence pictures.
Title (for children)   "Picture Perfect."
Curriculum area   Language arts (reading).   **Age range** 3 to 5.

What is our objective?   To expand problem-solving skills (table: 3-A-1).
What will we need?   The teacher will need a number of sets of sequence cards, with three cards in each sequence (the teacher can make these or use commercial cards or sequences from reading workbooks).
How will we do it?
1.   For each set of sequence cards, the teacher holds up the first and describes it briefly (e.g., "Here's an egg").
2.   Then the teacher holds up the second card and calls on one of the children to describe it. What the teacher should guide the children to give is a description of card 2 as a development of the situation in card 1 ("Now the egg is cracking").
3.   Concealing the picture on the third card, the teacher asks the class to volunteer ideas about what might be happening on it—again, the idea is to describe a reasonable development from cards 1 and 2 ("A bird will hatch").
4.   When the children have pooled ideas, the teacher shows the picture on card 3. Did the children predict it accurately? If their idea was different, was it nevertheless logical—that is, possible?

What else can we do? **Variation:** The children can draw their "predictions" about card 3—that is, each child makes a drawing to complete the sequence.   **Another activity:** Teacher and children can play "Prove It." The teacher holds up a picture showing some situation and makes a statement about it—the children are to "prove it" by finding evidence in the picture.

Description   Making a class toy catalog and labeling the entries by dictation.
Title (for children)   "Catalog Capers."
Curriculum area   Language arts (reading).   **Age range**   3 to 5.

What is our objective?   To use "word-attack" skills to identify written words (table: 3-A-3).
What will we need?   Catalogs, magazines, sales brochures; scissors and paste; scrapbook or looseleaf book and blank pages; marking pen for labeling.
How will we do it?
1.   The children use the catalogs, magazines, and fliers to find and cut out pictures of toys—just pictures, no text.
2.   The pictures are pasted in the class catalog, with room left for labels.
3.   In turn, the children dictate the labels for the pictures to the teacher, who writes them in the catalog.
4.   The catalog is displayed in the classroom, and the children take turns looking at it and "reading" the labels.
What else can we do?   **Other activities:** The teacher can bring in canned and packaged foods whose labels consist of a picture of the product and a term describing it—the children use the picture to "read" the label. Also, objects in the classroom can be drawn on cards, with a label—the children use the drawing to "read" the label, and match each card with the appropriate object in the room.

Description   Using pictures of nature scenes as the basis for making statements and asking and answering questions.
Title (for children)   "Naturally, It's Nature."
Curriculum area   Language arts (reading).   **Age range**   4 to 6.

What is our objective?   To expand problem-solving skills (table: 3-B-1).
Wht will we need?   To begin with: several pictures of scenes of nature, mounted and displayed by the teacher. Later: unmounted pictures, scissors, paste, and construction paper for the children. (The pictures can be from magazines, calendars, posters, etc.)
How will we do it?
1.   The teacher displays several mounted pictures of nature scenes.
2.   The children take turns making statements about a picture (their choice of scene) or answering questions about it posed by the teacher. E.g., a simple statement might be "There are pine trees and snow in this picture"; a question might be "Why are the leaves off the trees in this picture?"
3.   Then the children can choose from among the unmounted pictures—each child chooses one scene, mounts it, and makes up a question to ask about it.
4.   Taking turns, the children ask their classmates the questions they have thought up. The classmates must answer by finding evidence in the scene.
What else can we do?   **Follow-up:** A homework assignment—each child is to bring one picture from home and be prepared to ask a question about it that the other children can answer by examining it. **Another activity:** The teacher prepares sets of two cards in which card 1 shows cause (e.g., forest fire) and card 2 show effect (e.g., burned-out forest). (These can be made of mounted pictures from magazines.) The children must match all the cause-effect pairs.

Description   Working cooperatively to define words.
Title (for children)   "Definitely Defined."
Curriculum area   Language arts (reading).   **Age range**   4 to 6.

What is our objective?   To expand comprehension vocabulary on the basis of oral communication by others (table: 3-B-2).

What will we need?   Circles of, say, six chairs each; chart paper; tagboard; marking pen.

How will we do it?

1. Teacher and children discuss what a definition is. Then the children form "sharing circles" of about six children each.
2. The children in each "sharing circle" are to work cooperatively to define a word. The teacher "assigns" each circle its word by announcing the word orally and also giving the circle a tagboard card with the word written on it (even if not all—or not any—of the children are reading). The words to be defined should be "topical"—that is, meaningful to the children (e.g., "fun," "game," "home"). Each circle may be given the same word or a different word.
3. The children in each circle pool their ideas, and then each person in the circle defines the assigned word as he or she understands it.
4. The teacher writes each circle's definitions on a chart. The tagboard on which the word was written is pasted in place as the title of the chart.

What else can we do?   **Other activities:** The teacher can present incomplete phrases which the children are to "fill in"—e.g., "sweet as _____"; "soft as _____." Another good activity is the guessing game "I'm Thinking of Something"; the teacher provides clues in the form of descriptive terms ("round," "blue," "bouncy"), and the children guess the object.

Description   A team game—matching labels with objects in the classroom.
Title (for children)   "Label Lineup."
Curriculum area   Language arts (reading).   **Age range**   5 to 7.

What is our objective?   To use word-attack skills to identify written words (table: 3-C-3).

What will we need?   Three or four sets of labels (prepared by the teacher); each set consists of ten to fifteen sturdy labels for different objects in the classroom (DESK, TABLE, CHAIR, etc.). The sets are on different-colored stock but otherwise identical. (The children may have rolls of tape.)

How will we do it?

1. The class is divided into three or four teams; each team receives one set of labels.
2. On a signal from the teacher ("Go" or "Begin labeling" or whatever), the teams match their labels with the appropriate objects in the room. (They can tape their labels to the objects or simply place them on the objects.)
3. The first team to match all its labels with the right objects is the winner—but it must read back all the labels it has attached.
4. If any team can't finish labeling at the end, the other children may help.

What else can we do?   **Another activity:** (This is for individual children.) Each child gets a set of sticky tags labeled with names of body parts (ARM, HAND, etc.). The children see how quickly they can stick all the labels on the right body parts.

Description   A game involving use of reference materials to support given statements.
Title (for children)   "Facing Facts."
Curriculum area   Language arts (reading).   **Age range**   5 to 7.

What is our objective?   To read effectively to gather information (table: 3-C-4).
What will we need?   For each group: a book; pencil and paper for jotting down information. The teacher has prepared a set of "Facing Facts" cards—each card has a statement (the "fact") about the book that has been given to the groups; in addition to these cards, the teacher will need a timer.
How will we do it?
1. The class is divided into groups, and each group gets a copy of the same book.
2. The teacher hands each group a different "Facing Facts" card, which contains a statement that can be "proved" by recourse to the book. (E.g., "Grandmother lives far away.") The group must keep the card face down until the teacher says "Go."
3. The teacher says "Go," starting the timer. The groups have a given amount of time in which to "face the fact" and find supporting evidence in the book.
4. When the timer goes off (or the teacher says "Time's up"), the groups take turns reading their cards and the support they found for the facts.
5. The game continues with another "Facing Facts" card, and another, and so on.
What else can we do?   **Variation:** Each group can get a different book; in this case, the teacher will prepare a separate set of cards for each group.   **Another activity:** Each child gets a short paragraph or very short story; the children read silently and then take turns recounting or acting out what they've read.

Description   Using a simple "literature appreciation" form.
Title (for children)   "Formal Form Fill-In."
Curriculum area   Language arts (reading).   **Age range**   5 to 7.

What is our objective?   To develop appreciation of literature (table: 3-C-6).
What will we need?   Materials for making the "formal form"—one large poster and one 8½- by 11-inch master to be duplicated—and plenty of books and stories; a chalkboard.
How will we do it?
1. Teacher and children discuss what they think makes a book or story good, bad, or so-so.
2. The teacher keeps a running list on the chalkboard of children's ideas.
3. Teacher and children decide on a few simple basic ideas and put them together to make a "literature appreciation form." Each class will of course arrive at its own form; but the teacher should guide the children so that their form eventually includes data to identify the book (title, author) and the child filling out the form, the date on which the form is being filled out, and several literary criteria (e.g., Was it interesting? Did the ending make sense? Did the story have any surprises? Did I like the characters? Would I like to read more stories by this author?).
4. When the form is final, a large poster of it is made (by the teacher or a group); and the teacher makes an 8½- by-11-inch master and duplicates it in quantity. The copies are placed in the library area.
5. As the children read books and stories individually or in groups, they fill out the "formal form" to assess them.
6. From time to time, the class can read, compare, and discuss the filled-in forms.
What else can we do?   **Other activities:** Children can draw pictures to illustrate books and stories they like especially. A class trip to the local library is good.

Description   A class project—a collection of astounding facts about animals.
Title (for children)   "Believe It or Not."
Curriculum area   Language arts (reading).   **Age range**   7 to 9.

What is our objective?   To read effectively to gather information (table: 3-D-4).
What will we need?   For the class: a scrapbook or looseleaf book entitled "Believe It or Not—Animals." For the children: many resource books and magazines; pencils and note paper for collecting information; drawing materials and marking pens for writing in the class book.
How will we do it?
1. Children and teacher discuss how many interesting and unusual things can be learned about animals, and each child picks one animal to study about.
2. Over a period of time—a few days or a week—the children work independently, reading about "their" animals and taking notes on what they read.
3. When their research is complete, the children list as many interesting facts as they can about their animals and each child chooses, say, two or three unusual facts to put in the "Believe It or Not" book.
4. The children share their facts and then take turns writing the astounding ones in the class book. Each child illustrates his or her entries.
5. The book becomes a part of the class library.
What else can we do?   Variations: Other topics can also be used for "Believe It or Not" books—e.g., sports, places, history.   Other activities: Have children read paragraphs to identify the main idea; have children make up simple "bibliographies" for their reports in various subjects.

Description   A learning center for using the telephone directory.
Title (for children)   "Let Your Fingers Do the Walking."
Curriculum area   Language arts (reading).   **Age range**   7 to 9.

What is our objective?   To use reference materials (table: 3-D-5).
What will we need?   Well-defined area to serve as the "telephone center," with table and chairs, telephone books (white and yellow pages), paper and pencils, and task cards; a nonworking telephone is a nice addition. The task cards, made up by the teacher, contain such questions as "Who can you call to fix a broken refrigerator?" and "Where can I get a haircut?"—they can be kept in a file box.
How will we do it?
1. The teacher sets up the "telephone center," with telephone directories and task cards. Teacher and children discuss how telephone directories work.
2. As they work in the center, the children choose task cards and use the telephone directories to find the required information.
3. They fill in the "answers" on the file cards. If the task cards are kept in one file box, they can be transferred to a second file box as they are completed.
4. Periodically, the completed cards can be discussed by children and teacher.
What else can we do?   Follow-up' As the children become proficient, the tasks can be made more difficult—e.g., by the addition of some out-of-town directories.   Other activities: A "dictionary center" can be set up along the same lines, with the task cards requesting definitions, correct spellings, etymology, etc. Similarly, a "map center" can be set up, with atlases, road maps, and a globe—the task cards would request map-related information ("What lies west of California?" "Is Boston on a river?").

Resources for Language Arts

Bibliography for Teachers

Anderson, V. *Reading and young children.* New York: Macmillan, 1968. (Although basically a textbook, consideration is given to the beginnings of reading with various approaches presented and explained. Competencies and skills children are expected to achieve are described and practical ideas for teaching and evaluation presented. Focus is completely on the *young* child.)

Binder-Scott, L. *Learning time with language experiences for young children.* New York: McGraw-Hill, 1968. (Designed for teachers of young children. A great collection of language activities, including poems, finger plays, stories, rhymes, and riddles.)

Burrows, A., Jackson, D., & Saunders, D. *They all want to write* (3d ed.). New York: Holt, 1964. (This is a classic for those who want to encourage the love of writing in today's children. The authors distinguish between practical and personal writing and provide specific suggestions for developing skill in both in beginning writers.)

Chambers, D. *Storytelling and creative drama.* Dubuque, Iowa: Brown, 1970. (Both sections of this book provide specific examples of techniques in implementing activities with children. Suggested procedures and educational implications are discussed.)

Dorsey, M. *Reading games and activities.* Belmont, Calif.: Fearon, 1972. (This book contains hundreds of activities organized by skills to allow the teacher to vary programs and keep the child interested. Skills include visual and auditory perception, long and short vowel sounds, consonant blends, and vocabulary extension and comprehension.)

Durland, F. *Creative dramatics for children.* Kent, Ohio: Kent State University Press, 1975. (This manual for teachers includes source materials, techniques, problems, and suitable material for creative dramatics.)

Ehrlich, H., & Grastry, P. *Creative dramatics handbook.* Philadelphia: School District of Philadelphia Instructional Services, 1971. (This handbook offers many ideas for the teacher wishing to include creative drama in the curriculum with a fresh and practical approach.)

Gillies, E. *Creative dramatics for all children.* Washington, D.C.: Association for Childhood Education International, 1972. (Special features of this book are sections dealing with creative dramatics for children with special needs and for children for whom English is a second language.)

Jacobs, L. (Ed.). *Using literature with young children.* New York: Teachers College, 1965. (A collection of articles by several experts. This little book provides ideas for reading aloud, storytelling, presenting poetry, doing choral speaking, and other aspects of a literature program for young children.)

Johnson, E., Sickels, E., & Sayers, F. C. *Anthology of children's literature.* Boston: Houghton Mifflin, 1959. (From Mother Goose around the world to sacred writings, this book includes biographies, reading lists, and excellent suggestions for storytelling.)

King, J., & Katsman, C. *Imagine that: Illustrated poems and creative learning Experiences.* Pacific Palisades, Calif.: Goodyear, 1976. (This is a unique book of poems created by listening to children sharing their feelings and experiences, with illustrations and suggestions for activities designed to extend the meaning of the poems. Topics covered include such "universals" as our world around us, the senses, and feelings.)

Larrick, N. *A teacher's guide to children's books.* Columbus, Ohio: Merrill, 1963. (An invaluable guide to children's literature with practical suggestions for ways to arouse interest, and to relate books to personal and social growth, projects and activities; and ideas for appraising classroom reading activities and materials available. A detailed list of books and index are helpful.)

Lundsteen, S. *Ideas into practice.* Englewood Cliffs, N.J.: Prentice-Hall, 1976. (This teacher's guide aims at developing creative problem-solving skills in communication.)

McCaslin, N. *Creative dramatics in the classroom* (2d ed.). New York: McKay, 1974. (Specific exercises in pantomine, improvisation, play structure, and play preparation and production are offered. Suggestions are provided for using poetry, choral reading, and readers' theater. A good bibliography of books, films, and materials is included.)

McIntyre, B. *Creative drama in the elementary school.* Itasca, Ill.: Peacock, 1974. (Designed for the classroom teacher with little experience in drama. This book aims to help the teacher gain insight into the dramatic process and into how this process can stimulate children's language learning. Many examples and specific suggestions are included.)

Northwestern Regional Educational Laboratory. *CHILD: Coordinated helps in language development.* Portland, Ore.: Copy-Print Centers, 1971. (1206 S.W. Jefferson, 97201.) (This is a teacher's guide to a *direct* approach to improving language in the kindergarten. Lessons are arranged by instructional goals within a sequential order. Suggested materials are listed.)

Pilon, B. A. *Teaching language arts creatively in the elementary grades.* New York: Wiley, 1978. (The author presents a variety of activities designed to enhance language development. Appropriate activities for grades K through 6 in the areas of reading, writing, speaking, and listening are included.)

Possien, W. *They all need to talk: Oral communication in the language arts program.* New York: Appleton-Century-Crofts, 1969. (Specific teaching situations with appropriate techniques and procedure are provided to give children a wide range of stimulating experiences in the development of oral language skills.)

Povey, G., & Fryer, J. *Personalized reading: A chance for everyone.* Encino, Calif.: International Center for Educational Development, 1972. (Practical ideas for teachers interested in individualizing—or personalizing—their reading programs are presented by two teachers who tried and tested these ideas in the classroom. An excellent reference with many creative ideas.)

Schaff, J. *The language arts idea book: Classroom activities for children.* Pacific Palisades, Calif.: Goodyear, 1976. (This book contains lots of language activities in the areas of listening, speaking, vocabulary, and creative writing.)

Schimmel, N. *Just enough to make a story.* Berkeley, Calif.: Sisters' Choice, 1978. (The author believes that the skills of choosing, learning, and telling stories can be acquired, along with the attitudes that help a storyteller. This book includes a wealth of stories that lend themselves to this neglected art with ideas on how to tell them.)

Sealy, L. *Children's writing: An approach for the primary grades.* Newark, Del.: International Reading Assn., 1979. (An excellent source of material and activities geared to the beginning writer. The importance of reading and its relationship to other learning areas is included. The importance of the teacher in modeling is also discussed.)

Siks, G. *Creative dramatics.* New York: Harper and Row, 1960. (Chapters 5 to 8 of this classic provide practical ideas implementing a creative dramatics program with children aged 4 to 8.)

Spencer, Z. *FLAIR.* Stevensville, Mich.: Educational Service, Inc., 1972. (P.O. Box 219, 49127.) ("FLAIR" is a handbook of classroom ideas to motivate creative writing. Practical ideas and activities are included.)

Texas Education Agency. *Creative dramatics in the elementary school.* Austin, Tex.: Texas Education Agency, 1978. (A guide to creating a classroom atmosphere that encourages creative dramatics: materials and procedures. Available for $1 from Texas Education Agency, 201 E. 11th St., Austin, Tex. 78701.)

Veatch, J., Sawicki, F., Barnette, E., Elliott, G., & Blakey, J. *Key words to Reading: The language experience approach begins.* Columbus, Ohio: Merrill, 1973. (The answer to many of the critics of the language experience approach, this book provides ideas for changing the traditional reading program. How to begin, how to include literature, writing, and skill development are all dealt with and specific procedures suggested.)

Reference material:

Adventuring with books (Rev. ed., 1956). (Compiled and published by the National Council of Teachers of English, 704 S. 6th St., Champaign, Ill. 61820. A list of one thousand books recommended for K through grade 6, arranged under major subject headings.)

Bibliography of books for children (Rev. 1956). (Compiled and published by the Association for Childhood Education, International, 1200 15th St., NW, Washington, D.C. 20005. Another list of approximately one thousand books recommended for children from ages 4 to 12 arranged by major subject.)

Booklist, The: A guide to current books. (American Library Assn., 50 E. Huron St., Chicago, Ill. 60611.)

Horn Book Magazine, The: (A bimonthly, published by Horn Book, Inc., 585 Boylston St., Boston, Mass. 02116. A distinguished magazine devoted exclusively to the field of children's literature.)

Tarbert, G. *Children's book review index.* Detroit: Gale research. (Cites all reviews of children's books appearing in over 300 magazines and newspapers, general educational and literary journals, and certain subject areas. Each entry gives author's name, title of book, reviewing publication, date, and page of review.)

Poetry:

Brown, M. W. *Nibble nibble.* New York: Scott, 1959.
De Regniers, B. S., Moore, E., and White, M. M. *Poems children will sit still for.* New York: Scholastic, 1973.
Milne, A. A. *Now we are six* (Rev. ed.). New York: Dutton, 1961.
Stevenson, R. L. *A child's garden of verses.* New York: Airmont, 1969. (Many other modern reprints are available.)
Thompson, J. M. *Poems to grow on.* Boston: Beacon Press, 1957.

Journals:

Children's Theatre Review. (Children's Theatre Assn. of America, 1029 Vermont Ave., NW, Washington, D.C. 20005.)
Educational Theatre Journal. (American Theatre Assn. 1029 Vermont Ave., NW, Washington, D.C. 20005.)
Journal of Reading. (International Reading Assn., 800 Barksdale Rd., Newark, Del. 19711.)
Language Arts. (Official journal, National Council of Teachers of English, 1111 Kanyon Rd., Urbana, Ill. 61801.)
Reading Teacher. (International Reading Assn., 800 Barksdale Rd., Newark, Del. 19711.)

Book lists and sources of reviews of children's books:

Association for Childhood Education International. *Good and inexpensive books for children.* Washington, D.C.: ACEI, 1972. Author and title indexes, and classification by category—fiction, biography, etc. Includes list of publishers.)
Adell, J., & Klein, H. D. (Eds.). *Guide to non-sexist children's books.* Chicago: Academy Press, 1976. (Both current and retrospective titles. (Fiction and nonfiction.)
Bulletin of the Center for Children's Books. (University of Chicago, 5750 Ellis Ave., Chicago, Ill. 60637.)
Children's Book Council. *Choosing a child's book.* (Illustrator, P. Parnall.) (Free pamphlet.)
Ciancio P. (Ed.) *Picture books for children.* Chicago: ALA, 1973. (Pre-K through elementary. Compiled by National Council fo Teachers of English.)
Eakin, M. *Good books for children* (Rev. ed.). Chicago: University of Chicago: University of Chicago Press, 1962.
Eaton, A. T. *Treasure for the taking* (Rev. ed.). New York: Viking, 1957.
Gillispie, J. T. *Paperback books for young people: An annotated guide to publishers and distributors* (2d ed.). Chicago, Ill.: American Library Assn., 1977.
Madden, P., & Stocker, D. *Guide to children's magazines, newspapers, reference books* (Cohen, M.D., & Baron, B. D., Eds.). Washington, D.C.: Assn. for Childhood Education International (ACEI), 1977. (Well annotated for parents and teachers.)
Haviland, V. (Ed.). *Children's books.* Washington, D.C.: Government Printing Office, 1977. (Stock no. 030-001-0085-1.)
Horn Book. (585 Boylston St., Boston, Mass. 02116. Bimonthly magazine.)
Notable children's books. (American Library Assn., Children's Service Div., 50 E. Huron St., Chicago, Ill. 60611.)
Paperbound books in print. New York: Bowker. (Semiannual. Arranged by author, title, and subject.)

Reviews of children's books can be found in the spring and fall of each year in:

Christian Science Monitor.
New York Times.
Saturday Review.

Bibliography for Children

Criteria for evaluating picture books:

Is the subject interesting?
Is the story brief?
Is the background authentic?
What type of atmosphere is created?
What experience does the book offer?
Do the illustrations allow for imaginative contemplation?
Are the sounds of the words appealing?
Is the book a harmonious whole?
Will the child identify with the characters?
Are the words rhythmic?
Are the sentences short?

Kinds of books to include in filling a children's library:

Books of poetry and rhymes.
Storybooks and books of fairy tales and folktales.
Picture stories.
Stories about contemporary problems. (Birth, death, divorce, multicultural relations.)

A selection of ABC books:

Alexander, A. *ABC of cars and trucks.* New York: Doubleday, 1956.
The amazing adventures of Silent E Man. New York: Random House, Electric Company PopUp Series. (Ordering address: 457 Hahn Rd., Westminster, Md. 21157.)
Anno, M. *Anno's alphabet.* New York: Crowell, 1975. (Richly detailed illustrations.)
Berenstain, S., & Berenstain, J. *The B book.* New York: Random House, Bright and Early Book Series. (Ordering address 457 Hahn Rd., Westminster, Md. 21157.)
Bond, S. *Ride with me, through ABC.* New York: Scroll Press, 1968.
Cambique, S. *A is for angry.* (K. Hardin, Illustrator.) (Nonsexist, multiracial. Available from Children's Book and Music Center, 2500 Santa Monica Blvd., Santa Monica, Calif. 90404.)
Feelings, M. *Jambo means hello: Swahili alphabet book.* New York: Dial, 1974.
Fromen, R. *Angles are easy as pie.* New York: Crowell, 1976.
Fujikawa, G. *A to Z picture book.* (Available from Children's Book and Music Center, 2500 Santa Monica Blvd., Santa Monica, Calif. 90404.)
Ga'g, W. *The ABC bunny.* New York: Coward-McCann, 1933.

Geisel, T. S. *Dr. Seuss's ABC*. New York, Random House, Beginner Books. (Ordering address: 457 Hahn Rd., Westminster, MD. 21157.)

Lear, E. *ABC*. New York: McGraw-Hill, 1965.

Lionni, L. *Alphabet tree*. New York: Pantheon, 1968. (Beautifully illustrated. Accompanying record.)

Mendoza, G. *The Marcel Marceau alphabet book* (Photographs: M. Greene). New York: Doubleday, 1970.

Milgrom, H. *ABC science experiments* (Photographs: D. Crews). New York: Macmillan, 1970.

Milgrom, H. *ABC of ecology* (Photographs: D. Crews). New York: Macmillan, 1972.

Miller, B. *Alphabet world*. New York: Macmillan, 1971. Letter shapes in ordinary objects: coffee cups and traffic lights, for example.)

Munari, B. *ABC*. New York: World, 1960.

Tudor, T. *A is for Annabelle*. New York: McKay, Walck, 1954.

Turlay, C. N. *The kittens' ABC*. New York: Harper and Row, 1965.

Wildsmith, B. *Brian Wildsmith's ABC*. New York: F. Watts, 1962.

Some storybooks to have on hand:

Field Enterprises Educational Corp. *Childcraft* (Vols. I–IV: *Literature*). Chicago: Field Enterprises Educational Corp., 1964.

Geisel, T. S. Dr. Seuss books. New York: Random House, Beginner Books. (Ordering address: 457 Hahn Rd., Westminster, Md. 21157.)

Haviland, V. *The fairy tale treasury*. New York: Coward, McCann, and Geoghegan, 1972.

Humpty Dumpty's storybook. New York: Parents' Magazine Press, 1966. (From *Humpty Dumpty* magazine.)

Illustrated poems for children (K. Orska, Illustrator). Chicago: Rand McNally. (P.O. Box 7600, 60680.)

Minerik, E. H. *Little bear's friend* (M. Sendak, Illustrator). In *The Little Bear series*. New York: Harper and Row. (Ordering address: Keystone Industrial Pk., Scranton, Pa. 18512.)

Mother Goose rhymes. Various editions.

Rey, H. A. *Curious George* series. New York: Scholastic. (Ordering address: 904 Sylvan Ave., Englewood Cliffs, N.J. 07632.)

Rojankovsky, F. *The tall book of nursery tales*. New York: Harper and Row. (Ordering address: Keystone Industrial Pk., Scranton, Pa. 18512.)

Scarry, R. Richard Scarry books. (Several publishers, mostly Western, New York.)

Stoutenbery, A. *American tall tales*. New York: Viking, 1966.

Music, movement, and drama—books for children and their teachers:

Charlip, R. *Mother, mother, I feel sick*. New York: Parents' Magazine Press, 1966. (52 Vanderbilt Ave., 10017. Good for acting out.)

Coody, B. *Using literature with young children*. Dubuque, Iowa: Brown, 1979. (2460 Kerper Blvd., 52001.)

Emberly, B. & Emberly, E. *Drummer Hoff*. Englewood Cliffs, N.J.: Prentice-Hall, 1967. (07632. Good for reading into a tape recorder.)

Flint Public Library. *Ring a ring of roses*. (Flint, Mich.: Flint Public Library. (Asst. Director's Office, 1026 E. Kearsley St., 48502. A handbook of 400 finger plays.)

Glaza, T. *Eye Winker, Tom Tinker, Chin Chopper*. New York: Doubleday, 1973. (Finger plays, with music.)

Goodridge, J. *Creative drama and improvised movement for children.* Boston: Plays, 1970. (Practical suggestions for appropriate material for plays, and movement.)

Gray, V., & Percival, R. *Music, movement, and mime for children.* London: Oxford, 1962. (Paperbound. Lessons in music and movement illustrated by photographs of little children.)

Lowndes, B. *Movement and creative drama for children.* Boston: Plays, 1971. (Improvised movement as a creative act and as a way of expressing feeling.)

Sendak, M. *Where the wild things are.* New York: Harper and Row, 1963. (A classic for acting out.)

Stecher, M. B., et al. *Music and movement improvisations.* Vol. 4 of Threshold Early Learning Library (18 vols.). New York: Macmillan, 1970–1973. (Paper bound. Description of music activities. Photos. Songs.)

Storytelling records on the Pathways of Sound label (102 Mt. Auburn St., Cambridge, Mass. 02138.):

Uncle Remus. (Read by Morris Mitchell.)
Winnie-the-Pooh. (Read by Maurice Evans.)
More Winnie-the-Pooh. (Read by Maurice Evans.)
The most of Winnie-the-Pooh. (Read by Maurice Evans.)
E. B. White reads "Charlotte's Web."

From Children's Book and Music Center (2500 Santa Monica Blvd., Santa Monica, Calif. 90404), order Dance-a-Story records. Each title includes storybook with 7-inch long-playing record or with cassette. One side of record: music and narration; other side: music only. Titles and catalog numbers:

At the beach. (Record with book, PE 145; cassette with book, PE 568.)
Balloons. (Record with book, PE 140; cassette with book, PE 563.)
Brave hunter. (Record with book, PE 142; casette with book, PE 565.)
Flappy and floppy. (Record with book, PE 143; cassette with book, PE 566.)
Little duck. (Record with book, PE 144; cassette with book, PE 560.
Magic mountain. (Record with book, PE 139; cassette with book PE 562.)
Noah's ark. (Record with book, PE 138; cassette with book, PE 561.)
The toy tree. (Record with book, PE 144; cassette with book, PE 567.)

Learning Materials

Aids in learning the alphabet:

Wooden capital letters.
Magnetic alphabet board.
Alphabet puzzles. (Match capital and lowercase letters.)
Capital-letter templates.
Alphabet practice cards. (For copying sample letters.)
Stationery, pencils, pens, crayons.
Chalk, chalkboards.

Aids in learning to read words:

Phonic dictionary.
Phonics charts.
Photographic action cards with captions.

Handbooks on children's acting and books of stories to act out or read aloud:

Allstrom, E. *Let's play a story.* New York: Friendship Press, 1957. (A handbook on the uses of informal drama.)

Fitzgerald, B. *Let's act the story.* Palo Alto, Calif.: Fearon, 1957. (A handbook for the beginner.)

Fitzgerald, B. *World tales for creative dramatics and storytelling.* New York: Prentice-Hall, 1962. (Unusual stories for acting out.)

Iarusso, M. B. *Stories: A list of stories to tell and read aloud* (7th ed.). New York: New York Public Library, 1977. (Identifies over 450 individual stories and tales used successfully by librarians. Includes bibliographies of poetry and prose, as well as sound recordings, useful for storytelling activities.)

Kase, R. *Stories for creative acting.* New York: French, 1961. (Classic collection.).

Useful or essential items for playacting:

Stage.	Blocks.
Sheet or screen.	Boxes and cartons.
Costumes and hats.	Records. (For movement or mime.)
Accessories	Toy telephones.
Props.	Doorway Theatre for puppets.
Scarves.	(From Poppets, 1800 E. Olive
Puppets.	Way, Seattle, Wash. 98102.)
Puppet stage.	

Kits for dramatic play:

Doctor.	Cooking.
Grocery store.	Beauty shop.
Post office.	Pirate.
Police.	Painter.

Sources and Suppliers

General sources:

Library.
Curriculum laboratories.
Bookstore.
Toy store.

Teachers' supply store.
Garage sales.
Catalogs from stores, publishers, and manufacturers.

Manufacturers and publishers:

Aurora Products Corp.
Child Guidance Toys.
Childcraft.
Constructive Playthings.
Creative Playthings.
Dolch Sounding Material.
Educational Insights.
ETA and ABC School Supply.
Ideal.
Instructo.

Instructor Curriculum Materials.
Kenworthy Instructional Materials.
Milliken.
Milton Bradley.
Playskool.
Scholastic Book Service.
Trend Enterprises.
Uniworld Toys.
Weber Costello.
Wise Owl Publications.

Stores and supply houses:

Children's Book and Music Center, 2500 Santa Monica Blvd., Santa Monica, Calif. 90404.

Children's Learning Center, 4660 E. 62d St., Indianapolis, Ind. 46220.

Gale Research Co., Book Tower, Detroit, Mich. 48226. (Reprints about books and authors. Send for book list; 30-day approval period.)

Get Smart Educational Toys, Equipment and Supplies, 8898 Clairemont Mesa Blvd., Suite E., San Diego, Calif. 92123. (General education-supply house.)

Judy Co., Barclay School Supplies, 29 Warren St., New York, N.Y. 10007. (Learning games.)

Kaplan School Supply Corp., 600 Jonestown Rd., Winston-Salem, N.C. 27103. (Learning games.)

Scholastic Book Services, 904 Sylvan Ave., Englewood Cliffs, N.J. 07632. (Excellent inexpensive collection of children's paperback books.)

"Sing 'n' Sound," Play 'n' Talk International Headquarters, P.O. Box 18804, Oklahoma City, Okla. 73118.

Tucker's Yarn Shop, 950 Hamilton St., Allentown, Pa. 18101. (Bucilla Design No. 1888, ABC Sampler.)

Enrichment Materials

Sources for books, audiovisual materials, and information:

American Library Assn., Children's Service Div., 50 E. Huron St., Chicago, Ill. 60611.

Assn. for Childhood Education International, 3615 Wisconsin Ave., NW, Washington, D.C. 20016.

Assn. of Children's Librarians of Northern California, San Francisco Public Library, San Francisco, Calif.

Bank Street College of Education Bookstore, 69 Bank St., New York, N.Y. 10014.

Beckley-Cardy Co., Western Region, 25802 Clawiter Rd., Hayward, Calif. 94545. (A teacher's educational supply catalog. Lots of enrichment.)

Child Study Assn. of America, Inc., 9 E. 89th St., New York, N.Y. 10028.

Children's Record Guild, 27 Thompson St., New York, N.Y. 10013.

Educational Resources Information Center, 4936 Fairmont Ave., Bethesda, Md. 20014.

Encyclopaedia Britannica Educational Corp., Reference Div., 425 N. Michigan Ave., Chicago, Ill. 60611.
National Assn. for the Education of Young Children, 1834 Connecticut Ave., NW, Washington, D.C. 20009.
National Assn. for the Preservation and Prepetuation of Storytelling (NAPPS), Box 112, Jonesboro, Tenn. 37659.
Scholastic Records, 906 Sylvan Ave., Englewood Cliffs, N.J. 07632.

Children's book clubs:

Junior Literary Guild, Garden City, N.Y. (Picture Book, ages 5 to 6; Easy Reading, ages 7 to 8.)
Parents' Magazine's Book Clubs, Bergenfield, N.J. (Read Aloud Book Club, ages 2 to 6; Beginning Readers Book Club, ages 5 to 7; American Boy Book Club, ages 8 to 12; Calling All Girls Book Club, ages 8 to 12.)
Scholastic Book Clubs, Dept. RCC, 904 Sylvan Ave., Englewood Cliffs, N.J. 97632. (Lucky Book Club, grades 2 and 3.)
Weekly Reader Children's Book Club, Education Center, Columbus, Ohio 43216. (Age groups: 5 to 7.)

Resource guides and books and articles about children's books:

Commire, A. (Ed.). *Yesterday's authors of books for children: Facts and pictures about authors and illustrators of books for young people from early times to 1960.* Detroit: Gale Research. (Book Tower, 48226. Photographs of authors and artists, reproductions of book illustrations, and scenes from movies based on books.)
Locher, C., & Evory, A. (Eds.). *Contemporary authors.* Detroit: Gale Research. (Book Tower, 48226. Guide to current writers and their work in many fields, including movies and television.).
Multimedia for children's literature. *Instructor*, November 1971, pp. 50–57. (A resource guide for audiovisual materials in the language arts.)
Scott, L. B., May, M. E., & Shaw, M. S. *Puppets for all the grades.* Dansville, N.Y.: Instructor Publications. (14437.)
Viguers, R. H. *Margin for surprise: About books, children and librarians.* Boston: Little, Brown, 1964.

Resource books (finger plays, puppet plays, storytelling, drama, music, poems to read aloud):

Anderson, P. S. *Storytelling with the flannel board.* Minneapolis, Minn.: Denison, 1963.
Ellis, M. J. *Fingerplay approach to dramatization.* Minneapolis, Minn.: Denison, 1960.
Ellis, M. J. & Lyons, F. *Finger playtime.* Minneapolis, Minn.: Denison, 1960.
Haaga, A. & Randles, P. *Supplementary material for use in creative dramatics with younger children.* Seattle; University of Washington Press, 1952. (A program of lessons using music and literature with drama.)
McCall, A. *This is music for today.* Boston: Allyn and Bacon, 1971. (A little of everything in children's drama and music. Kindergarten and nursery school.)
Rasmussen, C. *Poems for play time.* Boston: Expression Co., 1942.
Rasmussen, C. *Let's say poetry together and have fun.* Minneapolis, Minn: Burgess, 1962.
Steiner, V. G., & Pond, R. E. *Finger play fun.* Columbus, Ohio: Merrill, 1970.
Wagner, J. A. *Flannel board teaching aids.* Palo Alto, Calif.: Fearon, 1960.
White, A. *A bouquet of poems.* East Orange, N.J.: Triad, 1966.

Records and cassettes:

All about the alphabet. (History of speech, from primitive sounds to the written word. Available from Children's Book and Music Center, 2500 Santa Monica Blvd., Santa Monica, Calif. 90404.)

Bert and I, and other stories from down east. (R. Bryan and M. Dodge. Bert and I, 35 Mill Rd., Ipswich, Mass. 01938. Also available from L. L. Bean, Inc., Freeport, Maine 04033.)

Birds, beasts, bugs, and bigger fishes. (Peter Seeger. Folkways FC 7011. New York, N.Y. 10023. Storytelling on record.)

Carl Sandburg's poems for children. ("Early Moon," "Buffalo Dusk," and others. Available from Children's Book and Music Center, 2500 Santa Monica Blvd., Santa Monica, Calif. 90404.)

Dance a story series. (RCA records.)

Frank Luther's ABC, 1 to 10. (Alphabet songs and counting in rhymes. Available from Children's Book and Music Center, 2500 Santa Monica Blvd., Santa Monica, Calif. 90404.)

Pick a pack o' poems. (Six records or cassettes with six filmstrips. Teacher's guide. Available from Children's Book and Music Center, 2500 Santa Monica Blvd., Santa Monica, Calif. 90404.)

Rootabaga stories. (Carl Sandburg. Caedmon TC 1089. 1995 Broadway, New York, N.Y. 10023.)

Spirit Cassette Kits. (Titles include *Get ready to read, Sight word fun,* and *Reading and thinking.* Hampden Publications, Inc., Baltimore, Md. 21211.)

Stallman, L. *Sound-word perception skills through music: When we were very young.* (Judith Anderson reads Milne's poems. Available from Children's Book and Music Center, 2500 Santa Monica Blvd., Santa Monica, Calif. 90404.)

Where the wild things are. (Tammy Grimes reads this and other Sendak stories. Available from Children's Book and Music Center, 2500 Santa Monica Blvd., Santa Monica, Calif. 90404.)

Videotapes in *Southern Appalachian video ethnography* series:

Ward, M. *Jack tales and others.* (Broadside Video, Elm and Millard, Johnson City, Tenn. 37601.)

Windham, K. T. *Ghost stories.* (Broadside Video, Elm and Millard, Johnson City, Tenn. 37601.)

Films:

Fixin' to tell about Jack. (16 mm, color, 25 min. Ray Hicks tells the tale of Soldier Jack, from Chan's *Jack tales.* Appalshop, Box 743, Whitesburg, Ky. 41858.)

Marcel Marceau pantomimes. (Sound, color, 13 min. Brandon Films, Inc., 200 W. 57th St., New York, N.Y. 10019.)

Playing: Pretending spontaneous drama with children. (Black-and-white, 20 min, Pittsburgh Child Guidance Center, Community Services Dept., 201 De Soto St., Pittsburgh, Pa. 15213.)

Puppets: Creative work and play. (Sound, black-and-white, 16 min. State University of Iowa, Extension Div., Bureau of Audiovisual Instruction, Iowa City, Iowa 55240.)

Story acting is fun. (Sound, black-and-white, 10 min. Florida State University, Div. of University Relations, Tallahassee, Fla. 32306.)

Additional sources of films:

Bailey Film Service, 6509 De Longpre Ave., Hollywood, Calif. 90028.)
University of Michigan, Audiovisual Center, Frieze Bldg., 720 E. Huron St.,
    Ann Arbor, Mich. 48104.)

Toys and games for language development:

Alphabet toys, such as alphabet rubber stamps and alphabet bingo.
Caldecott Reading Involvement Kits.
Hand Puppet Idea Bag. (A burlap bag filled with puppet-making materials.
    J. R. Holcomb Co., 3000 Quigley Rd., Cleveland, Ohio 44113.)

Kits and sources for kits:

Bank Street College of Education. *Early childhood discovery materials.*
    New York: Macmillan, 1973. (Ordering address: Front and Brown Sts.,
    Riverside, N.J. 08075. Language, perceptual, conceptual, and motor skills.
    Sets of interrelated materials. Open-ended and reinforcement materials.)
Dunn, L., Smith, J. O., & Horton, K. *Peabody language development pro-*
    gram: Level P. Circle Pines, Minn.: American Guidance Service, 1968.
    (Publisher's Bldg., 55014. Multimedia materials to aid in the development
    of perceptual and conceptual skills as well as language expansion. Teacher's
    manual, recordings, posters, mannequins, puppets, more.)
Educational Enrichment Materials, Dept. AN439258, 357 Adams St., Bed-
    ford Hills, N.Y. 10507. (Multimedia approach to children's literature.
    A filmstrip club offering bonus books and catalog cards for the class.)
Educational Insights. (Some products: The Reading Box, The Spelling Box,
    The Vocabulary Box.)
Houghton Mifflin, 777 California Ave., Palo Alto, Calif. 94304. (Offers a
    complete reading series: minibooks, writing helps, activity-card file box,
    story boards, records and cassettes, filmstrips, games, and more.)
Karnes, M. *Goal: Language development.* Springfield, Mass.: Milton Brad-
    ley, 1972. (443 Shaker Rd., East Longmeadow, Mass. 01028. 337 game-
    oriented activities for small groups or individuals to teach all sorts of
    perceptual and verbal skills. Manipulative materials and teacher's guide.)
Pushaw, D., Collins, N., Czuchna, Co., Gill, G., O'Betts, G., & Stahl, M.
    Teach your child to talk. New York: Cebeo Standard, 1969. (Ordering
    address: 11 Kerlick Rd., Fairfield, N.J. Preschool program for parents.
    Slides, tapes, film, manual.)
Spruegel, C., Nance, I., & Karnes, M. *Early childhood enrichment series:*
    Learning to develop language skills. Springfield, Mass.: Milton Bradley,
    1970. (443 Shaker Rd., East Longmeadow, Mass. 01028. Emphasizes
    labeling skills and verbal expression. Manipulative materials, teacher's
    manual.)

Community Resources

Performers and performances:

Radio and television.
Movies.
Theater. (Legitimate; little theater or community theater; high school or college plays.)
Local performers. (Actors; mimics; entertainers.)
Traveling circuses.
Puppet shows.

The printed word:

Libraries.   Newspapers.
Bookstores.   Print shops.
Magazine racks.

Materials:

Toy store.
Teachers' supply store.

Guest speakers:

Writers.   Operators.
Printers.   Tour guides.
Calligraphers.   Storytellers.

Community resources for kit making:

Thrift shops.   Hospitals.
Parents.   Lumberyards.
Local merchants.   Fabric shops.
Community workers.   Toy stores.
Craft supply stores.   Hardware stores.

Collect props, clothing, uniforms, accessories.

Section 5

AFFECTIVE DEVELOPMENT: ACTIVITIES AND RESOURCES

"Affective" development has to do with those aspects of children's experience that lead to well-adjusted, cooperative human beings—comfortable with themselves, able to express themselves openly and creatively, and capable of functioning effectively in social settings.

We begin, as before, with objectives and activities for infants and toddlers; we then present objectives, activities, and resources for older children. In the sections for older children, we have chosen social studies, music, and art to illustrate the affective domain. These three areas, of course, have a strong affective component and thus are good examples of affective approaches to the curriculum. But we are not suggesting either that social studies, music, and art are the only examples of the affective domain or that they do not have psycho-physical-motor, cognitive, and linguistic elements. Clearly, social studies, art, and music do have other components; and just as clearly, all the other areas of the curriculum have an affective component.

In fact, it is important to remember that the affective element is all-pervasive. Everything you do in setting up the environment, in interacting with children, and in teaching any subject has implications for the children's emotional, social, and creative development.

Objectives and Activities for Infants and Toddlers

From a very early age—possibly from the first moments of life—children are developing a concept of self and the ability to express themselves and relate to others through experiences, activities, and interactions. Early affective experiences lead naturally into later ones—into "informal" areas such as moral development and clarification of values and into "formal" subject areas such as social studies, art, and music.

We begin at the very beginning. What are some of the ways in which infants' and toddlers' affective development is fostered? Parents, caretakers, and teachers can provide the kind of nurturing and environment that will allow children to explore confidently and to experiment with themselves and others. An enriched environment, offering many opportunities for choosing among alternatives, making decisions, and solving problems; freedome within limits; and guidance by sensitive adults—all these help to ensure the wholesome development of young children.

In building sound emotional, social, and creative development, we need activities that emphasize awareness of the environment, a concept of the self and the world outside the self, independence, social awareness, the idea of different roles, the ability to deal with emotions, and the value of self-expression and creativity.

The table on the following pages (174–175) suggests objectives and activities for children from birth to 36 months; these constitute an "informal curriculum" for affective development in the very early years.

**Sequential Objectives and Activities for Affective Development:
Birth to 36 months (continued)**

LEVEL	OBJECTIVE	ACTIVITY
Birth to 1 month	1. To increase the sense of security. 2. To lay the foundation for identification of family roles. 3. To develop the concept that oneself is distinguishable from others. 4. To introduce music and rhythm, and to soothe the child.	1. Frequently touch and hold the child. 2. Maintain a regular daily routine with as many family members as possible participating. 3. Let the child touch your face, hair, fingers, etc. 4. Sing lullabys to the child.
1 to 3 months	1. To expand the concept of self. 2. To provide opportunities for smiling and reaching as a sign of recognition. 3. To make the child feel welcome and secure. 4. To stimulate rhythm.	1. Hold the child up to a mirror. 2. Present the child with familiar faces, objects, and actions. 3. Create a warm and pleasant environment (soft colors, good lighting, appropriate furniture and decorations); and hold the child firmly. 4. Provide the child with a variety of sounds (ticking clock or metronome, music box, wind chimes, etc.).
3 to 6 months	1. To develop self-confidence. 2. To develop selectivity. 3. To develop independence. 4. To develop facial expressions for various feelings.	1. Reward the child with a gentle touch, a smile, or words. 2. Place a variety of toys in the child's crib. 3. Allow the child to move freely on a rug. 4. Make faces at the child and encourage the child to imitate you.
6 to 9 months	1. To develop rhythm. 2. To develop self-expression. 3. To stimulate experimentation. 4. To develop creativity and expressiveness.	1. Clap for the child, or clap the child's hands together. 2. Move the child's body, arms, and legs to music. 3. Encourage the child to imitate you in such actions as clapping hands, pointing, and lying down. 4. Give the child objects for creating sounds (shakers, wooden spoons, etc.).
9 to 12 months	1. To develop awareness of the environment. 2. To develop the self-image. 3. To let the child use the body in new ways and develop the sense of things outside the self. 4. To stimulate social awareness and identification of significant others. 5. To encourage independence.	1. Demonstrate familiar sounds for the child; e.g., ring a doorbell, turn on a gush of water, dial a telephone, use a typewriter. 2. Show the child a mirror image or photographs of himself or herself. 3. Encourage the child to play with hand puppets. 4. Show the child pictures of familiar people and identify them: "Daddy," "Mommy," "Grandpa." 5. Allow the child to drink from a cup or hold a spoon.

174

LEVEL	OBJECTIVE	ACTIVITY
12 to 18 months	1. To further develop the concept of self, and to develop ideas of "mine" and "yours."	1. Take the child outside on a sunny day and play shadow games. ("Whose shadow is that?" "Stand on my shadow." "Catch my shadow.") You can create similar activities using a flashlight.
	2. To develop self-confidence and independence.	2. Have the child do some simple, useful tasks: clean up little messes; use a sponge to wipe off a table; put trash from a snack or meal in the trashcan.
	3. To encourage recognition of objects and develop the sense of causality and the ability to group logically.	3. Encourage the child to feel grass, smell flowers, listen to wind or wind chimes or the sounds of birds and animals, and so on.
	4. To develop the concept of adults' and children's roles, and to increase independence.	4. Give the child a doll and demonstrate how to rock it, kiss it, feed it, bathe it, dress it, etc.
	5. To encourage self-expression and develop rhythm.	5. Encourage the child to use rhythm instruments such as a drum or bells.
18 to 24 months	1. To develop warmth and security.	1. Have a special, loving bedtime routine: e.g., story, song, prayer, hug.
	2. To increase awareness of the body.	2. Form human figures out of clay for the child, or cut out and mount pictures from magazines (which can be made into puzzles).
	3. To develop pride and independence.	3. Let the child help with personal-care routines: combing and brushing the hair; brushing teeth; washing the face and hands.
	4. To increase self-confidence and build social responsibility.	4. Let the child do some useful jobs: e.g., dusting table tops, wiping down walls with a wet sponge, helping to set the table, putting away toys.
	5. To encourage self-expression and selectivity.	5. Let the child mix colors (food coloring and water) and encourage choice ("What's your favorite color?").
	6. To develop rhythm and cooperation.	6. Sing or chant along with the child.
24 to 36 months	1. To develop the self-concept.	1. Make a life-size tracing of the child; let the child color the outline in and add details.
	2. To encourage appreciation of, and movement to, various types of music.	2. Play recorded music—marches, waltzes, jazz, classical works, and popular songs—and join the child in responding to it.
	3. To increase awareness of the body and its parts, increase social awareness, and reinforce the concept of "mine" and "yours."	3. Name body parts, using the child's body, others' bodies (including dolls and pictures), and your own body to demonstrate.
	4. To stimulate exploration of roles and recognition of role models, encourage self-expression, and stimulate verbalization of ideas and feelings.	4. Encourage role playing, dramatic play, and sociodrama with humans or puppets. This can be done with or without simple props (hats, scarves, etc.).
	5. To increase independence and self-confidence, and to encourage selectivity.	5. Let the child dress—or help dress—himself or herself.
	6. To encourage free expression in various art media.	6. Let the child make "sculptures" with scraps of dough or peanut butter, or finger-paint with chocolate pudding.

Objectives and Activities for Older Children: Social Studies

Introduction: Objectives

Social studies is an interdisciplinary area; it is generally considered as including psychology, sociology, economics, anthropology, history, geography, and political science.

In arriving at objectives and activities for social studies, we have (1) selected certain broad concepts, (2) identified generalizations leading to each of these concepts, (3) arranged the generalizations in an effective sequence, and (4) designed experiences leading to each of the generalizations.

We have chosen the following broad concepts:

1. "People group together" (human behavior).
2. "People organize and set limits" (political science).
3. "People live on earth" (geography).
4. "People are aware of their heritage" (history).
5. "People manage resources" (economics).

These five major concepts make up the curriculum areas—the horizontal axis—on our table of objectives. The vertical axis, as before, is age levels. The objectives—categorized by curriculum area (or, in this case, concept) and age level—are the generalizations that lead to the broad concepts. Within each curriculum area, the generalizations are presented in order of increasing complexity.

How does this approach work? Consider, for example, curriculum area 2—or concept 2—"People organize and set limits." The first generalization at the first age level—that is, objective 1 at level A—is "I follow rules to help protect my freedom and safety and the freedom and safety of others." We suggest that this idea is appropriate for 3- to 5-year-olds. For 5- to 7-year-olds, the first objective is a more complex generalization: "Rules that people must obey (laws) protect us and our public places" (objective 1 at level C). For 7- to 9-year-olds (level D), still more complex generalizations are appropriate, involving the concepts of electing representatives to make laws and establishing agencies to enforce them.

We believe that the objectives in the table—the generalizations—are attained only after experience with a number or examples. Accordingly, content and activities need to be selected and arranged sequentially to correspond with the appropriate generalizations. The activities we present are keyed to the table of objectives and designed to provide experiences that will lead to the generalizations. As previously, we state the objective—the generalization, in this case—for each activity and give the "area, level, objective" key so that you can find it on the table ("1-A-1" means "area 1, level A, objective 1").

Before going on to the objectives and activities, we want to make some general comments on social studies.

First, although our remarks so far have focused on content—our major concepts and the generalizations leading to them—you need to realize that in many schools and preschools there is an attempt to balance content with process and with the wishes or goals of the community. "Process" has to do with the skills involved in social studies: e.g., reading maps and graphs; observing and recalling observations; classifying; analyzing; synthesizing; evaluating. The goals of the community, as reflected in a social studies program, are likely to be such things as avoiding stereotypes, stressing local concerns or a common local heritage, instilling good citizenship, and fostering individual interests.

Second, we believe that, whatever the specific makeup of a social studies program, continuity of experiences is important. Too often—especially in the primary grades—social studies is a haphazard collection of unrelated experiences. In a program like the one we recommend here, unity can be provided by means of themes which cut across the curriculum areas at each age level. For example, at level A (ages 3 to 5), we suggest "the family" as a unifying theme.

Third, the concept of a unifying theme brings us to the idea of a major unit of study. Curriculum areas which are tied together by an overall theme form such a unit. Let's return to our example of "the family" as a unifying theme—or unit—at level A. As the teacher and children develop this unit, generalizations (objectives) and activities from each of the curriculum areas will be involved. Developing a unit of study involves the following sequence of steps:

Initiation of the unit—that is, deciding on the unifying theme.
Arrangement of the environment in appropriate ways.
Exploratory questions—to determine what the children already know.
Planning by teacher and children.
Individual and group activities.
Related activities in other fields (e.g., music and art).
A culminating activity.
Evaluation.

Fourth, we must acknowledge that social studies is sometimes regarded as a nonessential, and that early childhood teachers sometimes wonder how to fit it into a day crowded with the teaching and learning of basic skills. We recommend that you try thinking about social studies units as a core from which many activities in reading, writing, mathematics, and other areas can emanate. The concepts of social studies should not be reserved for one period of the day; they represent knowledge, values, and attitudes that should permeate the climate of the classroom and the interactions that take place in it.

Fifth, and finally: remember that development in the area of social studies—as elsewhere—depends much more on what we get out of children than on what we put into them. Your major role as a teacher is to be a motivator, a resource, and a synthesizer. The children can and will do the rest.

	CURRICULUM AREAS	
	(1) PEOPLE GROUP TOGETHER (HUMAN BEHAVIOR)	**(2) PEOPLE ORGANIZE AND SET LIMITS** (POLITICAL SCIENCE)
LEVEL A (AGES 3 TO 5)	1. Although in some ways I am like other children, I am special—and so are all the people around me. 2. I am able to do many things, and I can solve many problems. 3. I can be responsible for my own behavior as I learn to care for myself. 4. It is all right to have different kinds of feelings.*	1. I follow rules to help protect my freedom and safety and the freedom and safety of others.* 2. When I play with others, I sometimes lead and sometimes follow. 3. Sometimes the choice of most of the people decides what we get to do. 4. Sharing or taking turns allows me to do and use more things.
LEVEL B (AGES 4 TO 6)	1. Families do things together. 2. Different people in my family help me in different ways. 3. Families differ in size and composition (which may change).* 4. All over the world, people have similar reasons for living in families. 5. Families' preferences can determine their food, clothing, and homes.	1. My family has rules to keep it running smoothly.* 2. Different members of my family help make decisions. 3. Different members of my family have different degrees of power in various areas. 4. All over the world, families have family rules. 5. Families' food, clothing, and homes are affected by different regulations.
LEVEL C (AGES 5 TO 7)	1. Religious, social, and service organizations in our neighborhood, community centers, and parks provide means for people in our community to be together.* 2. Schools are provided and supported in our community because people recognize the importance of education. 3. People who live in our community are responsible for making it a good place to live.* 4. All over the world, people have the same basic needs. 5. All over the world, people have similar reasons for living in communities.	1. Rules that people must obey (laws) protect us and our public places.* 2. Our community establishes ways to enforce laws and to deal with those who break them. 3. People need to be well-informed citizens and participate in running their communities. 4. All over the world, communities have rules or laws in order to run efficiently. 5. All over the world, people participate in running their communities.
LEVEL D (AGES 7 TO 9)	1. When larger groups of people come together, they can have more opportunities for such things as learning, recreation, social involvement, and shopping. 2. People make choices about living in urban or rural communities.* 3. The groups of people who make up our city and county are responsible for making it a good place to live. 4. All over the world, people live in urban or rural communities. 5. Migration between rural and urban areas and between states and nations creates many problems having to do with such things as housing, education, jobs, and cultural adjustment.	1. We select certain people to be our leaders in our city, county, state, and nation.* 2. We elect representatives to make plans and laws for our city and county. 3. We elect other representatives to make plans and laws for our state and nation. 4. We need to know who our government officials are and where our representatives meet.* 5. Government officials and agencies exist to implement services. 6. Courts exist to uphold our laws. 7. Law-enforcement agencies exist to enforce our laws. 8. People need to be well-informed citizens and to make their opinions known. 9. All over the world, there are systems to make, implement, and enforce laws. 10. All over the world, there are different methods for selecting leaders and governments.

*Asterisk signifies that an activity has been provided for this objective.

CURRICULUM AREAS		
(3) PEOPLE LIVE ON EARTH (GEOGRAPHY)	(4) PEOPLE ARE AWARE OF THEIR HERITAGE (HISTORY)	(5) PEOPLE MANAGE RESOURCES (ECONOMICS)

LEVEL A (AGES 3 TO 5)

(3) GEOGRAPHY	(4) HISTORY	(5) ECONOMICS
1. I know about my world. 2. I can describe special places in my world.* 3. I have ways of moving and traveling in my world.* 4. There are special things I can do because of the part of the world where I live.	1. As I grow, I change.* 2. The way I look and act is part of my heritage.	1. I take care of my possesions and things I use.* 3. I use things carefully and don't waste them. 4. I have a special job. My job is going to school.

LEVEL B (AGES 4 TO 6)

(3) GEOGRAPHY	(4) HISTORY	(5) ECONOMICS
1. My family and I have relatives and friends who live in different places.* 2. The members of my family have different ways of moving and traveling in their world. 3. There are special things my family does because of where the family lives. 4. All over the world, people have similar reasons for living in families. 5. Families' food, clothing, and homes are determined by environmental conditions and availability.	1. Family records tell me about my family's past.* 2. My family heritage is a result of the experiences and customs of all my ancestors. 3. All over the world, families have heritages and need to be aware of them. 4. Families' food, clothing, and homes can be determined by tradition.	1. When each person in my family does his or her special job, the family runs smoothly. 2. Homes and the way we choose them differ in many ways. 3. Families are supported in different ways. 4. All over the world, families manage their resources. 5. Families' food, clothing, and homes can be determined by cost and jobs.*

LEVEL C (AGES 5 TO 7)

(3) GEOGRAPHY	(4) HISTORY	(5) ECONOMICS
1. A map is a special kind of picture of a community or area.* 2. There are landmarks that make each community unique (e.g., churches, schools, shopping centers).* 3. In our community, there are different ways to travel. 4. Our community is similar to, and different from, others. 5. Natural conditions (soil, water, climate, etc.) have helped make our community what it is. 6. All over the world, communities use their environment and resources to supply their needs and wants.	1. Our community is constantly changing. 2. Maps and photographs can tell me about our community at different periods. 3. People in our community have different customs and traditions that help determine the character of the community. 4. The heritage of our community is the unique contributions made by its earliest settlers.* 5. All over the world, communities are constantly changing. 6. All over the world, communities need to be aware of the importance of their heritage.	1. Every family in our community depends on other people for services. 2. Some people in our community produce goods. 3. In our community, the work people do and the services provided are related to the resources available. 4. The money people get for doing work is called "income." 5. People use their income to buy things they want or need.* 6. All over the world, communities have divided up the jobs that need to be done. 7. All over the world, people have different ways of meeting their basic needs and wants.

LEVEL D (AGES 7 TO 9)

(3) GEOGRAPHY	(4) HISTORY	(5) ECONOMICS
1. Our community is one of many in our county; our county is one of many in our state; our state is one of fifty in our nation. 2. Our city and county have unique environmental features and natural resources. 3. Our city and county may be known for special products. 4. There are landmarks that make our city and county unique. 5. People from other parts of the world may come to share the unique features of our city and county. 6. All over the world, cities and counties use their environmental features and natural resources.*	1. Our city and county are constantly changing. 2. Maps, photographs, museums, and official records can tell me about my city and county at different periods. 3. The earliest settlers of our city and county made unique contributions.* 4. People from other parts of the world have enriched our city and county. 5. All over the world, cities are constantly changing. 6. All over the world, cities and counties are aware of, and record, their history.*	1. Taxes finance certain services in our city, county, state, and nation. 2. Planning and controls are needed to solve problems of housing, transportation, pollution, and use and conservation of natural resources.* 3. Ways of earning income change as technology changes. 4. Cooperation among cities, counties, and states is needed to regulate transportation, public safety, etc. 5. Different areas get different benefits from their natural resources. 6. All over the world, people sell or export products in excess of their needs.* 7. All over the world, people buy or import things they do not produce.* 8. The resources of the world are not equally distributed.

Description   A game involving recognizing and enacting various emotions.

Title (for children)   "Tell It Like It is."

Curriculum area   Social studies ("people group together").   **Age range**   3 to 5.

What is our objective?   "It is all right to have different kinds of feelings" (table: 1-A-4).

What will we need?   Large game board—say, six or eight faces (pictures or drawings) which express different emotions, set in a circle at the center of which a spinner is attached. The board can be made of poster paper or cardboard.

How will we do it?

1.   Children and teacher sit in a circle around the game board.

2.   Each child in turn spins the spinner. When it stops, the child examines the face it is pointing to and enacts the emotion that face seems to portray.

3.   The child explains the emotion he or she is enacting.

What else can we do?   **Variation:**   As they enact emotions, the children can examine their own faces in a mirror; or a tape recorder can be used so that they can hear changes in tone of voice.   **Another activity:**   Children and teacher can set up a "feelings area" where emotions can be acted out, with pillows to punch, soft cushions to snuggle in, dolls and stuffed toys, music, etc.

Description Making a class graph to show different family sizes.
Title (for children) "Are There Any More at Home Like You?"
Curriculum area Social studies ("people group together").   **Age range** 4 to 6.

What is our objective? "Families differ in size and composition (which may change)" (table: 1-B-3).
What will we need? Large piece of poster paper or construction paper; felt-tipped pens, or crayons; ruler.
How will we do it?
1. Children and teacher talk about how many people there are in their families (construe "family" as the immediate family).
2. The teacher sets up a large bar graph. The vertical axis is number of family members; the horizontal axis has the name of each child in the class, and there is a bar for each child.
3. Each child fills in his or her bar (with the teacher's help, if necessary) using a felt-tipped pen or crayon, to show how many people are in the family.

What else can we do? **Follow-up:** The children add to their bars if their families increase. **Other activities:** Graphs or charts can be made to show the composition of each child's family; each child can make a clothespin family (decorating the clothespins with felt-tipped pens, scraps of material, etc.) to represent his or her own family, or make a "family portrait" with construction paper, crayons, yarn, fabric, etc.

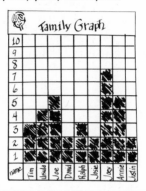

Description Making a felt and flannelboard "community" showing buildings, parks, and other meeting centers.
Title (for children) "Felttown" (or "Feltborough," or "Greater Felt," or "New Felt," or "San Felto"—whatever tickles the children).
Curriculum area Social studies ("people group together").   **Age range** 5 to 7.

What is our objective? "Religious, social, and service organizations in our neighborhood, community centers, and parks provide means for people in our community to be together" (table: 1-C-1).
What do we need? Large flannelboard; pieces of felt in different colors; cardboard outlines of buildings, vehicles, trees and shrubs, etc.; marking pen; poster paper.
How will we do it?
1. Children and teacher discuss their community—what kinds of buildings there are, what kinds of parks and streets, etc.—and plan a "felt community" which will represent it.
2. Using the cardboard outlines, the children cut out pieces of felt to form buildings and so on.
3. The felt pieces are arranged on the flannelboard; as each piece is put in place, children and teacher discuss what it represents and how that place or building serves the community.
4. To finish off the display, children and teacher make a sign with the name of the felt community (e.g., WELCOME TO FELTEAPOLIS).

What else can we do? **Variations:** As an introduction to this activity, teacher and children can visit some of the places that will be depicted; a three-dimensional community can be made from blocks and other building toys.

Description A clean-up campaign.
Title (for children) "Clean Scene."
Curriculum area Social studies ("people group together").   **Age range** 5 to 7.

What is our objective? "People who live in our community are responsible for making it a good place to live" (table: 1-C-3).
What will we need? Large litter bags (plastic or paper bags or gunny sacks); crayons, markers, and other materials for decorating the bags; poster paper and materials for making posters; paper and writing materials for leaflets.
How will we do it?
1. Teacher and children discuss a class project to help keep the community clean, deciding on the extent of their efforts (school building? plus playgrounds? plus surrounding streets?) and publicity (posters in the school? leaflets to take home? posters and leaflets in the neighboring area?).
2. Each child decorates his or her own litter bag.
3. In small groups, the children collaborate on making posters and leaflets; or the entire class can produce a leaflet which is to be photocopied in quantity. (The message could be something like "We're cleaning up; how about you?")
4. The children take a "field trip" through the area they've decided to concentrate on, picking up litter, putting up their posters, and distributing their leaflets.

What else can we do? **Follow-up:** After, say, a week or two, the children evaluate the success of their campaign: Is the area cleaner? Have other classes decided to join in? Has there been any response from the neighboring community? The class might want to give a report to the school. **Another activity:** A recycling campaign, run along similar lines.

Description A debate: "Urban Life versus Rural Life."
Title (for children) "A Hotly Debated Issue."
Curriculum area Social studies ("people group together").   **Age range** 7 to 9.

What is our objective? "People make choices about living in urban or rural communities" (table: 1-D-2).
What will we need? Two debating teams; research materials for the teams; ballots and pencils for the rest of the class; chalkboard or chart for tallying votes. (The teacher may need a set of rules for debating.)
How will we do it?
1. Teacher and class discuss what a debate is and how it is run. Two debating teams are chosen, and the topic is set: "Resolved: Urban life is better than rural life." One team will argue for ("pro"), and the other against ("con"). A date for the debate is set (say, a week hence).
2. The debating teams do research on rural life and urban life, and each team prepares its presentation.
3. The debate is held, with the rest of the class as audience.
4. After the debate, the class votes on where it's better to live, basing the votes on the facts and arguments presented by the debaters. Ballots are used.
5. The ballots are counted and the results tallied on a chart or the chalkboard. If the majority votes for urban life, the "pro" team wins; if the majority votes for rural life, the "con" team wins.

What else can we do? **Variation:** Before the debate, an opinion poll can be taken to see who prefers urban and rural life. Does the vote after the debate show that some people have changed their minds? **Another activity:** The children can make picture posters, with text or labels, to illustrate the advantages and disadvantages of urban and rural life.

Description Establishing, displaying, and following a set of class rules.
Title (for children) "Reasonable Rules."
Curriculum area Social studies ("people organize and set limits").   **Age range** 3 to 5.

What is our objective? "I follow rules to help protect my freedom and safety and the freedom and safety of others" (table: 2-A-1).
What will we need? Chalkboard; poster paper; marking pens; pictures from magazines, or drawings; construction paper.
How will we do it?
1. Teacher and children sit in a circle and discuss why rules are important.
2. The children suggest and discuss what rules the class needs to help it run smoothly and safely, and decide on some simple, basic rules (say, half a dozen to ten or so).
3. As each rule is decided on, the teacher writes it on a chalkboard or poster paper and illustrates each rule with a sketch.
4. When all the rules have been settled on, teacher and children cooperate to make an illustrated poster for each rule, using drawings or pictures from magazines in addition to the written rule. For rules stated negatively, put a red bar over the picture of the prohibited action, in the style of European road signs (the bar can be made of red construction paper).

What else can we do? **Follow-up:** The children can dictate stories to the teacher on the theme "The Day Nobody Followed Rules"; and, playing different roles, they can enact appropriate and inappropriate classroom behavior.

Description   Formulating and illustrating some "rules" for parents.
Title (for children)   "How to Be a Good Parent."
Curriculum area   Social studies ("people organize and set limits").   **Age range**   4 to 6.

What is our objective?   "My family has rules to keep it running smoothly" (table: 2-B-1).
What will we need?   Drawing paper; pencils and crayons; chalkboard.
How will we do it?

1. Teacher and children discuss what kinds of things family members do for each other, and particularly what things the children would like their parents to do. (The teacher can keep a running list of suggestions and ideas on the chalkboard or on poster paper.)
2. Each child chooses *one* thing he or she would like to suggest to parents as a "rule," and makes a drawing to illustrate it. Children who can write may state the rule briefly underneath the drawing (e.g., "Read to me at bedtime"; "Help me with my homework").
3. The children take their drawings home and talk about the proposed "rule" with their parents.
4. If they like, the children can share their experiences in class the next day.

What else can we do?   **Variation:** Children can dictate family rules to the teacher and illustrate them themselves.
Another activity: Playing roles of different family members, children can enact family problems and solve them with rules.

Description   Making posters depicting important laws.
Title (for children)   "Learn the Law."
Curriculum area   Social studies ("people organize and set limits").   **Age range**   5 to 7.

What is our objective?   "Rules that people must obey (laws) protect us and our public places" (table: 2-C-1).
What will we need?   Poster paper, construction paper, tagboard, pencils, crayons, marking pens. Optional: chalkboard.
How will we do it?

1. Teacher and children discuss what laws are and how serious they are.
2. Teacher and children identify some specific state and community laws in areas that touch children's lives—traffic, safety, littering, petty theft, etc. (The teacher can keep a running list of these on the chalkboard as they are discussed.)
3. Each child makes a poster stating and illustrating the law he or she thinks is most important. (The teacher may help younger children with the lettering.) Naturally, the laws will be worded in very simple terms ("No littering"; "No graffitti"; etc.).
4. The posters are displayed around the room or in the halls, or both.

What else can we do?   **Another activity:** The children can make traffic signs out of construction paper and poster paper. **Follow-up:** Children and teacher can visit the local police or fire station to discuss laws.

Description   Class elections.
Title (for children)   "Election Selection."
Curriculum area   Social studies ("people organize and set limits").   **Age range**   7 to 9.

What is our objective?   "We select certain people to be our leaders in our city, county, state, and nation" (table: 2-D-1).
What will we need?   Ballots, a ballot box, pencils. (Optional: materials for campaign posters.)
How will we do it?
1. Teacher and children discuss what an elective office is, how people are elected to such offices, and what duties and qualifications are involved.
2. To demonstrate on a small scale how the elective process works, the class elects a few officers—say, president, vice president, and secretary—after first establishing the duties each officer will have.
3. Three or four children volunteer to run for each office. (With older children, the activity can be made more sophisticated by having the class nominate candidates.)
4. Over the course of, say, a few days or a week, the candidates make speeches to the class describing their qualifications and what they'd do in office. (They and their friends may make and put up campaign posters.)
5. The class votes by secret ballot; then the ballot box is opened, the votes are counted, and the results are announced.
6. The class discusses how its election is like, and different from, a local, state, or national election.
What else can we do?   **Follow-up:** During a local election, visit a polling place; and keep a "log" of events leading up to election day.

Description   Writing to elected officials.
Title (for children)   "Keep Those Cards and Letters Coming."
Curriculum area   Social studies ("people organize and set limits").   **Age range**   7 to 9.

What is our objective?   "We need to know who our government officials are and where our representatives meet" (table: 2-D-4).
What will we need?   Reference materials (almanacs, etc.), for finding the names and addresses of officeholders and the correct forms of address; letter paper, pens, stamps; newspapers and magazines, for finding issues of interest.
How will we do it?
1. Teacher and class discuss who the community's representatives are at the national, state, and local level—e.g., the president, senators, congresspersons, state legislators, state governor, mayor, town council—and where each does his or her work (Washington? state capital? etc.).
2. Teacher and children take a week or so to find issues of interest and concern to the children in newspapers and magazines or their own experiences. They discuss these issues and which elected official would be involved with each.
3. Each child chooses an issue and an official, and writes to the official to state his or her views or urge some action. (Examples: To the president—"Why doesn't the Army pay my brother more?" To the mayor—"We need a traffic light on my corner.")
4. The children first write drafts of their letters and then copy them neatly, using the reference works to find addresses and forms of address (with the teacher's help).
What else can we do?   **Follow-up:** The children will almost certainly get answers to their letters, which they can share in class discussions.   **Another activity:** A bulletin-board display of names, titles, and pictures of elected officials.

Activities for Social Studies: "People Live on Earth"

Description   Making a class book of children's drawings illustrating places to visit.
Title (for children)   "Where in the World?"
Curriculum area   Social studies ("people live on earth").   Age range   3 to 5.

What is our objective?   "I can describe special places in my world" (table: 3-A-2).
What will we need?   Light-colored construction paper or drawing paper cut in circles about 1 foot in diameter (one for each child); crayons, colored pencils, felt-tipped pens; two pieces of construction paper, poster paper, or cardboard cut in a circle the same size as the drawing paper or slightly larger (for the front and back cover); hole puncher and yarn or string. Optional: A globe.
How will we do it?
1.   Teacher and children discuss places in the world they've visited or would like to visit. (Optional: The children can examine a globe.)
2.   Each child gets a round piece of drawing or construction paper and draws a picture of a place he or she knows about, has visited, or wants to visit.
3.   On a piece of heavy paper or cardboard (round), the teacher meanwhile draws a simple hemisphere map to represent the globe. This will be the front cover of the class book; it and the back cover can be laminated.
4.   Each child dictates to the teacher the name of the place he or she has drawn, and the teacher writes it—and some simple comments the child dictates—on the picture.
5.   The children's pictures and the front and back cover are put together with string or yarn drawn through two punched holes, and the book is put on the library table where all the children can use it.
What else can we do?   Variation: A similar book can be made with pictures cut from magazines.

Description An exhibition and demonstration of means of transportation assembled by the children.

Title for children) "Movement Mania."

Curriculum area Social studies ("people live on earth"). **Age range** 3 to 5.

What is our objective? "I have ways of moving and traveling in my world" (table: 3-A-3).

What will we need? Display area; table; bulletin board.

How will we do it?

1. Teacher and children discuss ways in which children and adults can get around in their world (trains, airplanes, bicycles, skates, etc.).
2. The children are asked to bring in pictures and models of means of transportation and actual means (roller skates, pogo sticks).
3. The things the children bring in are displayed (pictures can be mounted by the children), and the children examine them and talk about them. Older children can make simple labels or signs (TRAIN, BOAT).
4. A special "movement mania" day is held—the children take the usable exhibits out to the playground for races, contests, and games.

What else can we do? **Other activities:** A "transportation collage" can be made by mounting pictures of means of transportation on a map, in appropriate places; children and teacher can take a walk through the community to see how many means of transportation they can identify.

Description A display: world map and United States map and letters and postcards from friends and relatives around the world.

Title (for children) "Faraway Places with Strange-Sounding Names."

Curriculum area Social studies ("people live on earth"). **Age range** 4 to 6.

What is our objective? "My family and I have relatives and friends who live in different places" (table: 3-B-1).

What will we need? Large world map, large United States map, colored map pins, yarn or string; large wall for the display.

How will we do it?

1. Children and teacher examine maps of the world and the United States. The children name places where they have friends and relatives living, and find them on the map.
2. Over a period of time, the children collect letters (envelopes) and postcards sent by people they know from different places.
3. Teacher and children set up a display, with the letters and postcards surrounding the maps and connected to the appropriate points on the maps with map pins and yarn or string.

What else can we do? **Variation:** The exhibit could also include a third map, of the state or region (or even the city, if it's large enough)—with letters and cards from friends in the area. **Other activities:** If some of the children collect stamps, a display of stamps from around the world can be set up; or the class can start a joint stamp collection, asking friends and relatives in other countries to send stamps.

Description   Making a map of the neighborhood or community.
Title (for children)   "Map-a-Thon."
Curriculum area   Social studies ("people live on earth").   **Age range**   5 to 7.

What is our objective?   "A map is a special kind of picture of a community or area; and there are landmarks that make each community unique" (table: 3-C-1 and 3-C-2).

What will we need?   Very large piece of butcher paper; pencils, crayons, marking pens; construction paper and other construction materials (colored yarn, tinfoil, etc.); glue or paste; and an actual map of the area.

How will we do it?

1. Teacher and children examine a map of the neighborhood or community and then take a walk through it and make notes of points of interest.

2. Using a large piece of butcher paper, and using an actual map of the area as a guide, the children (with the teacher's help), draw an illustrated map of their community. First they put in the roads and streets; then they put in the points of interest—buildings, bodies of water, parks, woods, and so on. These points of interest can be made of construction materials, or drawn, or both.

3. The map is hung.

What else can we do?   **Variations:** A floor map can be made (instead of a wall map), and some of the points of interest can be made out of blocks and other building materials; the map (floor or wall) can be made more sophisticated by the use of map symbols and a key to them.   **Another activity:** The children can examine aerial maps of the area and identify places they know.

Description   Making a relief map from a salt, flour, and water mixture.
Title (for children)   "Cake Map."
Curriculum area   Social studies ("people live on earth").   **Age range**   7 to 9.

What is our objective?   "All over the world, cities and counties use their environmental features and natural resources" (table: 3-D-6).

What will we need?   Heavy cardboard, or thin plywood; flour, salt, and water; tempera paint and brushes. Optional: topographical maps, aerial photographs, or both. Useful but not strictly necessary: putty knives, tongue depressors, etc.

How will we do it?   Depending on how elaborate the map or maps are to be, this can be an activity for individuals, small groups, or the whole class.

1. Children and teacher discuss environmental features of the landscape and natural resources—mountains, valleys, lakes, rivers, etc. (They may examine maps and photographs.)

2. The children plan a relief map, or maps, of an imaginary area; or they may plan to map a real place—in the latter case, topographical maps or aerial photographs will probably be needed.

3. The relief map is made of a mixture of flour, salt, and water molded on a base of cardboard or plywood. Children can use their fingers for the modeling, or putty knives and similar tools—or both, of course. The paste is shaped to show mountains, hills, bodies of water, and so on.

4. When the paste has dried, it is painted in appropriate colors (tempera paints) and then allowed to dry again.

What else can we do?   **Other activities:** Graphs are useful in studying environment and natural resources—have the children graph rainfall, temperature, imports and exports, etc. Plan a class "trip" to anyplace in the world, and do research on its resources and topography; or study national parks and recreation areas.

Activities for Social Studies: "People Are Aware of Their Heritage"

Description A guessing game involving interviews with children.
Title (for children) "This Is Your Life."
Curriculum area Social studies ("people are aware of their heritage").   **Age range** 3 to 5.

What is our objective? "As I grow, I change" (table: 4-A-1).
What will we need? For the teacher: tape recorder or materials for taking notes; set of questions for the "interviews."
How will we do it?
1. Teacher and children discuss the concepts of one's past and one's future, and then the teacher takes the children aside one by one for a private interview.
2. The teacher asks the children a few simple questions about their past and future (e.g., "What did you do before coming to preschool?" "What do you want to be when you grow up?"), tape-recording the questions and answers (if no tape recorder is available, the teacher takes notes).
3. The teacher plays the tapes back for the class (or reads the notes), and the children guess who is being interviewed.
4. Children and teacher talk about how they've changed and how they expect to change (the teacher should be sure that each child gets a turn).
What else can we do? **Other activities:** A display of pictures of the children as babies and now; personal scrapbooks made by the children; "autobiographies" dictated to the teacher and illustrated by the children.

Description   Making a personal family tree.
Title (for children)   "Climbing My Family Tree."
Curriculum area   Social studies ("people are aware of their heritage").   **Age range**   4 to 6.

What is our objective?   "Family records tell me about my family's past" (table: 4-B-1).
What will we need?   For each child: drawing of a "family tree" on heavy construction paper (a master drawing by the teacher can be photocopied, and the photocopies mounted on construction paper); scissors; crayons or felt pens; paste or glue.
How will we do it?
1. The children are asked to bring in photographs of themselves, their parents, and their grandparents—but not to worry if there are any gaps in the collection.
2. When the children have brought the photographs, the teacher describes and explains the simple family tree the children will be making—a pyramid with four grandparents at the base, two parents in the middle, and the child at the top. Each child gets a "tree" to be filled in.
3. The children paste their photographs in the appropriate places on the tree; if they are missing any photographs, they make drawings of these people.
4. The family trees are displayed around the room; later, the children can take them home. (The charts may be laminated.)

What else can we do?   **Other activities:** Copies of actual family documents (e.g., birth and marriage certificates) contributed by the children can be displayed; or children can make their own "birth certificates."

Description   A class project—making an exhibit of ethnic groups which first settled the community, and their contributions to it.
Title (for children)   "Melting Pot."
Curriculum area   Social studies ("people are aware of their heritage").   **Age range**   5 to 7.

What is our objective?   "The heritage of our community is the unique contributions made by its earliest settlers" (table: 4-C-4).
What will we need?   Research materials; objects and documents for the exhibit (old photographs, artifacts, copies of documents, etc.); materials for making the displays (poster paper, construction paper, marking pens, etc.).
How will we do it?
1. As a whole, class and teacher consult research materials (or the library or a historical society) to find out which ethnic groups first settled the community.
2. The class is divided into groups, each group to study about one of these ethnic groups and find materials on it for the exhibit. The groups might concentrate on such things as local vocabulary, place names and street names, foods and restaurants, music, architecture and fine arts, local customs, and religions.
3. The information and collected materials are used to make an exhibit, to be set up where the whole school can enjoy it.

What else can we do?   **Another activity:** The children can make bar graphs to depict the ethnic makeup of the community from its origins to the present.

Description A class project—an exhibit of people who were early settlers of the community.
Title (for children) "Hall of Fame."
Curriculum area Social studies ("people are aware of their heritage").   **Age range** 7 to 9.

What is our objective? "The earliest settlers of our city and county made unique contributions" (table: 4-D-3).
What will we need? Research materials. For the exhibit: Modeling clay, photographs, paper, construction paper. marking pens, etc.
How will we do it?
1. As a whole, class and teacher discuss and study the earliest settlers of the area and compile a list of specific people who were among the early settlers.
2. Each child chooses one of the people on the list and then does research on that person, collecting—if possible—photographs or copies of documents, or other memorabilia, and writing a short report.
3. Working from old photographs, books of costumes, etc., each child makes a clay model of his or her subject.
4. The children's statues and reports are displayed in a "hall of fame." (Parents and other classes may be invited for guided tours through it.)
What else can we do? **Variation:** The children could paint and frame portraits of their subjects. **Another activity:** "Early Settlers Day," with the children in costumes of the early settlers.

Description Collecting representative objects, documents, etc., to preserve for posterity.
Title (for children) "Time Capsules."
Curriculum area Social studies ("people are aware of their heritage").   **Age range** 7 to 9.

What is our objective? "All over the world, cities and counties are aware of, and record, their history" (table: 4-D-6).
What will we need? For each group: a good-sized tin box, if possible (otherwise, a cardboard carton covered with tinfoil will do); large coffee cans will also do. Have available for all the groups: scissors, paper, writing materials, glue, etc.
How will we do it?
1. Teacher and children discuss what a time capsule is and where some famous ones have been buried (is there one somewhere in the community?); they also talk about what kinds of things people put into time capsules, and what significant aspects of their own life and community might be preserved in that way.
2. The class breaks up into groups; each group gets its own "capsule" (a tin box or can, or a carton), prepares a list of things to go in it, and collects or makes the items decided on.
3. Each group fills its capsule; when all the capsules are ready, the groups take turns presenting the capsules to the class and explaining the contents.
What else can we do? **Other activities:** The class can study early ways of recording history (hieroglyphs, etc.), mount and display copies of old documents, or prepare a newspaper for a typical day in the life of some earlier society (ancient Rome, Massachusetts Bay Colony, etc.).

Activities for Social Studies: "People Manage Resources"

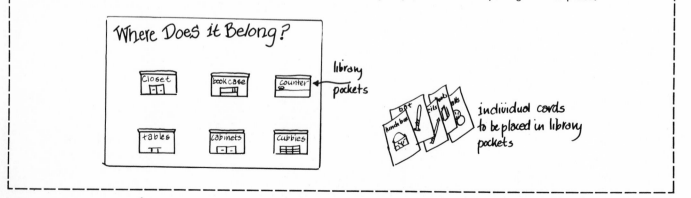

Description Identifying places where things are kept by using a pocket chart and illustrated cards.
Title (for children) "A Place for Everything and Everything in Its Place."
Curriculum area Social studies ("people manage resources"). **Age range** 3 to 5.

What is our objective? "I take care of my possessions and things I use" (table: 5-A-1).
What will we need? The teacher prepares a pocket chart by pasting or drawing on about six pockets pictures of storage places in the classroom (closet, bookcase, counter, cabinet, cubbies, etc.) and makes a set of cards (say, a dozen or so) with pictures or drawings of objects stored in these places (books, coats, etc.). For older children, labels (CLOSET; BOOK) are used in addition to the pictures.
How will we do it?
1. Teacher and children discuss how certain things are kept in certain places, and why this is important.
2. The children take turns using the pocket chart and cards: Each child takes the chart and a set of cards, and matches each item with its proper storage place.
3. To check their "answers," the children look around the classroom to see where things are. But this check works two ways—it can also show if anything in the classroom is out of place.
What else can we do? Other activities: A collage "map" or diagram of the classroom, with pictures of classroom objects pasted in place; "tours" of the room by the whole class or groups, to see if everything is in its place.

Description Finding pictures of uniforms and illustrating the jobs they represent.
Title (for children) "Clothing Match-Mates."
Curriculum area Social studies ("people manage resources"). **Age range** 4 to 6.

What is our objective? "Families' food, clothing, and homes can be determined by cost and jobs" (table: 5-B-5).
What will we need? Catalogs of clothing and uniforms, drawing or construction paper, scissors, crayons and markers, paste or glue.
How will we do it?
1. Teacher and children discuss jobs that require special clothing (e.g., baseball player, surgeon, nurse, pilot).
2. The children go through the catalogs and cut out pictures of uniforms and special clothes.
3. Each child chooses one picture, mounts it near the top (or in one corner) of a piece of drawing or construction paper, and draws a picture on the same sheet of paper to illustrate the corresponding activity.
4. The children discuss and display their pictures.
What else can we do? Other activities: Uniforms make a good addition to the dress-up corner (they can often be bought at thrift shops). Also, children and teacher can discuss how some kinds of clothes cost more than others, and cut out and compare prices in advertisements and catalogs.

Description Classifying pictures of products as necessities or luxuries.
Title (for children) "Needy or Greedy?"
Curriculum area Social studies ("people manage resources"). **Age range** 5 to 7.

What is our objective? "People use their income to buy things they want or need" (table: 5-C-5).
What will we need? Magazines and catalogs, bulletin board, butcher paper, scissors, glue or paste, marking pens.
How will we do it?
1. Teacher and children discuss the difference between things we need and things we just would like to have, citing some examples of each.
2. The teacher prepares a bulletin board for a display by covering it with butcher paper and using a marking pen to make two sections, one labeled NEEDY and the other GREEDY.
3. The children cut out pictures of various products from magazines and catalogs and paste them in the appropriate section of the display board.
What else can we do? Another activity: Set up a class store whose "merchandise" consists of objects or mounted pictures of things that represent necessities and luxuries, with prices marked. Give each child some play money and instructions to purchase necessities first and luxuries only if money is left after that. How well do the children establish priorities?

Description Identifying community problems and suggesting solutions.
Title (for children) "Future Shock."
Curriculum area Social studies ("people manage resources"). **Age range** 7 to 9.

What is our objective? "Planning and controls are needed to solve problems of housing, transportation, pollution, and use and conservation of natural resources" (table: 5-D-2).
What will we need? Magazines and newspapers; writing and drawing materials; research materials.
How will we do it?

1. Teacher and children examine newspapers and magazines to find articles about local problems (or national problems that also exist in the area) of housing, transportation, pollution, and natural resources. They decide on, say, three or four such problems that seem particularly evident or important.
2. Teacher and children take a "field trip" to see areas where these problems occur—e.g., a polluted lake, a factory belching smoke, a congested highway.
3. Each child chooses one of the problems and does some research on it. (The teacher should see that some simple articles or books are available.)
4. Each child prepares a short report on the problems he or she has chosen, illustrating it with drawings and suggesting a way to solve it.
5. The children share their reports.

What else can we do? **Another activity:** A community leader can be invited to talk to the class about how the community is handling some problem of housing, transportation, pollution, or conservation.

Description Making illustrated displays of imports and exports.
Title (for children) "What Goes In and What Comes Out."
Curriculum area Social studies ("people manage resources"). **Age range** 7 to 9.

What is our objective? "All over the world, people sell or export products in excess of their needs and buy or import things they do not produce" (table: 5-D-6 and 5-D-7).
What will we need? Research materials (books, maps, etc.) and materials for making the displays (magazines with pictures, construction and poster paper, marking pens, etc.).
How will we do it?

1. Teacher and children discuss what imports and exports are and what kinds of sources give information about them.
2. The children examine a world map, and each child picks a favorite country to study.
3. Working independently, the children do research on "their" countries and find pictures and other things for making their displays. (In addition to pictures, for example, they can use cotton balls to symbolize raw cotton, a swatch of wool for wool products, aluminum foil for aluminum, toy food or cans of food, and so on.)
4. Each child makes a display on poster paper (to hang or stand) in two parts: WHAT GOES IN and WHAT COMES OUT. The pictures and objects in the display should be augmented with printed or written labels.

What else can we do? **Variation:** This can be done by small groups instead of individuals. **Another activity:** Large outline maps can be used to illustrate imports and exports of different countries and regions.

Resources for Social Studies

Bibliography for Teachers

Canfield, J. *100 ways to enhance self-concept in the classroom.* Englewood Cliffs, N.J.: Prentice-Hall, 1976. (Numerous strategies are presented for teachers and parents to use to enhance self-concept. The strategies are drawn from many different approaches, such as values clarification, magic circle, effectiveness training, and achievement motivation. What makes the book unique is its criteria for selection related to the theme of enhancing self-concept. Highly recommended.)

Cole, A. *A pumpkin in a pear tree.* Boston: Little, Brown, 1976. (Gives simple directions for crafts, foods, games, and make-believe activities to help children understand and celebrate a variety of new and traditional holidays.)

Croft, D. *Be honest with yourself.* Belmont, Calif.: Wadsworth, 1976. (Another helpful booklet using typical incidents to stimulate discussion, study, and self-evaluation. A self-evaluation handbook designed for teachers, student teachers, parents, volunteers, and caretakers of children.)

Forte, I., & MacKensie, J. *Kid's stuff social studies.* Nashville, Tenn.: Incentive, 1977. (This attractively designed book contains numerous creative social studies activities to provide motivation, skill reinforcement, and enrichment for established elementary social studies programs. Grades 1 to 6.)

Seefeldt, C. *Social studies for the preschool-primary child.* Columbus, Ohio: Merrill, 1977. (Key concepts from each of the social science disciplines are identified and serve as the focus for fostering skills or social living and thinking and for clarifying values and attitudes. This book is directed at the 4- to 8-year-old child and offers practical ideas for activities and experiences.)

Seif, E. *Significant social studies in the elementary school.* Chicago, Ill.: Rand McNally, 1977. (An outstanding textbook showing how values clarification, decision-making skills, self-awareness, interpersonal communication, intergroup relations, consumer education, career education, environmental education, and citizenship education all can and should play a part in the elementary social studies curriculum.)

Shaftel, R., & Shaftel, G. *Role playing for social values: Decision-making in the social studies.* Englewood Cliffs, N.J.: Prentice-Hall, 1967. (This is one of the most complete presentations on the use of role-playing to learn about getting along with other people, to increase decision-making skills, and to learn more about society and its problems. Some of the themes for the role-play situations are honesty, responsibility for others, the law, being fair, the individual versus the group, surmounting prejudice, self-acceptance, and managing one's feelings.)

Simon, S. *I am lovable and capable.* Niles, Ill.: Argus Communication, 1974. ("A modern allegory on the classical put-down." A day in the life of Randy; the small events which make him feel more or less lovable and capable. The story has many uses. To the teacher, it is a vivid reminder of how we often fail to meet the emotional needs of students. It's an easy-to-read booklet which can serve as a basis for discussion and activities. The author suggests several classroom uses for the story at the end. This is a real classic.)

Zuckerman, D., & Horn, R. *The guide to simulations/games.* Garwood, N.J.: Didactic Systems, 1976. (Complete descriptions of over 600 simulations and games for education and human relations training, 210 of them in the social sciences and social studies.)

Journals and periodicals:

Social Education. (Official journal, National Council for the Social Studies, 1201 16th St., NW, Washington, D.C. 20036.)

Bibliography for Children

Criteria for selecting informational books:

Accuracy.	Presentation.
Style.	Coverage.
Clarity.	Reading level.

Where titles can be found:

Card catalogs. (School and public libraries; curriculum laboratories.)
Publishers' catalogs.
Bookstore catalogs.
Talk to children's librarian to learn about trade books on social studies topics.
Ask children what books they own.
Use the bibliographies in textbooks.

Some resource books:

Bernstein, J. (Ed.). *Books to help children cope with separation and loss.* Ann Arbor, Mich.: Bowker, 1977. (Selective, annotated list of children's books, films, filmstrips, and cassettes, books and chapters from books about bibliotherapy, and recent ERIC documents related to death and separation.)

Craft, D. J. *Parents and teachers.* Belmont, Calif: Wadsworth, 1979. (Excellent bibliography of books for children.)

Jones, C. *Learning for little kids.* Boston: Houghton Mifflin, 1979. (Excellent resource for books about alternative parenting roles, birth, death, divorce, adoption, moving, and lots more. Also materials, games, activities, and information.)

Materials other than books:

Kid's Magazine. (747 Third Ave., New York, N.Y. 10017. Written by kids for kids.)
Free pamphlets. (Children can write to organizations.)

Recordings.
Posters.
Films and filmstrips.
Multimedia kits.

Learning Materials

Maps, Globes, and Atlases

Types of materials:

School globes.
Wall maps.
Desk outline maps.
Simplified globes for primary grades.
Slate and chalkboard maps.
Road maps.
Historical and literary picture maps.

Mapmakers and map suppliers:

Ada-Air Photographic and Charting Services, U.S.A.F. Film Library Center, 8900 S. Broadway, St. Louis, Mo. 63118.
Aero Service Corp. 210 E. Courtland St., Philadelphia, Pa. 19120.
American Geographical Society, Broadway at 156th St., New York, N.Y. 10032.
American Map Co., Inc., 3 W. 61st St., New York, N.Y. 10023.
Civic Education Service, 1733 K St., NW, Washington, D.C. 20036.
George F. Cram Co., Inc., 730 E. Washington St., Indianapolis, Ind. 46202.

Denoyer-Geppert Co., 5235 Ravenswood Ave., Chicago, Ill. 60640.
Encyclopaedia Britannica, Inc., 425 N. Michigan Ave., Chicago, Ill. 60611.
Farquhar Transparent Globes, 3724 Irving St., Philadelphia, Pa. 19104.
John W. Gunter, Inc., 1027 S. Claremont, San Mateo, Calif. 94400.
Hagstrom Company, Inc., 311 Broadway, New York, N.Y. 10007.
C. S. Hammond and Co., Inc., 521 Fifth Ave., New York, N.Y. 10017.
D. C. Harris Co., Color-Graphics Div., Wooster, Ohio 44691.
Hearne Bros., National Bank Bldg., Detroit, Mich. 48232.
Historical Publishing Co., 717 E. Elm Ave., Monroe, Mich. 48161.
Hubbard Scientific Co., P.O. Box 105, Northbrook, Ill. 60062.

Interstate Commerce Commission, Washington, D.C. 20423.
Jeppensen and Co., 8025 E. 40th Ave., Denver, Colo. 80200.
Keystone View Co., Meadville, Pa. 16335. (Map slides.)
Library of Congress, Reference Dept., Map Div., Washington, D.C. 20540.
McConnell School Map Co., 610 E. Madison, Goshen, Ind. 46526.
McKinley Publishing Co., 809, 811 N. 19th St., Philadelphia, Pa. 19180.
Milton Bradley Co., 74 Park St., Springfield, Mass. 01100.

National Geographic Society, 16th and M Sts., NW, Washington, D.C. 20036.
A. J. Nystrom and Co., 3333 Elston Ave., Chicago, Ill. 60618.
Rand McNally and Co., P.O. Box 7600, Chicago, Ill. 60680.
Replogle Globes, Inc. 1901 N. Narragansett Ave., Chicago, Ill. 60639.
Social Studies School Service, 10000 Culver Blvd., Culver City, Calif. 90230.
Superintendent of Documents, Government Printing Office, Washington, D.C. 20402.
U.S. Bureau of the Census, c/o Superintendent of Documents, Washington, D.C. 20402.
U.S. Department of Commerce, Coast and Geodetic Survey, Washington, D.C. 20230.

U.S. Department of Commerce, United States Travel Service, Washington, D.C. 20230.

U.S. Department of the Army, Map Service, Corps of Engineers, Washington, D.C. 20315.

U.S. Department of the Interior, Geographic Names Board, Washington, D.C. 20240.

U.S. Department of the Interior, U.S. Geological Survey, Washington, D.C. 20242.

Ward's Natural Science Establishment, Inc., P.O. Box 1712, Rochester, N.Y. 14600, or P.O. Box 1749, Monterey, Calif. 93940.

Weber Costello Co., 1212 McKinley, Chicago Heights, Ill. 60411.

Welch Scientific Co., 7300 N. Linder Ave., Skokie, Ill. 60078.

Enrichment Materials

Use the following as resources:

Music books.
Art books (crafts).
Folk dance records.
Ideas for creative problem solving and role playing.
Catalogs (films, slides, filmstrips).
Curriculum labs and libraries (miscellaneous materials and kits).
Newspapers and political parties (election information).

Use the publications of the Educators' Progress Services (Randolph, Wis. 53956):

Educators' guide to free films.
Educators' guide to free filmstrips.
Educators' guide to free social studies materials.
Educators' guide to free teaching aids.
Educators' index of free materials.

Among the recommended kits, programs, and curricula are the following:

Andrew, J. L., et al. *Focus on self development.* Chicago, Ill.: Science Research Associates. (259 E. Erie St., 60611. Multimedia program for grades 1 to 3.)

Developmental Learning Materials. *Big box: Body and self-awareness.* Niles, Ill.: Developmental Learning Materials, 1974. (7440 Natchez Ave., 60648.)

Dinkmeyer, D. *Developing understanding of self and others (DUSO).* Circle Pines, Minn.: American Guidance Service. (Dept. EL-4, Publisher Bldg., 55814.)

Educational Research Council. *Concepts and inquiry: The educational research council social science program,* Boston: Allyn and Bacon. (470 Atlantic Ave., 02210. Spiraling concepts and subtopics which utilize texts, enrichment texts and supplements, and teacher's guide.)

Goldstein, H. *The social learning curriculum.* Columbus, Ohio: Merrill. (1300 Alum Creek Rd., 43216. Many components make up the ten-phase curriculum dealing with social skills and adaptive behaviors.)

Science Research Associates, Inc. *Our working world.* Chicago: Science Research Associates. (259 E. Erie St., 60611. Multimedia spiraling structure dealing with the themes of families, neighborhoods, and cities.)

TABA social studies curriculum. Menlo Park, Calif.: Addison-Wesley. (Sand Hill Rd., 94025. Stresses group processes in the search for answers to children's questions about key concepts.)

Community Resources

Fire department.
Police department.
Utility companies.
Local retailers.
Family members.
Trucking companies.
Bus companies.
Airlines.
Shipping firms.
Post office.
Supermarket.
Government agencies.
Government departments.
Clothing designers.
Clothing manufacturers.
Building contractors.
Hobby centers.

Airport.
Civil air patrol.
Banks.
Railroads.
Travel agents.
CB operators.
Recreational-vehicle dealer.
Restaurants.
Local officials.
Newspapers.
Representatives from ethnic groups.
Doctors, nurses, dentists.
Historical society.
Museums.
Conservationists.
Chamber of commerce.
Weather bureau.

Art for Older Children: Processes, Media, and Activities

Introduction: Processes and Media in Art

Why have we included art in this section on affective development? As we mentioned at the beginning of the section, we believe that art—like social studies and music—is a good example of the affective domain.

It's obvious, of course, that art involves both concepts (the cognitive element) and skills (the psycho-physical-motor element). Through art children develop concepts such as color, shade, balance, form, perspective, texture, and shape; and they develop skills such as eye-hand coordination, small-muscle control, visual acuity, and specific abilities in various media. There is also a linguistic element—consider the special terminology of art, for example, and the importance of description in this area.

What is it, then, that makes art such a good representative of the affective domain?

First, there are the important social values of art. In working on artistic activities, children learn such simple social values as sharing, taking turns, and participating in a group. As they develop in this area, they learn more sophisticated concepts, such as helping others and respecting the work of others. Eventually, we hope, they gain concepts about the ways in which art enriches a society and the place of art in society.

Second, there is the emotional component of art. Some of the emotional outcomes in this area are feeling good about oneself; channeling and expressing emotions; increased awareness of the emotions of others; and an increased sense of responsibility.

Third, there is the attitudinal component of art. Through early experiences with art, children can develop a lifelong interest in art and may even develop into creative artists as adults. And early experiences with art help develop willingness to experiment, confidence, and the freedom to be different.

Fourth, there is the fact that art is intensely personal. For example, consider three children who are fingerpainting: Andy is—perhaps unconsciously—improving his eye-hand coordination; Mike is learning how to blend colors; Jean is escaping temporarily from some negative aspect of her life. It's neither necessary nor desirable to set the same objective for all three children: for each child, the objective is personal and individual.

This fourth point raises two important questions: When we consider art as a part of the affective domain, what are our goals? What objectives can we set for children's development? Negatively, we can say what our goals are *not*: *not* to develop any specific concept or skill; *not* to concentrate on specific areas of expertise; and *not* to develop the Rembrandts or Picassos.

Positively, we can say what our goals *are*: to help children enjoy art in its many forms; to develop children's discrimination, that is, appreciation of and sensitivity to art; to give children opportunities to engage in creative exploration and experimentation; and to build a foundation for continued and more advanced experiences with art. These goals imply that our objectives for children will be of a somewhat special nature.

Accordingly, for art our "table of objectives" is not a table of objectives; instead, it is a table of *processes* and *media* through which our global goals can be achieved. We list media—tempera, modeling clay, etc.—and group them under three major processes:

1. Free exploration and experimentation.
2. Creation.
3. Appreciation.

In the first process—exploration—the children freely "mess around" with the materials of art. In the second—creation—they make artistic products; but here, as in process 1, the emphasis is still more on process than on product. The teacher demonstrates what the product is and how it can be made; but the children should work as independently as possible. The third process—appreciation—has to do with responding to art, with and without guidance.

Because a variety of experiences—in an open and supportive environment —is essential, the table includes a large selection of media to foster experimentation, creation, and appreciation. Once again, we have used the two-axis arrangement: curriculum areas (the horizontal axis) and age levels (the vertical axis). Our curriculum areas are:

1. Drawing and painting.
2. Collage and sculpture.
3. Design.
4. Crafts.

The age ranges, or levels, are—and it's important to remember this—only suggestions. The three basic processes (exploration, creation, appreciation) appear at each age level; and any of the media listed can work at almost any age.

The activities following the table of processes and media are grouped by curriculum area. For each of these activities, we identify the medium and the process; and each activity is keyed to the table by "curriculum area, age level, and process," so that "1-A-1" in these activities means "area 1, level A, *process* 1."

You will want to introduce the children to as many and as varied experiences as possible, provide a supportive climate with freedom to experiment, make artistic activities readily available to individual children and groups, demonstrate respect for the work of each child, help the children avoid frustration, and give the children as much control and responsibility as possible. Try our suggested activities, or create others, and enjoy them with your children—and remember that art "is its own excuse for being."

		CURRICULUM AREAS			
	PROCESSES	(1) DRAWING AND PAINTING	(2) COLLAGE AND SCULPTURE	(3) DESIGN	(4) CRAFTS
LEVEL A (AGES 3 TO 5)	1. Free exploration and experimentation	Pencils (large) Crayons Felt-tipped pens Fingerpaints Tempera Brushes (large) Toothbrushes	"Play dough" "Junk" Blocks Paper Glue Paste Scissors	Felt-tipped pens Paper Fingerpaints Scissors Paint Gadgets	Bags Crayons Felt-tipped pens String Beads, macaroni Paint Paper Glue Pins
	2. Creation	Free drawings and paintings Easel paints Screen stencils* Fingerpaints	"Play dough" painting sculpture* Block buildings "Free" constructions (one- and two-dimensional) Picture collages Junk collages	Finger prints* Mono paints Paper weaving	Masks Stringing beads "Glue-glob" pins* Stringing macaroni Paper-bag puppets
	3. Appreciation	Free viewing: Display classwork; assorted books; crafts. Guided viewing: Read well-illustrated children's books. Extended viewing: Informally examine different interpretations of one subject, by different artists working in different media.*			
LEVEL B (AGES 4 TO 6)	1. Free exploration and experimentation	Felt-tipped pens Soapflakes Chalk Fingerpaints Crayons Assorted brushes Sponges Glue	Modeling clay "Junk" Paper Natural objects Glue Paste Scissors Staplers	Junk and gadgets Vegetables and fruits Cloth Sponges Seeds, beans, etc. Paint Knives Glue Scissors	Rags Socks Spools String Seeds; beans; dry cereal String; ribbon Paper Glue Scissors
	2. Creation	Glue paintings Soap paintings* "Rainbow" drawings Brush and sponge paintings	Clay animals "Junk" collages and sculptures* Nature mobiles Nature collages Three-dimensional sculptures and constructions	Gadget printings Vegetable printings* Paper weaving* Sponge stamping Cloth weaving	Hand puppets Sock puppets Spool stringing Seed and bean jewelry Hat creations*
	3. Appreciation	Free viewing: Display large art books and classwork. Guided viewing: Read well-illustrated children's books; display prints, reproductions, and original works.* Extended viewing: Informally, examine the many subjects of art.			

*Asterisk signifies that an activity has been provided for this medium.

	PROCESSES	CURRICULUM AREAS			
		(1) DRAWING AND PAINTING	(2) COLLAGE AND SCULPTURE	(2) DESIGN	(4) CRAFTS
LEVEL C (AGES 5 TO 7)	**1.** Free exploration and experimentation	Crayons Colored pencils No. 2 pencils Straw Brushes String Sponges Feathers	Paper Hardening clay Cut-out pictures Beans; seeds; macaroni Glue Paste Scissors	"Ever-plastic" clay Yarn Cylinders Burlap Needle and thread Tin cans Glue and paste	Paper Wood Hardening clay Paint Paste Scissors Clips; pins
	2. Creation	Crayon resists, over- lays, and rubbings* "Air-blow" paintings Crayon etchings Gadget paintings sponges, feathers) Pencil drawings	Clay bowls Papier-maché vases Food collages* Picture collages (with themes) Free-form sculpture	"Eye-of-God" (*ojo de dios*) weaving Roller prints* Clay stamps Weaving with burlap and yarn Loom weaving	Puppets with wooden or papier-maché heads Papier-maché masks* Papier-maché, clay, and wooden jewelry
	3. Appreciation	Free viewing: Display art books and classwork; hold a schoolwide show; make multimedia displays. Guided viewing: Read well-illustrated children's books; display prints, reproductions, and originals; show slides and films. Extended viewing: Informally, examine the many media of art.			
LEVEL D (AGES 7 TO 9)	**1.** Free exploration and experimentation	Crayon Chalk Charcoal Pastels Pen and ink Watercolors Sand Starch and tissue	Clay Paper Soap Rocks Wood Paraffin Plaster Tiles Paste and glue	Yarn Needle and thread Wood Paper Glue Ink Paint Potatoes Knives Cloth	Wood Plaster Dowels Jute Drill Needle and thread Pins and cups String Paint Cloth
	2. Creation	Sketches in char- coal, ink, and pastels* Crayon meltings Sand painting Starch-and-tissue overlays Wet-chalk drawings	Carved or decorated soap* Clay sculptures Pottery Mosaics Molds Decoupage composites	Thread pictures Yarn-and-glue designs* Woodblock prints Ink prints Potato prints Stitchery Stencils	Marionettes* Rod and shadow puppets Wooden and plaster jewelry Sewn bookmarks
	3. Appreciation	Free viewing: Display art books and classwork; show filmstrips; hold an art show and judge entries. Guided viewing: Visit museums and galleries; view magazines, books, slides, and films.* Extended viewing: Informally, examine the various degrees of stylization and realism in art.			

Activities for Art: Drawing and Painting

Description Making a screen stencil with window screen, a toothbrush, and tempera paint.
Title (for children) "Peek-a-Boo Prints."
Curriculum area Art (drawing and painting).   **Age range** 3 to 5.

What is our medium? Screen stencils (creation; table: 1-A-2).
What will we need? Small pieces of window screen (one for each child), tempera paint, construction paper, old toothbrushes (several for each child), construction paper, and newspaper for covering the work tables.
How will we do it?
1. The teacher demonstrates (briefly) how a screen stencil is made and what it looks like when it's finished.
2. The children's work tables are covered with newspaper.
3. Each child gets a piece of construction paper, a piece of screen, a few toothbrushes, and thinned tempera paint (several colors).
4. To make the stencil, the screen is held in place over the construction paper, and one toothbrush is dipped into paint and then brushed across the screen. The process is repeated for each new color, with a fresh toothbrush each time.
5. Each child chooses how many colors, and which colors, to blend. The children can share and discuss the results.
What else can we do? **Variation:** Interesting stencil effects can be obtained by placing cutouts or flat objects (a leaf, e.g.) on the paper before applying the paint. **Other activities:** Using crayons on various textured surfaces—sandpaper, corrugated paper, paper towels, etc.—gives interesting results; the crests and troughs on the surface act as the "screen."

Description A class art show based on various interpretations of a single subject.
Title (for children) "And the Subject Is . . ."
Curriculum area Art (drawing and painting).   **Age range** 3 to 5.

What is our medium? Extended viewing (appreciation; table: 1-A-3).
What will we need? Duplicated notes to parents; drawing and painting materials for the children; reproductions of paintings and drawings from magazines, calendars, posters, etc.; area for the display; construction paper, poster paper, mounting frames, etc.
How will we do it?
1. Children and teacher discuss how different artists can treat the same subject differently. Together, they decide on a single subject for an art show.
2. When the subject has been chosen, the children take home notes to their parents (these have been written and duplicated by the teacher), informing them about the forthcoming show and asking for contributions of paintings, drawings, or reproductions on the subject chosen. Magazines, calendars, and posters are good sources; some parents may even be willing to lend framed paintings or reproductions.
3. Over a period of time (a week, perhaps), the children bring in their families' contributions; they also look through magazines in the classroom and cut out appropriate works.
4. When all the contributions are collected, children and teacher examine and discuss them; then, each child may make a drawing or painting to add to the collection.
5. The collection is displayed in various ways—some works can be put on easels, some hung, some arranged in looseleaf books or scrapbooks, some displayed flat on tables, etc. The teacher and older children collaborate on labels.
What else can we do? **Follow-up:** Other classes and parents can be invited to the show.

Description Painting with whipped soapflakes and food coloring or paints.
Title (for children) "Bubblerama."
Curriculum area Art (drawing and painting).   **Age range** 4 to 6.

What is our medium? Soap paintings (creation; table: 1-B-2).
What will we need? Ingredients for the "bubbles" mixture (½ cup soapflakes or detergent and 2 tablespoons liquid starch per child); food coloring or dry tempera paints (various colors); small containers; mixing bowl; paper; small brushes; spoon. For mixing the "bubbles," use an electric mixer or an eggbeater.
How will we do it?
1. Teacher and children whip the detergent-and-starch mixture until it becomes thick, stiff, "bubbles."
2. Each child gets several small containers; and paint or food coloring in several colors is put out for all the children. The "bubbles" are spooned out into the children's containers.
3. Each child chooses various colors to mix with his or her "bubbles"—one color per container.
4. When the "bubbles" have been tinted, the teacher shows how to paint pictures with them on paper, using brushes, fingers, or both; and then the children create their own pictures.
5. The pictures are left to dry overnight and then displayed.
What else can we do? **Variations:** The children can use different-sized brushes on the same picture; sponges can also be used; and of course brushes and sponges can be used together.

Description   Dipping crayon drawings into water and using tempera paint to make resists and prints.
Title (for children)   "Irresistible Prints."
Curriculum area   Art (drawing and painting).   **Age range**   5 to 7.

What is our medium?   Crayon resists (creation; table: 1-C-2).
What will we need?   Drawing paper (two sheets for each child), crayons, one or more basins of water, newspaper, thinned tempera paints, wide brushes.
How will we do it?
1. Each child draws a picture (abstract or representational) with crayon, coloring heavily.
2. The crayon drawing is crumpled and dipped into a pan or basin of cold water.
3. The excess water is squeezed out of the drawing, and the drawing is spread out on newspaper. (The teacher demonstrates steps 2 and 3; then each child does these steps himself or herself.)
4. The children then paint over their crayon drawings with thinned tempera paint, using a wide brush to cover the whole surface.
5. Then, immediately, each child presses a clean sheet of drawing paper on the painted surface.
6. The children peel away the second sheet of paper—this is the print. The first piece of paper—the crayon drawing— is the resist.

What else can we do?   **Another activity:** "Black magic" etchings—The children color a picture heavily with crayon and then color over it with black crayon. Then paper clips, fingernails, scissors, pencils, etc., can be used to "etch" a design or picture: the black is scratched off so that the original colors show through.

Description   Sketching faces of classmates in pen and ink.
Title (for children)   "Let's Face It."
Curriculum area   Art (drawing and painting).   **Age range**   7 to 9.

What is our medium?   Sketches in ink (creation; table: 1-D-2).
What will we need?   Drawing paper, india ink, pens (penholder-pen point).
How will we do it?
1. Children and teacher discuss the components of the face from an artist's point of view—lines, planes, angles, shadows, curves, etc.
2. The children work in pairs—the two children in each pair study each other's face and, as accurately as possible, sketch what they see (using pen and ink on drawing paper).
3. The children mat and mount their pictures and display them. Afterwards, they discuss their drawings and what they saw in each other's face.

What else can we do?   **Variation:** All the children can draw the teacher's face—it's then interesting to discuss what aspects different children emphasized, and other ways in which their sketches differ. **Other activities:** Charcoal can be used for drawing on white or light-colored paper, and shaded by using a finger wrapped in tissue paper. Chalk drawings (including colored chalks, charcoal, and pastels) can be "fixed" with liquid starch. Chalks can be dipped in water before being used for drawing—this produces deeper, darker colors.

Description Creating pictures with homemade "play dough."
Title (for children) "Doughy Doings."
Curriculum area Art (collage and sculpture).   **Age range** 3 to 5.

What is our medium? "Play dough" painting and sculpture (creation; table: 2-A-2).
What will we need? Basic recipe for play dough: 1 cup warm water, 1 cup salt, 2 to 3 cups flour, 2 tablespoons corn-starch, food coloring. This can be increased as necessary. In addition, you'll need: newspaper to cover the children's work tables; a piece of cardboard and a black felt pen for each child; popsicle sticks, tongue depressors, or the like for cutting and forming (at least one for each child); and implements for mixing the dough—measuring cup, spoon, bowl.
How will we do it?
1. The children help the teacher prepare several batches of play dough, working on newspaper-covered tables. Each batch is a different color.
2. Each child gets some dough of different colors, a piece of cardboard, a felt pen, and a molding tool.
3. Using the pen, each child makes a simple line drawing on his or her cardboard.
4. Each child pulls pieces of play dough from his or her lumps and presses them down to fill in the outline on the drawing, using different colors.
5. The children share their results.
What else can we do? Other activities: Some "play dough" recipes can be baked and then shellacked after the sculp-tures are finished; children can make animals from this kind of dough.

Description Making "mystery collages" by covering objects with aluminum foil.
Title (for children) "Curses! Foiled Again!"
Curriculum area Art (collage and sculpture).   **Age range** 4 to 6.

What is our medium? "Junk" collages and sculptures (creation; table: 2-B-2).
What will we need? A large assortment of "junk" for the collages—small objects such as nails, bolts, screws, seeds, pods, yarn, keys, odd pieces of wood, old pencil stubs, corks, coins, sponges, and rubber erasers—and a table to lay it out on. Each child will need: a piece of cardboard (8½- by 11-inch), white glue and water for thinning it, aluminum foil, a small paintbrush, scissors, a glue dish, and a soft cloth.
How will we do it?
1. Each child glues assorted "junk" onto a piece of cardboard, using undiluted glue. (The children help themselves to the "junk" from the table.)
2. When the glue dries so that the objects are firmly in place, each child makes a batch of thinned glue and, using a brush, "paints" the entire collage with it.
3. Then, the child presses aluminum foil all over the surface of the collage, molding it carefully over each object so that the shapes emerge.
4. The edges of the foil are glued along the back of the cardboard.
5. Finally, the foil is polished with a cloth.
6. The collages are displayed, and the children try to guess what the objects are. (Older children can keep a list of the objects in their own collages, to aid memory.)
What else can we do? **Another activity:** Small "junk" objects can be stuck into and onto modeling clay to create "found" sculptures.

Description Visiting a library and selecting books with illustrations of collages and sculptures to share.
Title (for children) "I Think You're Going to Like This One . . ."
Curriculum area Art (collage and sculpture).   **Age range** 4 to 6.

What is our medium? Guided viewing (appreciation; table: 2-B-3).
What will we need? Advance preparation: The teacher arranges for the children to visit a library with a good collection of art books; and the librarian selects beforehand—and makes available to the children when they arrive—a number of books with illustrations of sculpture and collages. Teacher and librarian also arrange for an area where the children can share and discuss these books.
How will we do it?
1. Teacher and children discuss or review collage and sculpture and then visit a library to examine books with illustrations of collages and sculptures.
2. The children are allowed free time to browse through the books.
3. Each child is given (or makes) a set of colored book markers (strips of construction paper, say) with his or her name written on them. When the children find illustrations of works that especially appeal to them, they mark the pages with their markers.
3. The books with markers are taken to the area that has been set aside for sharing and discussion.
4. The children take turns showing the illustrations they have marked and talking about what they like particularly about them—colors? lines? shapes? subjects?
5. The librarian and the teacher may contribute by telling the children something about the artists whose works the children have chosen.
What else can we do? **Follow-up:** Visit a museum or gallery to see some collages and sculptures.

Description Using beans, seeds, shells, dry pasta, etc., to create a "flower" collage.
Title (for children) "Full of Beans."
Curriculum area Art (collage and sculpture).   **Age range** 5 to 7.

What is our medium? Food collages (creation; table: 2-C-2).
What will we need? For each child: a cardboard disk (about the size of the lid of an oatmeal box), glue, glue brush. For the class or group: an ample assortment of beans, seeds, pods, small nuts, small shells, various small uncooked pasta (tubettini, orzo, small elbows, etc.), uncooked rice, and so on, and a table to hold them. The teacher will need safety pins (one for each child) and masking tape, and shellac and a sprayer.
How will we do it?
1. Each child gets a cardboard disk, glue, and a glue brush.
2. The children choose beans, seeds, etc., from the assortment—which can be spread out on a table. Then they coat the cardboard disks with glue.
3. Each child arranges the foods on the cardboard disk to form a flower shape, working from the center out and pressing down so that the items stick to the glue.
4. When each "flower" is finished, the teacher helps the child to spray it with shellac.
5. When the shellac has dried, the teacher helps each child to tape a safety pin the the back of the cardboard disk, so that the "flower" can be worn.
What else can we do? **Variations:** Similar materials can be used to make pictures, faces, etc.

Description Using collage to decorate bars of soap.
Title (for children) "Soap It to Me."
Curriculum area Art (collage and sculpture).   **Age range** 7 to 9.

What is our medium? Carved or decorated soap (creation; table: 2-D-2).
What will we need? For each child: a bar of soap (oval is best). For the group or class: an assortment of wallpaper and greeting cards; gold watercolor paint and thin brushes, paste. The teacher will need a hotplate, a shallow pan, and paraffin. Wrapping tissue is a nice addition.
How will we do it?
1. Choosing from the assorted pieces of wallpaper and greeting cards, the children cut out small pictures or designs that will fit on a bar of soap.
2. Each child pastes a cutout on one side only of his or her bar of soap.
3. Using the gold water paint and thin brushes, the children paint a design around the cutouts (e.g., a scroll design or a "frame").
4. When each bar of soap is decorated, the child dips the decorated side into warm paraffin (the teacher has this ready in a shallow pan on the hotplate).
5. The children can wrap their bars of soap—after the decoration has cooled and dried—to be used as gifts. (The design will remain intact as the soap is used.)
What else can we do? **Another activity:** Animals can be carved from soap (a design or guide can be marked on the soap first).

Activities for Art: Design

Description Making fingerprints with paint and then using them as the basis for a simple drawing.
Title (for children) "Do You Want to Make Something Out of It?"
Curriculum area Art (design).   **Age range** 3 to 5.

What is our medium? Finger prints (creation; table: 3-A-2).
What will we need? Construction paper, thinned tempera paints (various colors), black felt-tip pens (thin point), newspaper. For cleaning up afterwards: soap and water; paper towels.
How will we do it?
1. Each child gets a sheet of construction paper (white) and puts it on a "mat" of newspaper.
2. The children dip their fingers (one finger at a time) into the thinned tempera paint and then press the paint-coated fingertip gently onto construction paper.
3. Each child chooses different colors and different fingers to make a design on his or her construction paper—being sure to leave space between the prints.
4. The teacher shows the children how these prints can be made into little line drawings, illustrating how the shapes can suggest, e.g., an animal's body or a face.
5. The children make similar line drawings on their own designs, using black felt-tip pens.
6. The children share and talk about their ideas. What were they able to make out of their fingerprints?
What else can we do? **Another activity:** Fingerprints by themselves (without any drawing) can be used to make patterns and designs.

Description Printing designs with pieces of vegetables and fruits.
Title (for children) "Vegie Prints."
Curriculum area Art (design).   **Age range** 4 to 6.

What is our medium? Vegetable printings (creation; table: 3-B-2).
What will we need? Assorted fruits and vegetables; plastic knives; construction paper; newspapers; saucers or bowls with various colors of tempera paint.
How will we do it?
1. With the teacher's help, the children cut vegetables and fruits into slices, halves, quarters, or odd shapes.
2. Each child blots his or her "vegies" dry with newspapers (there can be a communal stack of newspapers for blotting) and then dips them into tempera paint—using different pieces and different colors.
3. As each piece of "vegie" is dipped into paint, the child presses it onto a piece of construction paper. Each child uses variation and repetition to create his or her own design.
What else can we do? **Follow-up:** When the children have got the knack of "vegie prints," they can use this technique to make their own wrapping paper, greeting cards, lunch bags, etc.

Description Designing and weaving paper placemats.
Title (for children) "Eager Weavers."
Curriculum area Art (design).   **Age range** 4 to 6.

What is our medium? Paper weaving (creation; table: 3-B-2).
What will we need? Construction paper in various colors, scissors, glue, pencils or marking pens. For younger children, the teacher can mark the guidelines on the construction paper; older children can do this themselves, following a model by the teacher.
How will we do it?
1. Each child gets two sheets of construction paper (two different colors). On one piece, parallel equidistant lines are drawn from edge to edge. On the second piece, parallel equidistant lines are drawn across, stopping at least 1 inch from either edge.
2. The children cut sheet 1 into strips, following the lines. Sheet 2 is folded in half perpendicular to the lines—then the children cut the doubled sheet along the lines, starting at the fold. When sheet 2 is unfolded, it is still in one piece, but with parallel cuts.
3. The strips made from sheet 1 are woven in and out of the cuts in sheet 2.
4. When the weaving is done, the children trim off any excess at the ends of the strips and glue the strips down at the edges.
5. They can then use their placemats at snack time or lunch.
What else can we do? **Variation:** The design can be varied by cutting on the diagonal or making the strips wavy.

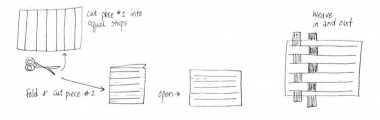

Description   Using a tin can decorated with heavy yarn to make roller prints.
Title (for children)   "Roll 'Em!"
Curriculum area   Art (design).   **Age range**   5 to 7.

What is our medium?   Roller prints (creation; table: 3-C-2).
What will we need?   Tin cans (soup size), thick yarn, glue, paint and paint tray, paper (or other surfaces for printing).
How will we do it?
1. Each child gets a tin can and removes the paper label.
2. Then, each child makes a design on his or her can by gluing strands of thick yarn around the outside.
3. When the glue has dried, the children take turns rolling their decorated cans in paint in a tray.
4. Then they roll the cans over paper to make designs (or over paper bags, wrapping paper, cardboard cartons, book covers, etc.).
5. More complex designs can be made by using two or more cans with different yarn patterns and colors.
What else can we do?   **Follow-up:** The children can collect cylindrical objects for use in making future roller prints— e.g., discarded hair rollers or rolling pins, spools, cardboard tubes, pencils.   **Another activity:**   Cardboard shapes can be glued to empty cardboard tubes; this will make interesting roller prints.

Description   Making designs by outlining drawn pictures with yarn.
Title (for children)   "Yarn It Anyway!"
Curriculum area   Art (design).   **Age range**   7 to 9.

What is our medium?   Yarn-and-glue designs (creation; table: 3-D-2).
What will we need?   Poster board, thick yarn in various colors, white glue (in squeeze bottles), pencils or felt-tip pens.
How will we do it?
1. On a fairly large piece of poster board, each child draws a simple, bold design or an outline-type rendition of an object. (Pencil or felt pen can be used for this.)
2. Using a squeeze bottle of glue, the child outlines the design or picture with glue.
3. Then the child presses a strand of thick yarn in place, following the glue line.
4. When the outer line of yarn is in place, the child makes another line of glue all the way around just inside it, and presses another strand of yarn in place. This process continues until the entire figure has been filled in with yarn. The child chooses the colors of the yarn and decides what kind of color pattern to make (alternating? 1-2-3, 1-2-3? 1-1-2, 1-1-2? etc.).
What else can we do?   **Another activity:** Yarn-and-glue can be used to outline or accent parts of the children's drawings of scenes or action.

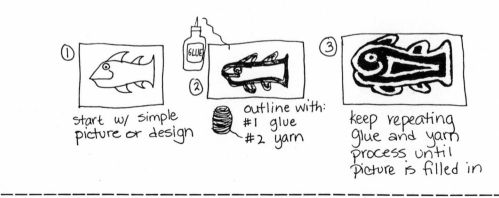

① start w/ simple picture or design

② outline with: #1 glue #2 yarn

③ keep repeating glue and yarn process until picture is filled in

Description Making jewelry from glue and decorating it with marking pens.
Title (for children) "Glue Globs."
Curriculum area Art (crafts).   **Age range** 3 to 5.

What is our medium? "Glue-glob" pins (creation; table: 4-A-2).
What will we need? White glue (clear-drying) in squeeze containers; wax paper; hair clips; fine-point felt pens. The teacher will need contact cement, and (if possible) a silver dollar.
How will we do it?
1. Each child (under the teacher's supervision) squeezes out of the glue bottle onto a piece of wax paper a glob about the size of a silver dollar. (The teacher can show an actual silver dollar as a model, or a disk of cardboard.)
2. The glue globs are left to dry for a day or two, on the wax paper.
3. When the globs are dry, each child peels his or hers off the wax paper and decorates it with colored marking pens (fine point).
4. As each child finishes decorating a glob, the teacher glues a hair clip to the back of it with contact cement.
5. The children can clip their jewelry to their clothing and model it.
What else can we do? **Variation:** Before each glob dries, a small object (or more than one object) can be pressed onto the surface—e.g., beads, sequins.

Description Making hats out of paper plates, crepe paper, and other assorted materials.
Title (for children) "The Glad Hatter."
Curriculum area Art (crafts).   **Age range** 4 to 6.

What is our medium? Hat creations (creation; table: 4-B-2).
What will we need? For each child: a paper plate and a 36-inch strip of crepe paper. For the class or group: glue or paste; staplers; stars, glitter, sequins; doilies; yarn; ribbon; paper (curling) ribbon.
How will we do it?
1. Each child gets a paper plate and (with the help of the teacher, if necessary) staples a crepe-paper strip to it (this will tie under the chin).
2. The glue, staplers, and decorative materials are set out where all the children can use them.
3. Each child chooses materials and decorates a hat ad lib.
4. The "glad hatters" can model their creations.
What else can we do? **Variation:** Small pieces of styrofoam in various shapes can also be used to decorate the hats.

Description Making "ceremonial" masks by molding papier-maché around balloons.
Title (for children) "Pop Goes the Mask."
Curriculum area Art (crafts).   **Age range** 5 to 7.

What is our medium? Papier-maché masks (creation; table: 4-C-2).
What will we need? Balloons, paint, brushes, commercial "instant" papier-maché and water, pins.
How will we do it?
1. Children and teacher examine and discuss pictures (and if possible samples) of ceremonial masks from one or more cultures.
2. To make their own versions of ceremonial masks, the children do the following;
    a. Each child blows up a big balloon and (with the teacher's help, if necessary) knots the end.
    b. One hemisphere of the balloon is then covered with "instant" papier-maché; the child leaves holes for the eyes, mouth, and nostrils and builds up the papier-maché to form brow ridges, nose, lips, ears, etc.
    c. The papier-maché is allowed to dry completely, and then each child pops his or her balloon with a pin (the teacher supervises the use of pins, of course).
    d. Next, the children paint their masks to add detail or decoration.
3. The complete masks can be displayed.
What else can we do? **Another activity:** The same method can be used to make heads for puppets (use smaller balloons for this, however).

214

Description Making cardboard marionettes with movable arms.
Title (for children) "Merry Marionette."
Curriculum area Art (crafts).   **Age range** 7 to 9.

What is our medium? Marionettes (creation; table: 4-D-2).
What will we need? Sheets of heavy cardboard, crayons or marking pens, scissors, hole punchers, paper fasteners, string.
How will we do it?
1. On a sheet of cardboard, each child draws an outline of a human figure without arms and then colors it in.
2. These figures are cut out. A hole is punched at each shoulder.
3. On another sheet of cardboard, each child draws (in outline) two arms (with hands) and colors them in.
4. The two arms are cut out. At the shoulder end of each arm a hole is punched, and the arms are attached to the shoulders with paper fasteners.
5. Now a hole is punched in the top of each figure's head, and one hole is punched in each hand.
6. A string is run through the hole in the head; and a string is run through the hole in each hand.
7. Each child ties the head string to his or her wrist, a string from one hand to the thumb, and the string from the other hand to the little finger.
8. The children learn how to make their own puppets move.
What else can we do? Follow-ups: Obviously, the children can use these puppets for puppet shows. **Other activites:** "Shadow puppets" are figures (or the hands) manipulated in front of a back-lighted screen or curtain; "rod puppets" are pictures mounted on cardboard attached to dowel rods.

Description A slide and film show of crafts around the world.
Title (for children) "That's Pretty Crafty."
Curriculum area Art (crafts).   **Age range** 7 to 9.

What is our medium? Guided viewing (appreciation; table: 4-D-3).
What will we need? Considerable advance preparation—books and articles for the children; arrangements with a local library and perhaps with shops that sell crafts; contributions from parents. The teacher will need a camera and other equipment for making slides, and a slide projector; a motion picture or filmstrips from a library or film library, and a projector; and a "script" for the show.
How will we do it?
1. Teacher and children discuss various crafts—e.g., clothing, pottery, jewelry—and some outstanding examples from around the world. The children talk about trips they or their parents have made to places where craftwork is produced. The class decides on several categories of crafts to learn more about.
2. The teacher prepares for the crafts presentation by arranging to make slides at local shops or a museum, borrowing or renting films or filmstrips, and asking parents for contributions that can be photographed for slides.
3. As the nature of the materials to be presented takes shape, the teacher formulates a "script" for the show, being sure to have an organizational theme (e.g., raw materials to finished product? places? craftsmen and craftswomen?), and provides books and articles for the children to read.
4. The show is presented to the children. It is a good idea to have the children take brief notes and prepare short reports afterwards.
What else can we do? Follow-up: A visit to a craft shop, museum, or private collection. **Another activity:** A display of good illustrated books on crafts.

Resources for Art

Bibliography for Teachers

Association for Childhood Education International. *Art guide: Let's make a picture.* Washington, D.C.: ACEI, 1969. (Teaching ideas for a variety of art media blend with material directed at helping the child to notice what makes a picture. A good bibliography of art books and audiovisual materials is included.)

Baker, L. *The art teacher's resource book.* Reston, Va.: Reston, 1979. (An excellent resource manual. Covers all the materials and techniques used in most elementary art curriculums. Clear descriptions and illustrations ensure that teachers can successfully organize and implement exciting art programs for young children.)

Bland, J. *Art of the young child.* New York: Museum of Modern Art. (Practical suggestions for encouraging children's art development, as well as for specific art materials, are provided.)

Blond, A. & Janusz, L. *Spectrum of visual arts of young children.* Sepulveda, Calif.: Double M, 1976. (Innovative arts and crafts projects for children aged 2 to 8. Each activity includes descriptions, materials and equipment required, and detailed easy-to-follow directions for adult supervision and participation by children.)

Cherry, C. *Creative art for the developing child.* Belmont, Calif.: Fearon, 1972. (The author claims that all the activities in this book can be pursued by a 4-year-old without adult assistance, although they can effectively be used with children aged 2 to 6. Activities are grouped into sections for the various media, such as print making, woodworking, crayons, paste and paints. An introductory chapter provides excellent background for the teacher in setting up a creative art program.)

Enthoven, J. *Stitchery for children.* New York: Van Nostrand Reinhold, 1968. (The author suggests materials suitable for children beginning at age 2, stressing creative expression. Various materials and stitches are described.)

Fiarotta, P. *Sticks and stones and ice cream cones.* New York: Workman, 1973. (This is a good collection of innovative crafts ideas using paper, empty boxes, cans and other "junk" items. See also *Snips and snails and walnut whales* by the same author for parent-child activities.

Frank, M. *I can make a rainbow.* Nashville: Incentive, 1976. (A delightful collection of arts and crafts activity ideas for children and their grown-up friends. Using natural and everyday around-the-house materials, the author describes over 200 activities. Highly recommended!)

Haskell, L. *Art in the early childhood years.* Columbus, Ohio: Merrill, 1979. (Fundamental techniques used in providing art experiences for young children are included in this volume, arranged by age level for 4- to 8-year-olds. Emphasis is placed on using found objects to help cope with the high cost of art materials.)

Herberholz, B. *Early childhood art.* Dubuque, Iowa: W. C. Brown, 1974. (Attention is given to the child as an appreciator of art as well as a creator. Many activities are described in sufficient detail for the novice to carry them out with young children.)

McGrath, R., & Graham, B. *Tools, wood and glue: An invitation to grow.* Buffalo, N.Y.: D.O.K., 1976. (Tailor-made for teachers who want to try some woodworking projects in their classroom. This book contains instructions for twenty-four woodworking activities, a list of suggested basic woodworking tools, materials, and supplies, and hints on storage.)

Romberg, J. *Let's discover* series. New York: Center for Applied Research in Education, 1974. (521 Fifth Ave., 10017. Arts and crafts discovery units, each with many suggestions for use with children. Titles include *Let's discover crayons, Let's discover mobiles, Let's discover paper, Let's discover papier-maché, Let's discover printing, Let's discover puppets, Let's discover tempera, Let's discover tissues, Let's discover watercolor,* and *Let's discover weaving.*)

Journals and periodicals:

Arts and Activities. (8150 N. Central Park Ave., Skokie, Ill. 60076.)
School Arts. (Davis Press, Inc., Printers Bldg. Worcester, Mass. 01608.)

Bibliography for Children

Types of books to include:

Arts and crafts activities books.
Well-illustrated children's books. (Look for Caldecott Award winners.)
Biographies of great artists.
Good books of art prints or reproductions.
Art portfolios and catalogs from art shows, galleries, and auctions.

Books and series:

About us. Childcraft Annual. 1973. (Field Enterprises Educational Corp., Chicago.)

Haskell, L. *Art in the early childhood years.* Columbus, Ohio: Merrill, 1979. (Includes outstanding bibliography in all areas of art.)

Look again. Childcraft Annual. 1968. (Field Enterprises Educational Corp., Chicago.)

Pluckrose, H. (Ed.). *Starting points* books. New York: Van Nostrand Reinhold, 1971. (Titles include *Let's paint, Let's crayon, Let's print, Let's make a picture, Let's model, Let's make soft toys, Let's draw,* and *Let's make puppets.*)

Raboff, E. *Art for children series.* New York: Doubleday. (Some titles are *Marc Chagall,* 1968; *Paul Klee,* 1968; and *Pablo Picasso,* 1968.)

Wilson, J. *Weaving is for anyone.* New York: Van Nostrand Reinhold, 1966.
Wilson, J. *Weaving is fun.* New York: Van Nostrand Reinhold, 1970.
Wilson, J. *Weaving is creative.* New York: Van Nostrand Reinhold, 1972.

Books dealing with color and lines:

Alexander, D. S. *Discovering colors.* Glendale, Calif.: Regal, 1974.
Hoban, T. *Circles, triangles, and squares.* New York: Macmillan, 1974.
Mendoza, G. *Norman Rockwell's Americana ABC's.* New York: Dell, 1975.
O'Neill, M. *Hailstones and halibut bones.* New York: Doubleday, 1961.
Samson, A. S. *Lines, spines, and procupines.* New York: Doubleday, 1969.
Yolen, J. M. *See this little line?* New York: McKay, 1963.
Zaidenberg, A. *How to draw people.* New York: Vanguard, 1952.

Materials and Sources

Suggested Basic Materials

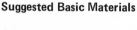

Binney and Smith, Inc., 380 Madison Ave., New York, N.Y. 10017.
Craftool Co., Inc., 1 Industrial Rd., Wood Ridge, N.J. 07075.
Crafts Advisory Committee, Troy Yarn, 603 Mineral Spring Ave., Pawtucket, R.I. 02862.
Creative Hands Co., 4146 Library Rd., Pittsburgh, Pa. 15234.
Crystal Craft Tissue, Dept. S-3, Middletown, Ohio 45042.
Milton Bradley Co., Springfield, Mass. 01101.
Permanent Pigments, Inc., 2700 Highland Ave., Cincinnati, Ohio 45212.
School Arts, Items of Interest Editor, Printers Bldg., Worcester, Mass. 01608.

Enrichment Materials

General sources for art prints, unusual pictures, and photographs:

Camera shops	Libraries
Photography magazines	Book clubs
Art museums.	Galleries.
Sidewalk art sales.	

For art books and collections, visit:

Libraries.	Museums.
Bookstores.	Private collections.
Galleries.	

For colors, collect:

Books.	Slides.
Movies.	Songs on color themes.

Write to the following for books, films, reproductions, and filmstrips:

Aim Instructional Media Services, Inc., P.O. Box 1010, Hollywood, Calif. 90028. (Film loops.)
Bowmar Artworlds, 4563 Colorado Blvd., Los Angeles, Calif. 90039. (Multimedia kits. Grades K through 3.)
Children's Books and Music Center, 2500 Santa Monica Blvd., Santa Monica, Calif. 90404. (Catalog of books and multimedia materials.)
Creative Hands Bookshop, 103 Printers Bldg., Worcester, Mass. 01608. (Extensive art book list.)
Educational Insights, Inc., Inglewood, Calif. (*The art box: Primary* is a kit with 150 art activities.)
International Film Bureau, Inc. 332 S. Michigan Ave., Chicago, Ill. 60604. (Color films about the lives of famous artists.)

Metropolitan Museum of Art, New York. (Portfolios; Metropolitan Seminars in Art. Reproductions.)

Sandak, Inc., 4 E. 48th St., New York, N.Y. 10017. (Slide sets; art history catalog.)

School Arts, 50 Portland St., Worcester, Mass. 01608. (An art education magazine for teachers.)

Society for Visual Education, Inc., 1345 Diversey Pkwy., Chicago, Ill, 60614. (Art slide sets with sound, and other products.)

Community Resources

Sources for supplies and places to visit:

Paint stores.
Artists.
Art shows.
Art museums.
Art galleries.
Art studios.
Craft supply shops.
Printers.
Decorators.
Artisans.

Libraries.
Factories and manufacturers. (Discards.)
Local art associations.
Colleges.
Local art supply vendors.
The local and surrounding environment. (As subjects for children's art.)
Fabric shops.
Lumberyards.
Children's homes.

Where to look for art:

Calendars.
Playing cards.
Stationery.
Greeting cards.
Old and new texts.
Old and new periodicals.

Children's books.
Photographs.
Magazines.
People's homes.
Advertisements.

Music for Older Children: Processes, Experiences, and Activities

Introduction: Processes and Experiences in Music

Much of what we've said about art as a part of the affective domain applies equally to music.

Music, like art, certainly contains cognitive and psycho-physical-motor components. Melody, harmony, tempo, and rhythm are among the many concepts that children develop through music; and moving in rhythm, playing an instrument, and reading music are among the many skills they can develop. As with art, there is also a linguistic element: a specialized terminology is appropriate both for musical activity and for musical description.

But music—again like art—is especially appropriate to represent the affective domain because of its social, emotional, and attitudinal components, and because it is so personal. We described these aspects of art earlier, but it's worthwhile to restate them briefly here for music:

Music helps children develop certain *social values*—e.g., sharing, taking turns, cooperating with others, participating in group activities, respecting others' work.

Activities in music have certain *emotional outcomes*—e.g., feeling good about oneself; expressing and channeling emotions; being aware of others' emotions; taking responsibility.

Music fosters certain *attitudes*—e.g., a lifelong love of music and perhaps a lifelong participation in music making; self-confidence; willingness to experiment.

Music is *personal*. Each child responds individually to music, so that many different things can and will happen as a result of a single music activity.

When approaching music as part of the affective domain, we must ask (as we did with art): What are our goals as teachers, and what do they imply about our objectives for children? Our goals are *not* to develop specific concepts or skills or to try to produce or nurture musicians. Rather, we want to help children enjoy various forms of music, help them develop discrimination as listeners (appreciation of music and sensitivity to it), allow them to express themselves through different musical forms, give them opportunities for creative exploration and experimentation in music, and build a foundation for later, more advanced musical experiences. We also want to create an environment conducive to these goals: one in which children are free to experiment and are supported in their experimentation, many activities are available, and children have as much responsibility and experience as little frustration as possible.

To achieve these global goals, we do not need or want to think in terms of fixed, specific objectives; instead, we want to think in terms of process—what the children experience, and how. Our "table of objectives" for music reflects this orientation: it is a table, not of objectives, but of *processes* and *experiences*.

We identify three basic processes for music:

1. **Creating** (that is, making up one's own music—chants, songs, etc.).
2. **Performing** (that is, interpreting one's own music and that of others).
3. **Appreciating**, or **responding** to, the music of others.

On our table, the experiences are grouped under these three major processes; they include such things as chanting, humming, and rhyming; listening to music and discussing it; dancing and watching others dance; and playing instruments.

These processes and experiences are arranged along our usual two axes: curriculum areas (the horizontal axis) and age levels (the vertical axis). For music, our curriculum areas are:

1. Vocalization.
2. Instrumentation.
3. Movement.

The activities which follow the table of processes and experiences are grouped in these three curriculum areas. For each activity, we identify process and experience and give a key to the table. The key reads, for music activities, "curriculum area, age level, *process*"—so that "1-A-1" means "area 1, level A, *process* 1."

Remember that our age levels are only suggestions: many of these experiences will be effective with children at various ages. And don't forget that our activities are only samples. We hope that you will create other activities of your own and that you and the children will enjoy music for its own sake.

	PROCESSES	CURRICULUM AREAS		
		(1) VOCALIZATION	(2) INSTRUMENTATION	(3) MOVEMENT
LEVEL A (AGES 3 TO 5)	**1.** Creation	Rhyming Chanting Humming	Using body sounds* Using sounds made by objects Putting sounds together	Moving freely to music Moving freely without music Dancing to simple rhythms and syncopated rhythms
	2. Performance	Songs: transitional, spontaneous, echoing, and personally invented* Individual and informal singing*	Instruments: percussion and rhythm, with or without accompaniment	Marching* Acting out to music* Dancing to simple rhythms
	3. Appreciation	Repeated listening to recorded vocal music (individually and in groups)* Singing by the teacher (the children listen)	Watching and listening to short live performances on solo instruments Listening to recorded music (of various types and tempos) as background for different actions	Observing natural movements of plants, animals, etc. Watching a demonstration by a dancer (ballet, disco, etc.)
LEVEL B (AGES 4 TO 6)	**1.** Creation	Imitating sounds and songs Making up words to familiar music* Matching pitch (which can be set by the teacher or an instrument)	Constructing simple instruments* Experimenting freely with sound Examining real instruments and trying them out	Moving freely with props and music "Glued-feet" movement to music Individual movement to music, in response to suggestions Miming to music Dramatizing to music*
	2. Performance	Songs: improvisational, cumulative, and scale-wise* Individual and informal group singing*	Clapping or tapping a beat Playing rhythm instruments with or without accompaniment*	Playing group musical games* Exercising while chanting Movement with a partner
	3. Appreciation	Listening to recorded music of our different heritages Watching and listening to a short live performance by a vocal group	Watching and listening to short live performances by instrumental groups Discussing how different kinds of music make one feel	Watching other classes dance at festivals, etc. Watching a short, live presentation of movement or dance

*Asterisk signifies that an activity has been provided for this experience.

	PROCESSES	CURRICULUM AREAS		
		(1) VOCALIZATION	(2) INSTRUMENTATION	(3) MOVEMENT
LEVEL C (AGES 5 TO 7)	1. Creation	Making up words and music*	Constructing instruments* Playing to different beats* Experimenting with groups of rhythm instruments	Interpretive dancing Experimental movement to varied tempos*
	2. Performance	Joining in repeated parts of songs* Songs: from a music book* Informal group singing Action songs*	Playing specific parts Forming a rhythm band with or without musical accompaniment	Exercises to chanting Exercises to music* Chanting and musical games Simple folk dances
	3. Appreciation	Repeated listening to recorded vocal music of different types and tempos Listening to live or recorded vocal presentations	Repeated listening to recorded instrumental music Watching and listening to live performances by soloists or orchestral sections*	Watching short live and filmed dance performances Learning about a day in the life of a dancer
LEVEL D (AGES 7 TO 9)	1. Creation	Making up and writing down lyrics and music* Writing narratives to music*	Constructing instruments Selecting sound effects and background music* Experimenting with orchestration Recognizing instruments by sound	Freely exercising to music Freely dancing to current music Learning popular and ballroom dance steps
	2. Performance	Song: rounds; two- and three-part songs; choral reading; singing in large groups	Playing a simple instrument Giving a class presentation	Performing simple folk dances Presenting a dance show*
	3. Appreciation	Listening to recorded or live folk music from other countries Learning about the life of a professional vocalist	Watching and listening to a live orchestra or band performance Repeated listening to recorded instrumental music	Attending a live dance performance Meeting dancers who will demonstrate their art

Activities for Music: Vocalization

Description Listening and responding to "Little Sir Echo."
Title (for children) "Follow the Leader."
Curriculum area Music (vocalization).   **Age range** 3 to 5.

What will we experience? Songs: echoing; and individual and informal group singing (performance; table: 1-A-2).
What will we need? Recording or sheet music of "Little Sir Echo," by Laura R. Smith and J. S. Fearis. The sheet music is copyright 1917 by Bregman, Voco, and Conn, Inc. (J. S. Fearis and Bros.). The recording is from "We All Live Together," Vol. 1, Youngheart Music Ed. Service, P.O. Box 27784, Los Angeles, Calif. 90027 (telephone 213-663-3223).
How will we do it?
1. The children listen to the music of "Littel Sir Echo."
2. Following the "leader" (the record or the teacher), the children make the appropriate echo responses.
3. Once they know the song, the children can take turns being leader and echo.
What else can we do? **Follow-up:** The children can make up their own words for each other to echo.

Description   Using tape recordings of classroom songs to improve performance.
Title (for children)   "Kiddie Chorus."
Curriculum area   Music (vocalization).   **Age range**   3 to 5.

What will we experience?   Repeated listening to recorded vocal music (appreciation; table: 1-A-3).
What will we need?   Words and music of favorite classroom songs; tape recorder. Optional: instrument or instruments to accompany the singing.
How will we do it?
1. Teacher and children discuss what kinds of things make group singing sound good (e.g., everyone on key, everyone singing together, no one singing too loud).
2. The class decides on, say, two or three favorite songs to sing together and record. (They may decide on a simple instrumental accompaniment if they are used to it, but the emphasis should be on choral singing.)
3. The children may "rehearse" each song once or twice. Then they sing the songs and the teacher tapes their performance.
4. The tapes are played back, one song at a time.
5. After listening to each song several times, the children assess their performance and suggest ways to improve it—using the criteria they discussed earlier.
6. The children put their ideas into practice on new, "final" performances, which are taped again.
7. The teacher makes a collection of best performances on one tape, which can then be used as background music for ordinary activities or special events or shows.

What else can we do?   **Other activities:** A tape can be made of favorite selections from classroom records; and children can learn new songs by listening to tapes repeatedly.

Description   Finding new words for favoite tunes.
Title (for children)   "Lyrics by Us!"
Curriculum area   Music (vocalization).   **Age range**   4 to 6.

What will we experience?   Making up words to familiar music (creation; table: 1-B-1).
What will we need?   Imagination.
How will we do it?
1. Teacher and children discuss how different words can be used with the same tune. (They might sing an example or two; e.g., "Frère Jacques"—"Christmas Bells.")
2. When the children have the idea, they try making up their own words for tunes they know.
3. The teacher can jog their imaginations by making up some simple lyrics for everyday activities. E.g., to the tune of "Row, Row, Row Your Boat," the children might sing, "Let's, let's, let's clean up;/ Let's clean up right away./ If we do, we will go out/ Because it's time to play."

What else can we do?   **Follow-up:** The children will enjoy tape-recording their new songs and playing them back; and the songs can be put on rebus charts so that the children can read and sing them repeatedly.

Description Adding "verses" onto a basic song to make a cumulative song about daily activities.
Title (for children) "Come On In—The Song's Fine."
Curriculum area Music (vocalization). **Age range** 4 to 6.

What will we experience? Songs: improvisational and cumulative; individual and informal group singing (performance; table: 1-B-2).

What will we need? A musical instrument for the accompaniment (piano, xylophone, autoharp, etc.), and a simple tune to get the children started.

How will we do it?

1. Near the end of the school day, teacher and children discuss what they did and what happened during the day.
2. The teacher plays a simple, catchy tune and starts the children off by singing a brief phrase about one thing that happened ("We made brown bear puppets, tra-la," or whatever).
3. The first child repeats the teacher's phrase and sings an additional one of his or her own ("We made brown bear puppets, tra-la; and Juan's mother came to help us, dum-de-dum").
4. The next child repeats the first two phrases and adds another, and so on around the group.

What else can we do? **Variation:** This can be an activity for the end of the week rather than the end of the day. **Follow-up:** When the children have gotten the hang of this, one of their efforts can be recorded. **Another activity:** The cumulative song is also appropriate for holidays (e.g., "What is Halloween about? About black cats, te-tum. And broomsticks, la-la-la. And witches, tiddley-pom. Etc.").

Description Using "props" while singing verses of a song.
Title (for children) "I Know an Old Lady Who Swallowed a Spider."
Curriculum area Music (vocalization). **Age range** 5 to 7.

What will we experience? Joining in repeated parts of songs (performance; table: 1-C-2).

What will we need? Sheet music for "I Know an Old Lady" (copyright Peer International Corp., 1619 Broadway New York, New York 10019); a shoebox with the old lady's face drawn on the lid and a large open mouth cut out; and the "verse cards" (one card per verse per child)—small cards, each with a picture or drawing of one animal mentioned in the song (fly, spider, bird, dog, horse, etc.).

How will we do it?

1. Each child gets a complete set of "verse cards." The children sit in a circle with the shoebox in the middle.
2. The children listen to the music for "I Know an Old Lady" and then sing it through.
3. As each animal is mentioned, the children drop the appropriate "verse card" into the mouth on the lid of the shoebox.

What else can we do? **Variation:** A similar setup can be used for singing "Old MacDonald"—the lid of the shoebox could have an open barn door, and the "verse cards" will again be all the animals mentioned in the song. **Another activity:** The teacher can sing the verse of a familiar song and then point at the children to indicate that they are to sing the refrain.

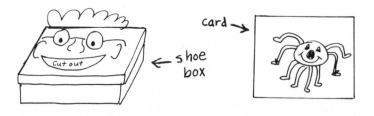

226

Description   Singing songs and making up actions to go with the words.
Title (for children)   "Actions Speak Louder . . ."
Curriculum area   Music (vocalization).   **Age range**   5 to 7.

What will we experience?   Songs: from a music book; action songs (performance; table: 1-C-2).
What will we need?   A selection of children's songbooks and records of songs. Optional: one or more instruments for accompaniment.
How will we do it?
1. The children choose from the songbooks and records several songs that they think could be illustrated with simple actions while being sung.
2. Children and teacher go through the songs one by one and pool their ideas to come up with appropriate actions for each.
3. The children perform their songs, using the actions they've made up.

What else can we do?   **Variation:** The class can be divided into groups; each group chooses a song and makes up actions for it; then the groups take turns singing and performing for the rest of the class. **Other activities:** Use old favorite actions songs such as "I'm a Little Teapot" and "Eensie-Weensie Spider"; for some of these, props can be used along with the traditional actions. Hap Palmer's records have actions included.

Description   Making up simple songs about various subjects.
Title (for children)   "A Jingle, a Jangle."
Curriculum area   Music (vocalization).   **Age range**   7 to 9.

What will we experience?   Making up and writing down lyrics and music (creation; table: 1-D-1).
What will we need?   Music manuscript paper; piano or xylophone.
How will we do it?
1. Teacher and children discuss the components of a "jingle"—a short song with a simple tune, a regular meter, and words that rhyme. To get the idea, the class sings a few jingles.
2. The children try their hand at composing some jingles, working individually. They'll probably begin with a little rhyme and then set it to music, but some may want to start with the tune. Those who want to can compose at the keyboard.
3. When each child has his or her jingle "set," the children take turns singing their songs to the teacher, who reproduces the melody on the keyboard and writes it down. The children then write in their own words.
4. The children take turns singing their jingles to the class; the written versions are collected in a class book, which can be illustrated by the children.

What else can we do?   **Follow-up:** The children's jingles can be tape-recorded and used as background music or for singing along, played at open house, and used in dramatic presentations.

Description   Using parts of the body to create a rhythmic accompaniment to tunes.
Title (for children)   "Body Band."
Curriculum area   Music (Instrumentation).   **Age range**   3 to 5.

What will we experience?   Using body sounds (creation; table: 2-A-1).
What will we need?   Records of tunes with a clear beat; or sheet music and a piano.
How will we do it?
1. Teacher and children use parts of the body to beat time as they listen to music.
2. The teacher gives directions to the children, who follow them as the music goes along—e.g., "Clap your hands. Stamp your feet."
3. The children take turns giving directions and demonstrating "new" sounds—e.g., "Smack your lips. Click your tongue. Tap your elbow."
What else can we do?   Variation: Teacher or children can point to pictures of the body parts while giving directions.
Follow-up: When the children have gotten the idea, the music can be omitted and they can make up "tunes" consisting entirely of the "body beats."   **Another activity:**   The teacher can make up simple "body beats" for the children to repeat (e.g., "tum-te-TUM, tum-te-TUM"; "TEE-TEE-tum, TEE-TEE-tum").   Then the children can make up such beats for each other to repeat.

Description Making a "ta-maraca."
Title (for children) "Shake 'n' Sound."
Curriculum area Music (instrumentation).   **Age range** 4 to 6.

What will we experience? Constructing simple instruments (creation; table: 2-B-1).
What will we need? Two paper plates for each child, pinto beans, crayons, crepe paper, and a stapler. Since the little instrument made in this activity is a sort of cross between a tambourine and a maraca, it is a good idea to have a real tambourine and maraca on hand.
How will we do it?
1. Teacher and children examine a tambourine and a maraca (or pair of maracas)—the teacher demonstrates how they are used, and the children can try them out.
2. Now the children make their own combination "tambourine-maraca" or "ta-maraca," as follows.
    a. The children decorate the backs (bottoms) of two paper plates with crayon.
    b. A few crepe-paper streamers are stapled to the top of one of each child's plates.
    c. Beans are placed on one plate (a good handful), and then the second plate is stapled to it, face to face. Be sure the streamers hang out.
3. The children play their "ta-maracas." They may want to use them to accompany recorded music or their own songs.
What else can we do? **Other activities:** Another simple instrument the children can make is "nail chimes"—suspend several steel nails with string from a 12-inch dowel or a coat hanger. An instrument that more closely simulates the maraca can be made by covering a lightbulb with papier-maché; when the papier-maché is dry, tap the bulb on a table—it will break, and the fragments will create the shaker.

Description Using a familiar song to practice rhythmic accompaniment.
Title (for children) "Old MacDonald Had a Band."
Curriculum area Music (instrumentation).   **Age range** 4 to 6.

What will we experience? Playing rhythm instruments with or without accompaniment (performance; table: 2-B-2).
What will we need? Assorted rhythm instruments.
How will we do it?
1. The teacher introduces and demonstrates basic rhythm instruments (drums, bells, tambourine, maracas, rhythm sticks, etc.), and the children take turns trying them out.
2. The assorted instruments are laid out on a table or on the floor, and the children form a circle around them.
3. The teacher leads the children in singing this version of "MacDonald's Farm": "Old MacDonald had a band,/ Ee-i-ee-i-o./ And in this band he had a drum (a bell, some sticks, etc.),/ Ee-i-ee-i-o." As the teacher says "a drum" or whatever, he or she points to a child.
4. The child who's been chosen must quickly select the instrument named from the assortment. If the child chooses correctly, he or she gets to play the instrument during the next lines: "With a bang, bang here/ And a bang, bang there (or a rattle-rattle, or whatever);/ Here a bang, there a bang, everywhere a bang, bang./ Old MacDonald had a band,/ Ee-i-ee-i-o." (If the child's choice is incorrect, the instrument is put back in place and the teacher starts the verse again and chooses another child.)
5. When all the instruments have been handed out in this way, the "band" plays as an ensemble.
What else can we do? **Follow-up:** The band can accompany an instrument (the teacher at the piano, e.g.); or the children can play along with a record.

Description   Making a simulated kazoo.
Title (for children)   "Can You Kazoo?"
Curriculum area   Music (instrumentation).   **Age range**   5 to 7.

What will we experience?   Constructing instruments; and playing to different beats (creation; table: 2-C-1).
What will we need?   For each child: paper-towel tube, wax paper, rubber band. For the group or class: at least one real kazoo or "hum-a-zoo." The teacher will need an implement for poking holes in the cardboard tubes.
How will we do it?
1.   The teacher demonstrates a kazoo (or "hum-a-zoo"), and the children can examine it and try it out.
2.   Then the children make their own simulated kazoos, thus:
   a.   Each child gets a cardboard tube.
   b.   The child stretches wax paper over one end of the tube and pulls it taut. The taut paper is fastened in place with a rubber band.
   c.   The teacher helps each child poke holes in the tube.
3.   The children play their "kazoos" by humming (not blowing) through the open end. Teacher and children make up beats to hum.
What else can we do?   Other activities: Two more rhythm instruments children can make are shakers (fill assorted containers—cans with lids, plastic tubs, etc.—with beans, dried peas, or rice) and coconut clappers (cut a coconut in half, clean it out, let it dry, sandpaper it, and decorate it).

Description   Chanting and using rhythm instruments to produce varied rhythms.
Title (for children)   "That's My Beat."
Curriculum area   Music (instrumentation).   **Age range**   5 to 7.

What will we experience?   Playing to different beats (creation; table: 2-C-1).
What will we need?   Chalkboard or "experience chart" paper; chalk or marking pen. Each child will need a pair of rhythm sticks.
How will we do it?
1.   Teacher and children discuss notation for beat or rhythm (various systems are possible); and the teacher writes the words to a simple chant on the chalkboard or "experience chart" paper, indicating the beat with the system they have discussed. Here is an example: "FOUR little MONkeys JUMPing on the BED. (Rest.) ONE fell OFF and BUMPED his HEAD. (Rest.) MAMma called the DOCtor; the DOCtor SAID, (Rest.) THAT'S what you GET for JUMPing on the BED."
2.   Teacher and children chant the words, following the stresses indicated.
3.   Then they create the beat by clapping, stamping, hands on thighs, or whatever.
4.   The children then use rhythm sticks to create the beat as they "read" the stress notations.
What else can we do?   Follow-up: The class is divided into sections—all the children in each section have the same rhythm instrument (drums in one section, sticks in the next, and so on). The teacher draws a sketch of each instrument next to one line of the chant. As the class chants, each section plays the line indicated for its instrument. When the class is becoming proficient, chants of more complexity can be used, and the children can accompany records (Ella Jenkins's records—on the Folkways label—are good; two titles are "Adventures in Rhythm" and "Call and Response Rhythmic Group Singing").

Description A demonstration of instruments by orchestra musicians.
Title (for children) "Here to Make Music."
Curriculum area Music (instrumentation).   **Age range** 5 to 7.

What will we experience? Watching and listening to live performances by soloists or orchestral sections (appreciation; table: 2-C-2).

What will we need? Advance preparation by the teacher or school with a local professional symphony orchestra; if your area has no orchestra, a similar program can be arranged with amateur musicians. You'll also need an ample space for the presentation—the ideal setup is a large room where the musicians can sit in the middle with the children all around; a stage is also possible, but this is more formal and gives less chance for interaction.

How will we do it?

1. The teacher or school arranges with a local orchestra for several musicians to come and give a lecture-demonstration-concert presentation. Most regional and city orchestras are old hands at this; but if you are arranging a presentation with amateur musicians, you may want to take a greater part in shaping it. As a rule, six instruments at a time are about as many as the children can absorb without confusion.

2. The musicians show their instruments, talk about them, play them, encourage questions from the children, and may play some selections as an ensemble. (The teacher can tape this.)

3. As preparation and follow-up, the teacher will want to have some pictures of the instruments to display in the classroom and will discuss the instruments with the children—e.g., how each fits into the orchestra.

What else can we do? **Follow-up:** Continue having such presentations (at reasonable intervals) until all the instruments of the orchestra have been covered. At some point, class or school can attend a children's or young people's concert if the area orchestra has such programs.

Description Making up sound effects and finding music to go with a favorite story.
Title (for children) "Crash, Bang, Boom."
Curriculum area Music (instrumentation).   **Age range** 7 to 9.

What will we experience? Selecting sound effects and background music (creation; table: 2-D-1).

What will we need? Records or tapes of instrumental music of various kinds; an assortment of instruments (horns, drums, etc.) and objects for sound effects (sheet metal for thunder, leather-soled shoes for footsteps, etc.); and books and stories.

How will we do it?

1. This can be a project for the class or for groups.

2. The children discuss what kinds of music seem to be appropriate for various things that happen in books and stories, and what kinds of objects can be used to approximate specific sounds. (The teacher may guide them with questions.)

3. The children decide on a story to embellish with music and sound effects.

4. The children go through the story, trying out music and creating sound effects to go with it. It may take several run-throughs before their presentation is "set."

5. If this activity has been done by groups, each group can present its embellished story to the class, with narration, music, and sound. If it has been a class activity, one or more children can read the story while others handle the sound effects and music.

6. The children's presentations can be tape-recorded and played back.

What else can we do? **Other activities:** The children can be asked to use ordinary classroom materials to recreate sounds (thunder, cars, etc.); the teacher can play short instrumental recordings and ask children to think of poems or stories to go with them.

Activities for Music: Movement

Description   Playing imaginary instruments to march music.
Title (for children)   "Pantomine Parade."
Curriculum area   Music (movement).   Age range   3 to 5.

What will we experience?   Marching (performance: table: 3-A-2).
What will we need?   Record or tape of march music played by a band, pictures of the band instruments (or actual instruments if possible), large open area for marching, one or two flags.
How will we do it?
1. The teacher shows how the band instruments are played—that is, what motions are involved in playing each. (If pictures are being used, this demonstration will be pantomined.)
2. The children mimic the movements for each instrument.
3. Then the teacher tells the children to pick an instrument and pretend to play it in the "pantomime parade."
4. For the parade, the teacher chooses one or two children to lead the way with flags; the others line up behind, each ready to play his or her imaginary instrument.
5. The teacher starts the band music, and the children march around, "playing" their instruments.
What else can we do?   Follow-up: As the children get used to marching, the teacher can give some orders ("About face," "Right," "Left," etc.) for the whole group or sections.   Another activity: Marching outdoors is fun. Since it's not always easy to have music outdoors, the children can simply march to a beat or chant ("Hay foot, straw foot" or whatever).

Description   Acting out the words of a song.
Title (for children)   "The Rabbit Song."
Curriculum area   Music (movement).   **Age range**   3 to 5.

What will we experience?   Acting out to music (performance; 3-A-2).
What will we need?   Rebus chart with words and movements for the "Rabbit Song." Optional: an instrument for accompaniment.
How will we do it?
1. The teacher plays or sings the "Rabbit Song," and the children sing it through once or twice to learn the words and tune. (See step 2.)
2. Next, the children learn and add the movements, which go as follows. The words will fit to the tune (the verse, not the refrain) of "Little Brown Jug" if the tune is pushed and pulled a bit. "In a cabin in the wood (use hands and index figures to shape a roof)/ A boy and girl at the window stood (cup hands around eyes like binoculars)./ Saw a rabbit hop along (close fist, and extend index and middle fingers as rabbit ears);/ Who knocked at the door (knock on air with clenched fist)/ and sang this song./ (Tune da capo.) 'Help me, help me,' the rabbit said (wave arms in air),/ 'Or the hunters will shoot me dead' (make gun with thumb and index finger)./ 'Come live with us,' the children replied (beckon with hand),/ 'We'll be happy here inside' (stroke one hand with the other, and hug yourself)."
3. A leader can point to the chart as the children sing.
What else can we do?   **Follow-up:** Like "John Brown's Baby," this song can be done with words progressively omitted, so that just the movements remain.   **Other activities:** Many movement songs are available on records; counting songs are fun (the fingers are used to show "how many").

The Rabbit Song

Description   Using props to act out a song.
Title (for children)   "The Hokey Pokey."
Curriculum area   Music (movement).   **Age range**   4 to 6.

What will we experience?   Dramatizing to music (creation; table: 3-B-1).
What will we need?   Various "props"—paintbrushes, pencils, balls, etc.
How will we do it?
1. The children learn the tune for "The Hokey Pokey."
2. Teacher and children look around the room for objects they can use for new verses to the song—e.g., "You put your paintbrush up,/ You put your paintbrush down,/ You put your paintbrush up,/ And you swish it all around"; and "You put your ball up,/ You put your ball down./ You put your ball up,/ And you bounce it all around."
3. The children sing their new verses and act them out with the objects they've chosen.
What else can we do?   **Another activity:** "This Old Man" is also a good acting-out song.

Description Changing the volume of a song in a searching game.
Title (for children) "Hide and Sing."
Curriculum area Music (movement).   **Age range** 4 to 6.

What will we experience? Playing group musical games (performance; table: 3-B-2).
What will we need? A small object to hide.
How will we do it?
1. This is a searching game—one child looks for a hidden object while the rest sing a song. If the searcher is "getting warmer," the children sing louder; if the searcher is "getting colder," the children sing softer.
2. One child is chosen to leave the room or hide his or her eyes.
3. A second child is given the object and hides it somewhere in the classroom.
4. The searcher comes back into the room or uncovers his or her eyes, and starts looking for the object.
5. The others sing a favorite song (e.g., "Yankee Doodle"), loudly or softly as appropriate, until the object is found.
6. For the next round, a new hider and a new searcher are chosen. A new song can be chosen, too.

What else can we do? Other activities: "Hot Potato" can be played to music; another good musical game is an old favorite—"Musical Chairs."

Description Dancing or moving freely to music played at various speeds.
Title (for children) "Mixing Movements."
Curriculum area Music (movement).   **Age range** 5 to 7.

What will we experience? Experimental movement to varied tempos (creation; table: 3-C-1).
What will we need? If the teacher can play an instrument: a piano, xylophone, or whatever; and some tunes to be played at various tempos. If not: records of tunes that can be played at different speeds (33, 45, and 78 rpm) and still sound recognizable; or records of different tunes, some fast, some slow, some moderate.
How will we do it?
1. Either the teacher plays a tune at various tempos; or a recording of a tune is played at different rpm settings; or at least three tunes of contrasting tempos are played on a record player (fast, slow, moderate).
2. Children dance or move to the music, varying the *tempo* of their movements to match the music. The movements they do should remain the same—what changes is the speed at which they move.

What else can we do? Variation: Instead of music, a drum can be used to set the tempos. **Another activity:**
Children and teacher can discuss how tempo affects mood. Then the children can listen to music of different kinds and show by moving what moods it induces in them.

234

Description Doing "mirror movements" to music.
Title (for children) "Mirror, Mirror . . ."
Curriculum area Music (movement).   **Age range** 5 to 7.

What will we experience? Exercises to music (performance; table: 3-C-2).
What will we need? A full-length mirror for the demonstration; records of music (instrumental or songs); ample open area.
How will we do it?
1. Using one child as a "model," the teacher shows the children how the mirror reflects his or her movements— being sure to get across the idea that left and right are reversed.
2. The children form two circles, one inside the other, so that each child in the outer circle has a "partner" in the inner circle.
3. As the music is played, the children in the outer circle make individual movements to it—anything simple and identifiable enough to be repeated and copied.
4. The children in the inner circle are the "mirrors"—each child imitates the movement his or her partner is making. The "mirror" child should try to do exactly what the partner is doing, so that the children look like a mirror image of each other. The "mirror" child will have to remember to reverse left and right.
5. This is trickier than it sounds. The children should have plenty of time to get the idea, starting with simple movements.
6. From time to time, rotate the circles so that the children get different partners.
What else can we do? **Variation:** From time to time, the teacher can stop the music and tell the children to "freeze" (does each pair form a mirror image?); as the children get better at this, they can try to make their movements more and and more expressive of the music.

Description Learning basic dance steps for various kinds of music, and giving a show.
Title (for children) "Gotta Dance!"
Curriculum area Music (movement).   **Age range** 7 to 9.

What will we experience? Presenting a dance show (performance; table: 3-D-2).
What will we need? If possible, some movies or videotapes of dancers doing various steps (e.g., you may be able to rent filmed dance instructions); books of dance instructions; if possible, someone to demonstrate dances (a dance teacher, a parent, a high school or college student, etc.); plenty of recorded music for various dances (ballroom, disco, and so on); drawing or poster paper and marking pens for making diagrams of various steps (a chalkboard is also good for this); if possible, a piano and someone who can play it (with the necessary sheet music); full-length mirror for practice; clear area or areas.
How will we do it?
1. This is a fairly elaborate project—allow plenty of time to make the necessary arrangements beforehand, and give the children ample time for learning.
2. It is probably most practical to divide the class into groups, each of which will learn, say, one or two dance steps.
3. The class as a whole studies various kinds of dances—using films, books, a demonstrator, etc. Then each group chooses one or two dances to learn.
4. The groups work separately, with as much guidance as can be provided, and using books, records, and sheet music. As they progress, the groups can take turns giving "progress reports" to the class—demonstrations with diagrams or whatever they find appropriate.
5. When all the groups are proficient, they get together to create and present a class show for parents or the school.
What else can we do? **Variations:** This same setup can be used for learning folk dances.

Resources for Music

Bibliography for Teachers

Bayless, K., & Ramsey, M. *Music: A way of life for the young child.* St. Louis: Mosby, 1978. (Excellent coverage of music in the lives of young children from infancy through kindergarten, as well as music and the child with special needs and music in other curriculm areas. A valuable resource section and autoharp instruction are also included.)

Burnett, M. *Melody, movement and language: A teacher's guide of music in game form for the pre-school and primary grades.* San Francisco: R and E, 1973. (Musical games for children are used to develop the basic elements of Orff "Schulwerk.")

Cherry, C. *Creative movement for the developing child: A nursery school handbook for nonmusicians.* Belmont, Calif.: Fearon, 1971. (Materials offered include a broad repertoire and range of creative rhythms.)

Gelineau, R. P. *Experiences in music* (2d ed.). New York: McGraw-Hill, 1976. (A comprehensive book for classroom teachers.)

Hart, L. *Music in motion.* Mill Valley, Calif.: Music in Motion, 1973. (Box 331, 94941.) (This book provides activities and songs dealing with attitudes, appreciation and value judgments while building skills of listening, singing, moving, and playing simple instruments.)

McLaughlin, R., & Wood, L. *Sing a song of people.* Glendale, Calif.: Bowmar, 1973. (This is an integrated program involving music and social studies with clearly stated objectives in the cognitive and affective domains. Teacher's resource book provides background information and suggested activities.)

Raebeck, L. *New approaches to music in elementary school.* Dubuque, Iowa: Wm. C. Brown, 1974. (Includes singing experiences, rhythmic experiences, instrument experiences, listening experiences, and books and sources for music materials.)

Wheeler, L., & Raebeck, L. *Orff and Kodaly adapted for the elementary school.* Dubuque, Iowa: W. C. Brown, 1972. (Focusing on rhythm, melody, movement, improvisation, and instrumental experiences, this book attempts to adapt the ideas of Carl Orff and Zoltan Kodaly so that American teachers can understand and use them.)

Winslow, R., & Dalling, L. *Music skills for classroom teachers.* Dubuque, Iowa: W. C. Brown, 1970. (This book, designed for general elementary teachers, is a reference and source book which develops basic skills and techniques helpful in teaching music. Piano, guitar, and autoharp sections are included, as is a section on music listening and a collection of songs.)

Journals and periodicals:

American Music Teacher. (Journal of the Music Teachers National Assn. 2113 Carew Tower, Cincinnati, Ohio 45202.)

Music Educator Journal. (Music Educators National Conference, 1902 Association Dr., Reston, Va. 22091.)

Bibliography for Children

Carnes, K., & Pastne, J. *The child's book of the symphony.* New York: Howell, Soskin, 1941.

Greene, C. *Let's learn about the orchestra.* New York: Harvey House, 1967. Instruments, orchestra leaders, and physical layout.

Jenkins, D. *This is rhythm.* New York: Oak Publications, 1962. (For children of any age; descriptions of instruments; songs, poems, rhythms.)

Surplus, R. W. *The alphabet of music.* Minneapolis, Minn.: Learner, 1963.

Young Keyboard Jr. (1346 Chapel St., New Haven, Conn. 06511.)

Songbooks:

Commins, D. B. *The big book of favorite songs for children.* New York: Grosset and Dunlap, 1951.

Curry, W. L., et al. *Songs for early childhood.* Philadelphia: Westminster, 1958.

Eberhart, A. M. *Swinging on a tune* (C. Marshall, Ed.). Emporia, Kans.: Emporia State Press, 1975.

Landeck, B. & Crook, E. *Wake up and Sing.* New York: Morrow, 1969.

McLaughlin, R., & Wood, L. *The small singer songbook.* Los Angeles: Bowmar-Noble, 1969.

McLaughlin, R., & Wood, L. *Sing a song of people songbook.* Los Angeles: Bowmar-Noble, 1973.

MacCarteney, L. P. *Songs for the nursery school.* Florence, Ky.: Willis Music, 1938.

Palmer, H. *The Hap Palmer songbook: Learning basic skills through music.* (Vol. 1.) Baldwin, N.Y.: Educational Activities, Inc., 1971. (1937 Grand Ave., 11510.)

Richards, M. H. *Pentatonic songs for young children.* Belmont, Calif.: Fearon, 1967.

Seeger, R. C. *American folk songs for children.* New York: Doubleday, 1948.

Smith, B. *Let's sing this-a-way.* La Salle, Ill.: Open Court, 1971. (A songbook for young children. Fully illustrated with regular and picture musical notation.)

Wood, L. *Rhythms to reading songbook.* Los Angeles: Bowmar-Noble, 1972.

Materials and Sources

Materials include:

Instruments.	Record player.
Songbooks.	Headsets.
Records.	Cassette recorder.
Audiovisual equipment.	Microphones.

Three sample instrument selections:

1. Bongo drum, hand drum, triangle, pair of claves, clave tone block with striker, gourd tone block with striker, handcastas, sand blocks, bells on a handle, wrist bells, liberty bell, finger cymbals with wooden handles, and tambourine.
2. Double Mexican bongo, cowbell with striker, pair of wooden maracas, castanet on handle, pair of claves, tambourine, and guiro.
3. Bongo drum, hand rhythm drum, hand snare drum with mallet, clave tone block with mallet, gourd tone block with striker, liberty bell, wrist bells, wood maracas, jingle clogs, triangles and strikers, pair of junior cymbals with knots, castanets on a handle, handcastas, sand blocks, rhythm sticks, and tambourines.

Musical resource collections:

Choate, R. A. *Beginning music.* In *New dimensions in music* series. New York: American Book, 1970.

Choate, R. A. *Music for early childhood.* In *New dimensions in music* series. New York: American Book, 1970.

Records

Records of general interest:

American folk songs for children. Pete Seeger. Folkways 7001.
Best of Burl's for boys and girls. Burl Ives. MCA 2-4034.
Birds, Beasts, bugs, and bigger fishes. Pete Seeger. Folkways 7010-7-11.
Bowmar Orchestral Library, Series 1 and 2.
Burl Ives sings "Little White Duck" and other children's favorites. Harmony 9507.
Golden Records music appreciation records. (Titles include *Peter and the wolf, A child's introduction to the Nutcracker Suite, Sleeping beauty and Swan lake, Saturday morning children's concert, Music of the great composers,* and *Gilbert and Sullivan.*
Papa Haydn's Surprise and Toy symphonies. Disneyland.
Know the orchestra. Bowmar. (With filmstrip and study prints.)
Learning basic skills through music. Hap Palmer.
Modern times for rhythms and instruments. Hap Palmer.
Movement exploration. Educational Activities, Inc.
Movin', Hap Palmer.
Patriotic and morning time songs. Hap Palmer.
Play your instruments and make a pretty sound. Ella Jenkins. Folkways 7665.
RCA Victor Music Service Basic Record Library.
Rhythms of childhood. Ella Jenkins. Folkways 7653.
The small listener. Bowmar.
You'll sing a song, and I'll sing a song. Ella Jenkins, Folkways 7644.

Many recordings are available of the following favorite classics:

Anderson, L. *Sleigh ride.*
Anderson, L. *The syncopated clock.*
Bizet, G. *Children's games.*
Debussy, C. *Children's corner suite.*
Grainger, P. *Country garden.*
Ghys. *Amaryllis.*
Grieg, E. *Peer Gynt suite No. 1.*
Grofé, F. *Grand Canyon Suite.*
Haydn, F. J. *Symphony No. 94 in G major (Surprise).*
Haydn, F. J. *Toy symphony.*
Herbert, V. *March of the toys.*
Moussorgsky, M. *Ballet of the unhatched chicks.*
Offenbach, J. *Barcarolle from Tales of Hoffmann.*
Pierne, G. *March of the little lead soldiers.*
Poldini, E. *The dancing doll.*
Prokofiev, S. *Peter and the wolf.*
Rimsky-Korsakov, N. *The flight of the bumblebee.*
Saint-Saens, C. C. *Carnival of the animals.*
Saint-Saens, C. C. *Danse macabre.*
Tchaikovsky, P. I. *Nutcracker suite.*
Waldteufel, E. *The skater's waltz.*

Some action songs are included in these albums:

On top of spaghetti. Tom Glazer. Wonderland 267.
Songs to grow on. Woody Guthrie. Folkways.

Albums containing folk songs:

Ella Jenkins song book.
On top of spaghetti. Tom Glazer. Wonderland 267.
Peter, Paul and Mommy. Peter, Paul, and Mary. Warner Bros. S-1785.
Songs to grow on. Woody Guthrie, Folkways.
We all live together, Vol. II. Greg Seelsa and Steve Millang.

Music to relax to:

Nocturne. Leonard Bernstein, conductor. Columbia M-30573. (Orchestral collection.)
Pachelbel, J. *Canon in D.* (Various recordings.)
Spectrum suite. Steve Halpern.

Good song sources:

American folk songs for children. Pete Seeger, Folkways 7001.
Best of Burl's for boys and girls. Burl Ives. MCA 2-4034.
Early early childhood songs. Ella Jenkins, Folkways 7530.
Ella Jenkins song book.

Creative movement:

Creative movement and rhythmic expression. Hap Palmer.
Dance a folk song. Ann Barlin and Paul Barlin.
Movin'. Hap Palmer.

Dance:

We all live together, Vols. I to III. Greg Seelsa and Steve Millang.

Physical skills:

Clap, snap and tap. A. Brazelton and G. De Santis.
Getting to know myself. Hap Palmer.
Learning basic skills through music, Vol II. Hap Palmer.

Music of feeling:

Free to be you and me. Marlo Thomas. Arista 4003.
The homesick snail. Rick Master.
Imagination and me. Joe Wayman and Don Mitchell.

Songs and music for teaching other subjects:

Big Bird sings. Sesame Street S22068.
Health and safety. Hap Palmer.
Learning basic skills through music, Vol, I. Hap Palmer.
Math readiness. Hap Palmer.
Witches' brew. Hap Palmer.

Sources and Suppliers

For instruments:

ABC School Supply, Inc., P.O. Box 13085, Atlanta, Fa. 30324.
Childcraft Education Corp., 20 Kilmer Rd., Edison, N.J. 08817.
Children's Book and Music Center, 2500 Santa Monica Blvd., Santa Monica, Calif. 90404.
Eduquip-McAllister Corp., 1085 Commonwealth Ave., Brighton, Mass. 02215.
Hammatt and Sons, 1441 N. Red Gum, Bldg. E., Anaheim, Calif. 92806.
Hohner, M., Inc., Education Div., Andrews Rd., Hicksville, N.Y. 11802.
Kaplan School Supply Corp., 600 Jonestown Rd., Winston-Salem, N.C. 27103.
Lyons, Inc., 223 W. Lake St., Chicago, Ill. 60606.
Northern Supply Co., P.O. Box 920, Bangor, Maine 04401.
Peripole, Browns Mills, N.J. 08015.
Rhythm Band, Inc., P.O. Box 126, Fort Worth, Tex. 76101.

For records:

AA Records, 250 W. 57th St., New York, N.Y. 10019.
Capitol Records, Inc., 1370 Avenue of the Americas, New York, N.Y. 10019.
Columbia Records, Inc., 545 Madison Ave., New York, N.Y. 10022.
Disneyland Records, 800 Sonora Ave., Glendale, Calif. 91201.
Educational Activities, Inc., Freeport, N.Y. 11520.
Educational Recordings of America, P.O. Box 231, Monroe, Conn. 06468.
Folkways Records, 43 W. 61st St., New York, N.Y. 10023.
Folkways Scholastic Records, 50 W. 44th St., New York, N.Y. 10036.
Golden Records Educational Div., Michael Brent Publications Inc., Port Chester, N.Y. 10573.
Honor Your Partner Records, P.O. Box 392, Freeport, N.Y. 11520.
Kimbo Educational, P.O. Box 477, 86 S. 5th Ave., Long Branch, N.J. 07740.
A. B. Le Crone Co., 819 NW 92d St., Oklahoma City, Okla. 73114.
Lyons Band, 520 Riverview Ave., Elkhart, Ind. 46514.
MCA Records, 100 Universal City Plaza, Universal City, Calif. 91608.
Mercury Record Corp., 35 E. Wacker Dr., Chicago, Ill. 60601.

RCA Records, Educational Sales, P.O. Box RCA 1000, Indianapolis, Ind. 46291.
Scott, Foresman and Co., 1900 E. Lake Ave., Glenview, Ill. 60025.
Sing 'n' Do Records, Kimbo Educational, P.O. Box 55, Deal, N.J. 07723.
Vox Productions, Inc., 211 E. 43d St., New York, N.Y. 10017.
Youngheart Music Education Service, Box 27784, Los Angeles, Calif. 90027.

For general music materials:

Bowmar Publishing Corp., P.O. Box 3623, 622 Rodier Dr., Glendale, Calif. 91201.
Classroom Materials, 93 Myrtle Dr., Great Neck, N.Y. 10022.
Columbia Records, Inc., 545 Madison Ave., New York, N.Y. 10022.
Disneyland Records, 119 Fifth Ave., New York, N.Y. 10003.
Educational Activities, Inc., Freeport, N.Y. 11520.
Educational Record Sales, 157 Chambers St., New York, N.Y. 10007.
Folkways Scholastic Records, 701 Seventh Ave., New York, N.Y. 10036.
Greystone Corp., Institutional Trade Div., 100 Sixth Ave., New York, N.Y. 10003.
Hargail Music Press, 157 W. 57th St., New York, N.Y. 10019.
Jim Handy Organization, 2821 E. Grand Blvd., Detroit, Mich. 48211.
MCA Inc., 445 Park Ave., New York, N.Y. 10022.
Mercury Record Corp., 35 E. Wacker Dr., Chicago, Ill. 60601.
Pepper, J. W., and Son, 231 N. Third St., Philadelphia, Pa. 19106.
Schwann, W., 137 Newbury St., Boston, Mass., 02116.
Sing 'n' Do Co., Inc., P.O. Box 279, Ridgewood, N.Y. 11227.
Sound Book Press Society, Inc., 36 Garth Rd., Scarsdale, N.Y. 10583.

Enrichment Materials

Categories of materials:

Songbooks and music instruction books.
Books about sound and sounds.
Films on music and movement.
Poster and prints (composers, performers, instruments).
Television presentations.
Actual concerts.
Homemade instruments.
Ethnic instruments.
Kits, programs, and curricula.

Songbooks and other music books:

Hoenack, P. *Let's sing and play book.* (Child's music for use with recorders and small wind instruments.)
Langstaff, N., & Langstaff, J. *Jim along Josie.* New York: Harcourt Brace Jovanovich, 1970. (Singing, dancing, and acting-out games.)
Ludwig & Ludwig. *Colors and chords for the autoharp.* (For very young children.)
Songs I can play. (Songs to play on xylophone or bells.)
We all live together. Vol. I. Younghart Music. (Record and book. Sing-alongs, call-and-response and resting music, and rhythm and movement activity.)
Kaufman, L. *What's that noise?* New York: Lothrop, 1965.
Showers, P. *The listening walk.* New York: Crowell, 1961.

On creating instruments:

Hawkinson, J., & Faulhaber, M. *Music and instruments for children to make.* Chicago: Al Whitman, 1969. (560 W. Lake St. Simple, to be made at home or at school.)

Some homemade instruments:

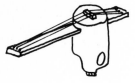

Bathtub tuba. (Use a rubber shower-spray hose by itself. Those who are talented at playing brass instruments can make music with almost any rubber hose.)

Bleach bottle banjo. (Make two slots in a plastic bleach bottle that will enable a wooden board to be pushed through the bottle parallel to and near the bottom. The bottom of the bottle will serve as the top of the instrument, and the board will serve as the fingerboard and tail. Stretch strings from one end of the board to the other, using a block of wood glued to the bottom of the bottle as a bridge.)

Flowerpot bells. (Suspend several flowerpots of different sizes upside down from a wooden board.)

Kits, programs, and series:

Crook, E., et al. *Silver Burdett music.* Morristown, N.J.: Silver Burdett, 1974.

Gillett, D. K. *Comprehensive musicianship program.* Menlo Park, Calif.: Addison-Wesley. 1974. (Moving, singing playing basic instruments, listening, improvising, experimenting. Uses an ensemble approach. Grakes K and 1.)

Smith, B., & Harter, T. C. *Teacher's guide to the Open Court kindergarten music program.* LaSalle, Ill.: Open Court, 1970. (Set comes with teaching records. Wonderfully illustrated traditional songs.)

Sur, W. R., et al. *This is music.* Rockleigh, N.J.: Allyn and Bacon, 1967. (07647. Books, accompaniment, and recordings, Grades K through 8.)

And these kits from Bowmar-Noble:

Bowmar listening center. (Listening, reading and movements. Interpreting the meaning of poetry and music.)

Johnny Mann presents: Nursery rhymes. (Narration and singing of old favorites.)

Primary rhythms. (Basic and interpretive movement.)

Primary songs. (Musical literature for children.)

Rhythms to reading. (Listening, singing; reading readiness and musical sensitivity.)

Small musician series. (Singing, dancing, and listening to develop musical background.)

Community Resources

Music store.
Local symphony orchestra.
Local chamber group.
Bands.
Orchestras.
Recitals.
College and high school programs.
Special musical programs (Orff, Yamaha).
Instrumental class or rehearsal.
Singers.
Music studio.
Recording studio.
Television station.
Children's concerts.
Concerts.
Library.
Museum.

Section 6

MULTICULTURAL APPROACHES TO THE CURRICULUM

In this section we provide concepts, activities, and resources specifically geared to a multicultural approach to teaching and learning. We give this material as a separate section for several reasons: to stress its importance; to encourage teachers and caretakers to think specifically about multicultural approaches; to make it easy for our readers to find, and refer to, the multi- cultural material.

But—and this is a very important "but"—we don't want to suggest, by providing this separate section, that what we might call "multiculturalism" is somehow a separate part of the curriculum. It is not. Multicultural ideas should permeate the curriculum, at all levels and in all areas. Don't set aside a special time or place for "doing something multicultural." Instead, you and your children should try to make multicultural approaches an integral part of everything you do.

Concepts and Activities

Introduction: Concepts for Children

As we think about multicultural approaches to the curriculum, we want to be very sure what it is we are trying to do. It's easy—and true—to say that we want children to recognize and appreciate cultural diversity, to enjoy it and understand how it enriches human life. But when we examine this more closely—when we consider what specific ideas we want children to form—then some questions arise.

Too often, multicultural approaches, however well-intentioned they may be, take the form of symbols that are little more than clichés, or even stereotypes. When we are working with young children, we tend to present ethnic and national diversity in terms of shamrocks and edelweiss; sombreros, beaded moccasins, wooden shoes; Chinese kites, piñatas; African drums, Indian dances, castanets—the easily recognizable symbols. These symbols, in addition to being easily recognizable by children, are lovable and appealing and lend themselves readily to use in children's activities— art, music, games, and so on. Moreover, all of them have some foundation in fact. But it cannot be denied that they are all, to some degree, hackneyed, and that they tend to give children a simplistic idea of what other cultures are like.

We need to ask ourselves how we can present cultural diversity to children without subjecting them to a barrage of clichés. How do we draw the line between respecting diverse heritages and simply perpetuating stereotypes? We can't give a definitive answer to this question; we can only suggest that each teacher give it thoughtful consideration. In the last analysis, it's probably a question that must be continually asked and asked again, and answered only tentatively.

Below, we suggest some concepts for children that we consider appropriate for a multicultural approach, grouped under seven broad areas:

1. Psycho-physical-motor.
2. Science.
3. Mathematics.
4. Language arts.
5. Social studies.
6. Art.
7. Music.

In a sense, these concepts represent our tentative answer to the question we've just posed. We have tried to make them as general as possible and to stress that there are similarities as well as differences among cultures. These concepts are not meant to be exhaustive—in fact, we list only three in each of the major areas. Teachers and caretakers will certainly want to add concepts of their own—the concepts we list are only examples of the kinds of basic ideas we believe children need to attain.

Following the list of concepts are some sample activities. For these activities, the format is somewhat different from that in the preceding sections. First, you'll notice that we have no "table of objectives." Instead, each of the activities is aimed at one of the concepts in our list. Second, for these activities the "curriculum area" is broader than usual—we have simply grouped the activities in the seven major areas noted in the list of concepts, so that "curriculum area" is in each case one of these areas. Third, we have not indicated different age ranges. These concepts can be introduced in simple ways very early on, and they continue to be appropriate almost indefinitely.

Remember that these activities are only examples; they are meant to give you an idea of what the multicultural approach is like. You will want to make up activities of your own, and to adapt some of the activities presented in earlier sections so that they will reflect multicultural ideas. This is an area in which your own imagination and the needs of your own children are especially important.

Multicultural Concepts for Children

IN THE PSYCHO-PHYSICAL-MOTOR DOMAIN:

1. Dances and games of each culture have unique characteristics, but there are also similarities from culture to culture.
2. People from different cultures have different ways of meeting the needs of mental and physical health.
3. There are similarities and differences in the way different cultures meet basic nutritional needs.

IN SCIENCE:

1. Different cultures approach science in different ways and emphasize different aspects of it.
2. Scientific discoveries can be, and are, made by people from many different cultures.
3. In a cultural context, science is a constant: its principles do not differ from culture to culture.

IN MATHEMATICS:

1. Different cultures approach mathematics in different ways and emphasize different aspects of it.
2. Most cultures have their own systems for dealing with time, money, quantity, measurement, and other mathematical concepts.
3. In a cultural context, mathematics is a constant: its principles do not differ from culture to culture.

IN LANGUAGE ARTS:

1. Different cultures have different vocabularies; many have different languages; and some have different alphabets.
2. Many words we use are derived or adapted from other cultures.
3. The folk tales of different cultures have many thematic similarities.

IN SOCIAL STUDIES:

1. Each of the disciplines that make up the social studies lends itself to cross-cultural comparison.
2. Each culture has its own celebrations and symbols; and many cultures have their own traditional dress.
3. Each culture has its own history and its own heroes and heroines.

Multicultural Concepts for Children (continued)

IN ART:

1. Each culture has its own artists and art forms.
2. Often, the art of a culture depends on the natural materials available.
3. Often, the art of a culture is related to ceremonial events.

IN MUSIC:

1. Each culture has characteristic melodies, modes, rhythms, harmonies, and so on.
2. Each culture has its own music, songs, instruments, composers, and performers.
3. Often, the music of a culture is related to ceremonial events.

Multicultural Activities for Psycho-Physical-Motor Development

Description   Learning and playing children's games from around the world.
Title (for children)   "Worldwide Olympics."
Curriculum area   Psycho-physical-motor (multicultural).

What concept are we aiming at?   "Dances and games of each culture have unique characteristics, but there are also similarities from culture to culture."

What will we need?   Some research materials for finding out about games in different nations and cultures; equipment for the games selected, or materials for making it; a good-sized area for the "Olympics"; small flags of many nations (packets of these are available in most teachers' supply stores).

How will we do it?

1. Teacher and children discuss various games from different cultures. With younger children, the teacher may simply demonstrate several games (over a period of time) and have the children learn them. Older children can divide into groups to do some research on their own, learn the games they discover, and demonstrate them to the class.

2. Here are a few examples:
   a. Japanese tag—This is like our tag, but the player who is tagged must hold the spot where he or she was tagged.
   b. Chinese jacks—The jacks are 4-inch-square pieces of cloth, filled with raw rice and tied closed with yarn.
   c. Israeli "klass"—This is like hopscotch, but the marker is pushed with a toe while the player hops. Hebrew letters can be used on the course.
   d. Mexican "bola"—This is a 1-foot stick or dowel with a paper cup tacked to one end and a 15-inch string with a ball attached tied to the top. Object: make the ball land in the cup.

3. When a number of games have been learned, have an international Olympics. Divide the class into "national teams" and play all the games. Give flags to the winners.

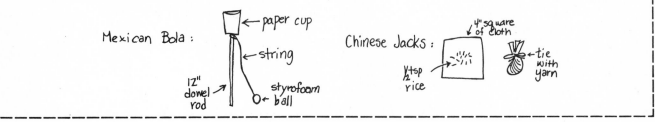

Description Making Greek "worry beads."
Title (for children) "What—Me Worry?"
Curriculum area Psycho-physical-motor (multicultural).

What concept are we aiming at? "People from different cultures have different ways of meeting the needs of mental and physical health."

What will we need? 2- by 4-inch squares of cardboard (one for each child); wooden beads (one for each child); short macaroni (tubettini); yarn; scissors; tape.

How will we do it?

1. Teacher and children talk about how "worry beads" are used and may examine a set.
2. To make the worry beads, do the following:
   a. Each child winds a long piece of yarn around the square of cardboard ten to twelve times.
   b. The top of this skein is tied off with another piece of yarn, about 6 inches long, and taped.
   c. The ends of the 6-inch yarn are threaded in opposite directions through the large wooden bead, which is pulled tight to the cardboard.
   d. The macaroni is threaded on both sides of the 6-inch yarn, leaving enough yarn free to tie the ends in a secure knot.
   e. Now the original skein of yarn is snipped open along the bottom of the cardboard (discard the cardboard). This makes a fringe.
3. The children use their worry beads and discuss their reactions.

What else can we do? Another activity: The children can learn some simple Indian Yoga positions and try them. How well do they relieve stress?

colored macaroni →
bead →
yarn →

Greek Worry Beads

Description Making stir-fried vegetables in a wok.
Title (for children) "Wok's Up?"
Curriculum area Psycho-physical-motor (multicultural).

What concept are we aiming at? "There are similarities and differences in the way different cultures meet basic nutritional needs."

What will we need? Gas range; wok; stirrer; vegetables (it is nice to use Chinese vegetables if any are available—e.g., snow peas, bean sprouts—but western vegetables will also do—e.g., celery, leeks, green peppers, broccoli); oil and seasonings (soy sauce, if possible); paper plates or bowls; napkins; chopsticks.

How will we do it?

1. Teacher and children discuss the Chinese method of cooking vegetables: "stir frying." (The teacher can refer to a cookbook if necessary.) How does it differ from the standard western method (boiling)?
2. The children, with the teacher's supervision, make some stir-fried vegetables (it's nice to have an aide or volunteer to help with this), as follows:
   a. Wash and trim the vegetables and then slice or chop them (bean sprouts and snow peas do not get chopped or sliced, however).
   b. Heat some oil in the wok.
   c. When the oil is hot, add one kind of vegetable at a time; stir it with a stirrer or long chopstick; put on the lid of the wok. The vegetables cook quickly. Remove at once from the wok, and keep warm.
   d. Continue making the vegetables, batch by batch.
3. When all the vegetables are done, the children sample them, eating them with chopsticks. (The teacher may want to demonstrate the use of chopsticks.)
4. The children share their reactions. How are the results different from American-style vegetables?

What else can we do? Other activities: The children can make some other simple dishes—e.g., blackeyed peas (American black), latkes (potato pancakes; Eastern Europe and Israel), baklava (Greece).

Multicultural Activities for Science

Description Charting the different aspects of science emphasized by cultures with different climates and topography.
Title (for children) "Elementary, My Dear Watson."
Curriculum area Science (multicultural).

What concept are we aiming at? "Different cultures approach science in different ways and emphasize different aspects of it."
What will we need? Maps and other research materials, especially books and articles emphasizing geography—climate, topography, location. For making the chart: poster paper and marking pens.
How will we do it?
1. Teacher and children select three or four areas that differ markedly geographically—different parts of the world, different climates, different topography.
2. After examining the geographical elements of each place and discussing them, the children try to surmise what people in each place would have had to do to survive, and what aspects of science they would have concentrated on.
3. The children keep notes, or a list, of their predictions (for children who are not yet writing, the teacher can do this) and then check them against reality—older children can use reference materials themselves; for younger children, the teacher might read excerpts or show pictures. For instance, if the children surmised that American Indians would emphasize ecology, the Japanese would emphasize oceanography, and the Arabs would emphasize desert botany and zoology, they'd be right.
4. The children make a chart (young children help the teacher make it) showing each culture, its important geographical elements, and the results for science. The chart can be illustrated with pictures or simple drawings.
What else can we do? **Follow-up:** Continue the activity with other areas of the world.

Description   Learning about scientists from different cultures, and reporting on their discoveries.
Title (for children)   "Science Stars."
Curriculum area   Science (multicultural).

What concept are we aiming at?   "Scientific discoveries can be, and are, made by people from many different cultures."
What will we need?   This is an activity for children who read; the teacher should make available reading materials at the appropriate level on scientists and their contributions. In addition: construction paper, pictures of many scientists, paste, and a bulletin board.
How will we do it?
1. Teacher and children discuss scientists around the world (past and present) and mount pictures of as many as possible on construction-paper stars. Each picture is labeled (ALBERT EINSTEIN, MARIE CURIE, ISAAC NEWTON, GALILEO, etc.), and the "stars" are displayed on a bulletin board.
2. Each child chooses one "star" to learn about and over a period of time (say, a week or two) gathers information about him or her.
3. The children prepare simple reports on "their" scientists and present them to the class.
4. The display of "stars" can be expanded to include the reports, or excerpts from them.

What else can we do?   **Variation:** This can be a group project instead of an individual project—each group chooses a "star."   **Another activity:** The children can do research on, and make a chart showing, contributions to science from different cultures (e.g., paper from China—an interesting chart might show how the Chinese made paper and how it is made today).

Description   Discovering scientific methods of problem solving.
Title (for children)   "How Did You Know?"
Curriculum area   Science (multicultural).

What concept are we aiming at?   "In a cultural context, science is a constant: its principles do not differ from culture to culture."
What will we need?   A number of "problems" made up by the teacher; depending on what the problems are, various materials may be needed to solve them.
How will we do it?
1. The teacher divides the class into groups and tells the children that each group will be given a series of problems to solve in a set time. No other explanation is given.
2. The problems are given one at a time, and the time allotted to solve them should depend on their difficulty—which in turn depends, of course, on the children's age and sophistication. (E.g., "Go out to the playground and find out which direction the wind is coming from. You have 5 minutes.")
3. Each group reports its findings to the teacher in two parts:
   a. What's the answer?
   b. How did you find it? (How do you know?)
4. When all the problems have been solved, the class reconvenes. The teacher lists the answers and the methods for each problem, and the class and teacher discuss them.
5. What similarities emerge? What does this tell us about "scientific method"? The teacher should try to guide the children's discussion so that the steps of scientific problem solving emerge and it becomes apparent that these would be the same all over the world.

What else can we do?   **Another activity:** Children who read can study (individually or in groups) the steps that led to several discoveries—how are they similar?

Multicultural Activities for Mathematics

Description Using various methods of counting.
Title (for children) "Does This Count?"
Curriculum area Mathematics (multicultural).

What concept are we aiming at? "Different cultures approach mathematics in different ways and emphasize different aspects of it."
What will we need? Pictures of typical scenes in various cultures (e.g., fishing village, flock of goats, items in a store); cup of beans for each child.
How will we do it?
1. Teacher and children talk about what kinds of things people have to count—the teacher can show pictures to give some ideas, and the children can contribute ideas of their own (miles between cities, times at bat, possessions, etc.).
2. The teacher narrows the discussion by asking what the children think people in different cultures might want to count (again, pictures can get things started)—e.g., people who depend on the ocean for their living, people in the desert, people in the jungle.
3. Next, teacher and children discuss different ways of counting in different cultures—e.g., on the fingers, on joints of fingers, by making marks on the ground, by using objects (e.g., 1 stick for each sheep), by using an abacus. If the children are sophisticated enough, the concept of larger units can be added (1 *long* stick for each 10 sheep).
4. Each child gets a cup of beans to count using various methods.

What else can we do? **Follow-up:** Children can check these methods of counting against a hand calculator, counting objects in the room; a chart can be made of THINGS TO BE COUNTED and WAYS OF COUNTING THEM (showing methods of various cultures).

Description Comparing systems of measurement.
Title (for children) "Take Me to Your Liter."
Curriculum area Mathematics (multicultural).

What concept are we aiming at? "Most cultures have their own systems for dealing with time, money, quantity, measurement, and other mathematical concepts."

What will we need? Containers and measuring instruments marked with both United States and metric units (e.g., a thermometer with degrees Celsius on one side and degrees Fahrenheit on the other; a ruler with both centimeters and inches; a container marked in both liters and quarts); objects to measure; chartboard and felt pens.

How will we do it?

1. Teacher and children talk about the changeover in the United States from our present system to the metric system used in other parts of the world.
2. Children use the dual measuring instruments to measure various things in the classroom (e.g., dimensions of the room, volume of dry and liquid ingredients, indoor and outdoor temperature).
3. Metric equivalents for United States units of measure are written on the board.
4. The children make a three-column chart. In the first column is a picture symbolizing what is being measured, in the second its measurement in United States units, in the third its measurement in metric units.

What else can we do? Other activities: Have parents and friends contribute foreign money so that the children can set up an international exchange; have the children discuss different cultures' calendars and draw some samples (e.g., Aztec, Hebrew, Chinese).

Description Counting in different languages.
Title (for children) "Only the Names Have Been Changed."
Curriculum area Mathematics (multicultural).

What concept are we aiming at? "In a cultural context, mathematics is a constant: its principles do not differ from culture to culture."

What will we need? The teacher will need some foreign-language phrasebooks to find the names (and pronunciations) of numbers in various languages—these can be written on a chart by the teacher or the class. The children will need objects to count.

How will we do it?

1. Teacher and children talk about the names for numbers in different languages. If the teacher has not prepared a chart, the children do so.
2. The chart is posted, and the children use it to count in the various languages, thus:
   a. The children take turns counting objects aloud in English (e.g., pencils, chips, beans).
   b. The teacher counts the same items in another language.
   c. Using the chart as a guide, the children identify the language and the country; then they repeat the numbers in that language.
3. When the children are familiar with the chart, they can use it in various ways. For instance: they can do follow-the-dots number pictures with foreign number words instead of numerals; and they can try counting independently in various languages and comparing the results with counting on the fingers, on a calculator, or on an abacus to learn that the results remain the same.

What else can we do? Follow-up: It's interesting to expand the chart by adding as many languages as possible—in addition to the usual German, French, Spanish, and Italian, have Vietnamese, Laotian, Hebrew, etc.

Description   Labeling objects in the classroom in foreign languages.
Title (for children)   "Lingo."
Curriculum area   Language arts (multicultural).

What concept are we aiming at?   "Different cultures have different vocabularies; many have different languages; and some have different alphabets."
What will we need?   Foreign-language phrasebooks or dictionaries; index cards; tape; marking pens.
How will we do it?

1. Children and teacher discuss some foreign languages—they may focus on (but need not confine themselves to) languages spoken by the families or ancestors of the children.

2. Using the dictionaries and phrasebooks, the children find the foreign-language equivalents for as many objects in the classroom as they can, make labels for these things in the foreign languages, and tape them in place. (Don't forget that in many other languages, the article is needed as well as the noun; e.g., PEN = LA PLUME.) Each label should identify the language: e.g., LA PLUME (FRENCH).

3. After the labels have been in place for a while, another set can be made and used as flash cards—can the children read the cards and give the English translation without looking around the room at the labeled objects?

What else can we do?   Variation: This labeling can be a team project or game—each team gets a language and reference materials for it, and labels as many objects as possible in that language; which team labeled the most objects?

Another activity: The children can make bilingual or multilingual picture dictionaires.

Description Making a class dictionary of words in English which are derived from other languages.
Title (for children) "Derivation Dictionary."
Curriculum area Language arts (multicultural).

What concept are we aiming at? "Many words we use are derived or adapted from other cultures."
What will we need? Dictionaries; a looseleaf book and blank pages for it.
How will we do it?
1. The teacher explains how to find derivations of words in the dictionary.
2. To practice finding derivations, the children look up several words the teacher lists.
3. When the children have the hang of this, they work independently to find derivations of words of their own choice. Each child keeps a list of words and derivations.
4. The lists are pooled and duplications are omitted.
5. The remaining list entries are put in alphabetical order, and the children take turns copying entries into the class dictionary (the looseleaf book).
6. The dictionary becomes part of the class library—and words can always be added to it.

What else can we do? **Another activity:** It's interesting for the children to look up derivations of their own given names—for this, they'll need a dictionary that includes names. A similar activity is to make a chart showing forms of the children's names in several languages (JOHN—JEAN—JUAN—JOHANNES; PETER—PIERRE—PEDRO—PIETRO; MARY—MARIA—MARIE; etc.).

Description Collecting folk tales from different cultures and noting thematic similarities.
Title (for children) "Once Upon a Time . . ."
Curriculum area Language arts (multicultural).

What concept are we aiming at? "The folk tales of different cultures have many thematic similarities."
What will we need? A good assortment of folk tales from various cultures; writing paper, posterboard, pencils, crayons, marking pens.
How will we do it?
1. Each day, a story from the collection is chosen and the teacher reads it to the children. (It's a good idea to set aside a special time for this—always after lunch, for instance.) The children can take notes as it is read.
2. Children and teacher discuss elements of the plot, types of characters, and theme. These are summarized on a chart, which also indicates the name of the tale and its culture or country of origin.
3. As more stories are read and discussed and the chart grows, the children can compare elements of the tales and point out similarities.
4. It's possible then to make up a new chart, on which similar stories are grouped together—for example, themes might be used as headings ("COOPERATION," "HOW IT STARTED," "THREE WISHES," etc.) and stories and cultures listed as appropriate under them.
5. The stories can be typed up and duplicated, and each child can get a set to "bind" in posterboard covers and take home. Older children can group the stories according to the themes they identified and may even make a table of contents listing the themes.

What else can we do? **Another activity:** Proverbs from different cultures can be collected and analyzed similarly.

Multicultural Activities for Social Studies

Description   A game involving identification of similarities and differences among cultures.
Title (for children)   "Same or Different?"
Curriculum area   Social studies (multicultural).

What concept are we aiming at?   "Each of the disciplines that make up the social studies lends itself to cross-cultural comparison."
What will we need?   The teacher should prepare a list of statements about various cultures which the children have studied—quite simple for younger children; more sophisticated for older children. Poster paper and marking pens can be used to make a sign for each team; and the statements can also be written on posters. The score can be kept on the chalkboard.
How will we do it?
1.   The class is divided into two groups. Group 1 gets a sign reading "SAME"; group 2's sign reads " DIFFERENT."
2.   The teacher reads a list of statements about cultures the class has studied (each statement can be displayed as it is read). Examples:
    a.   In Laos, houses are made of wood.
    b.   In Korea, rice is served at most meals.
    c.   In Israel, people read from right to left.
    d.   In Mexico, people speak Spanish.
    e.   In Iran, there is a lot of oil.
3.   After reading each statement, the teacher calls on one child in the SAME group to name a culture where the situation is similar, and then calls on one child in the DIFFERENT group to name a culture where the situation is different.
4.   Each team gets one point for each correct answer.
What else can we do?   **Another activity:** It's interesting to compare how holidays are celebrated in different cultures—e.g., the new year.

258

Description Making and clothing paper dolls, using traditional costumes.
Title (for children) "Oh, You Beautiful Doll."
Curriculum area Social studies (multicultural).

What concept are we aiming at? "Each culture has its own celebrations and symbols; and many cultures have their own traditional dress."
What will we need? Good pictures of several traditional costumes—e.g., sombrero, serape, huaraches, and charro suit (Mexican); kimono, obi sash, zori sandals, tabis (Japanese). These should be large and show as much detail as possible. The children will need patterns for cutting out paper dolls (each child gets one), scissors and paste, marking pens, and plenty of materials for making costumes—construction paper, scraps of fabric, feathers, scraps of leather, and so on. Optional: folders.
How will we do it?
1. Teacher and children examine the pictures of costumes and discuss them.
2. Each child gets scissors and paste and a pattern for cutting out paper dolls. The materials for making costumes are laid out where all the children can choose from them.
3. Each child chooses one or more of the costumes to use as a guide and dresses a paper doll, or dolls, appropriately.
4. The dolls can be displayed, with brief descriptions written or dictated by the children. (Alternatively, each child can make up a folder to keep, containing the doll or dolls and the description.)
What else can we do? **Another activity:** Each child chooses a culture and fills in a one-year calendar showing its feasts (or fasts), holidays, and celebrations, along with brief descriptions.

Description A class research and writing project on heroes and heroines in different cultures.
Title (for children) "World Book of Heroes and Heroines."
Curriculum area Social studies (multicultural).

What concept are we aiming at? "Each culture has its own history and its own heroes and heroines."
What will we need? Pictures of heroes and heroines of different cultures (e.g., Martin Luther King, Sun Yat Sen, Pancho Villa); research materials; writing paper and pens or pencils; construction paper or poster paper for the front and back cover of the book, and a stapler (alternatively, a looseleaf binder or spring binder can be used).
How will we do it?
1. To begin, a bulletin board is divided into sections, one for each of several cultures (the class decides beforehand which cultures will be studied), and pictures of heroes and heroines are mounted under the appropriate culture and labeled. These people can be historical or contemporary, or both.
2. Each child chooses one hero or heroine to study.
3. Working individually, the children do research in simple encyclopedias, biographies, articles, and so on.
4. Each child prepares a short report on his or her subject and shares it with the class.
5. All the reports are "bound" in construction-paper covers or a looseleaf book or spring binder. This is called the "World Book or Heroes and Heroines"—it becomes part of the class library.
What else can we do? **Other activities:** Class "World Books" can also be made for famous athletes, scientists, and so on.

Multicultural Activities for Art

Description   A class project—a multicultural art show.
Title (for children)   "Global Gallery."
Curriculum area   Art (multicultural).

What concept are we aiming at?   "Each culture has its own artists and art forms."
What will we need?   This is a rather long-term project. Class and teacher will need pictures of, and books about, various forms of arts and crafts (e.g., Japanese daruma dolls, origami, fans; Chinese scrolls, paper cuts; African wood-carving; American Indian basketry and rugs; Mexican pottery, yarn painting, and bark painting; Indian batik) and as many concrete examples as possible. They will also want to consult experts if possible—e.g., people in the community who make or deal in such things; museum employees or private collectors. The children will, finally, need various materials for making their own versions of some of these art forms; an area for display; and materials for making the display—easels, tables, bulletin boards, poster paper, marking pens, etc.

How will we do it?
1. Over a considerable period of time, children and teacher study and discuss art forms in several different cultures. They may hear talks by experts, visit museums or shops, etc.
2. As each culture is studied, the children make their own versions of some of its characteristic or traditional art forms.
3. The children may also collect actual examples (illustrations or objects) of the art forms they are studying—e.g., parents may contribute them.
4. The children's art and the collected art are then displayed in a special area, with labels and brief descriptions written by the children (very young children can dictate these).

What else can we do?   Follow-up: Other classes and parents can be invited to visit the art show.

Description   Using natural materials to create art forms.
Title (for children)   "It's Only Natural."
Curriculum area   Art (multicultural).

What concept are we aiming at?   "Often, the art of a culture depends on the natural materials available."
What will we need?   (This depends on the cultures being studied.) "Natural" art and crafts materials—e.g., shells, straw, clay, bark, berries—and if possible some experts from the community; books (illustrated) on the arts and crafts being studied; the necessary tools; concrete examples of the arts and crafts.
How will we do it?
1. The teacher shows and explains some examples of arts and crafts made by various cultures from natural indigenous materials—e.g., sand paintings, reed or straw baskets, batik colored with berry dyes, bark paintings, wool weavings, clay pottery.
2. The children decide on, say, two or three forms they would like to work in; or the class can be divided into groups, each of which will work on a different form.
3. With the help of illustrated books, experts (if possible), and the teacher, the children recreate some of these natural art forms. As they work, they learn about the culture which produced the form using readily available materials. How do these arts and crafts reflect the natural resources of the cultures that produced them?
What else can we do?   **Follow-up:** The children's artwork—or pictures of it—can be displayed along with examples of the materials from which it is made and labels or brief descriptions identifying the cultures which originally produced it.

Description   Recreating ceremonial masks from various cultures.
Title (for children)   "Who Was That Masked Man?"
Curriculum area   Art (multicultural).

What concept are we aiming at?   "Often, the art of a culture is related to ceremonial events."
What will we need?   Pictures and (if possible) examples of ceremonial masks, and some research materials telling how they were or are used; papier-maché, paint, brushes, balloons.
How will we do it?
1. Teacher and children examine examples of ceremonial masks used in various cultures and discuss how they are used—e.g., African, Mexican, Japanese, Greek, Chinese, Native American.
2. Using pictures of these masks as guides, the children recreate their own versions (they should try for accuracy), as follows:
    a. Wet papier-maché is spread over part of the surface of an inflated balloon.
    b. The papier-maché is molded to form brow ridges, nose, ears, lips, etc.; and holes are made in it for eyes and mouth.
    c. The papier-maché is allowed to dry, and then the balloon is punctured and removed.
    d. The masks are painted or decorated as appropriate.
3. The masks are displayed around the room, with labels to identify the cultures.
What else can we do?   **Variations:** Mexican tin masks can be recreated with aluminum foil; Chinese theater masks can be recreated with colored construction paper.   **Follow-up:** The children can enact some of the ceremonies in which their masks figure (simplified versions may be appropriate, of course).

Description   Matching music and instruments with names of cultures.
Title (for children)   "Name That Culture."
Curriculum area   Music (multicultural).

What concept are we aiming at?   "Each culture has characteristic melodies, modes, rhythms, harmonies, and so on; and its own music, songs, and instruments."

What will we need?   Tapes or recordings of music from various cultures (vocal and instrumental); assorted pictures of musical instruments from different cultures, or the instruments themselves; a set of "culture cards" for each child (these are index cards labeled by the teacher or the children with the names of each culture under study and illustrated by the children.)

How will we do it?

1. Over a period of time, teacher and children hear and discuss examples of music from various cultures (records or tapes). As they study each example, they examine an illustration of the instrument or instruments they are hearing (or the instruments themselves, if possible) or pictures of singers. (This study can be made more elaborate by having visits from singers or instrumentalists.)

2. As each culture is studied, each child gets a "culture card" for it (labeled "INDIA" or "MEXICO" or whatever). The children illustrate their own cards with a sketch of an instrument, or a costumed singer, or whatever will aid memory.

3. When the children have heard and studied musical examples from, say, ten cultures or so (a smaller number for younger children; more for older or musically sophisticated children) and have made "culture cards" for all the cultures, they play a game: The teacher plays a selection or holds up an instrument, and the children hold up the card labeled with the appropriate culture.

What else can we do?   Other activities: The children can learn songs from different cultures and make a simple version of musical instruments from various cultures.

Description Hearing and assessing musical performers from different cultures.
Title (for children) "International Auditions."
Curriculum area Music (multicultural).

What concept are we aiming at? "Each culture has its own music, songs, instruments, composers, and performers."
What will we need? Records or tapes of music performed by vocalists and instrumentalists from various cultures, primarily soloists or small groups; some posters or fliers advertising musical events, and materials for the children to make their own posters and fliers.
How will we do it?
1. Over a period of time, children and teacher listen to musical selections by soloists and small groups from many cultures. As they hear each piece, the performer and culture are identified ("PABLO CASALS—SPAIN," for example). The performers need not still be alive, and the music should be a mixture of old and new, light and serious.
2. With repeated listening, the children should be able to identify the performers and their cultures.
3. Each child chooses one or more of the international performers and makes a poster or flier for him or her—on the model of a real poster if the child likes.
4. Finally, all the pieces are played one by one. As each selection is played, the children who made posters for that performer share their reactions—Why do I like him or her especially? How does his or her music make me feel?
What else can we do? **Follow-up:** The children's posters and fliers can be displayed in the halls; older children can do some research about the performers they liked best and prepare short reports, which can be "bound" in construction-paper covers and shared. **Another activity:** The same setup can be used to study composers of several cultures.

Description Enacting various ceremonies from different cultures.
Title (for children) "Masters of Ceremonies."
Curriculum area Music (multicultural).

What concept are we aiming at? "Often, the music of a culture is related to ceremonial events."
What will we need? Some good research materials with illustrations and descriptions of ceremonies involving music from several different cultures; recordings or tapes of some appropriate music; materials for making costumes and recreating instruments.
How will we do it?
1. Teacher and children discuss ceremonial events that involve music (e.g., weddings, funerals, coming-of-age celebrations, births, graduations).
2. The class is divided into four to six groups. Each group chooses a different ceremonial event from one culture to enact (e.g., Japanese wedding; Native American harvest ceremony; American wedding).
3. With the help of the teacher and research materials, each group prepares a simple reenactment of the ceremony it has chosen, with music. (If people from the community can be enlisted to help, so much the better.) The groups should be given ample time to prepare their presentations—find the music, make instruments and simple costumes or masks, rehearse the ceremony, etc.
4. When all the groups are ready, they take turns enacting their ceremonies for the class, using tapes or records of the appropriate music (e.g., chants for a Native American festival; "Pomp and Circumstance" for an American graduation).
What else can we do? **Follow-up:** The children's presentations can be tape-recorded (or videotaped if the equipment is available) and played back for later discussion.

Multicultural Resources

Bibliography for Teachers

Burger, H. *Ethno-pedagogy: Cross-cultural teaching techniques.* Albuquerque, N. Mex.: Southewestern Cooperative Educational Laboratory, 1971. (Discusses practical steps for teachers who are working in multicultural classrooms.)

Children and intercultural education. Washington, D.C.: ACEI, 1974. (Three-booklet kit, 72 pp.)

Cole, A., Haas, C., Heller, E., & Weinberger, B. *Children are children are children.* Boston: Little, Brown, 1978. (Units are provided for the study of Brazil, France, Iran, Japan, Nigeria, and the Soviet Union. Each unit includes suggestions for activities exploring customs of the country. Material is well organized so that the book serves as a reference and guide for teachers.)

Grove, C. *The intensively annotated bibliography on cross-culture problems in education.* New York: Teachers College, 1975. (Paragraph-length annotations are included for over 100 references.)

Hansen-Krening, N. *Competency and creativity in language arts: A multiethnic focus.* Reading, Mass.: Addison-Wesley, 1979. (This book is a resource text for teachers interested in using multiethnic materials in teaching basic language skills and in integrating this teaching with the arts—the common base for teaching children from many different cultures and ethnic groups. Model lessons and materials are included.)

Lee, N., & Oldham, L. *Hands on heritage.* Long Beach, Calif.: Hands On Pub., 1978. (7061 Mariner Way, 90803. Includes activities for art, cooking, and recreation, with a special section on festivals for China, Greece, Israel, Japan, Mexico, Native Americans, and West Africa. An excellent annotated bibliography is a key feature.)

Litsinger, D. *The challenge of teaching Mexican-American students.* New York: American Book, 1973. (Although the major portion of this book is devoted to a description of the background and culture of the Mexican-American student, practical teaching ideas are provided in Chapter 5, with emphasis on bilingual education in Chapters 6 and 7. A selected list of resources is valuable.)

Marquevich, P., & Spiegel, S. *Multi-ethnic studies in the elementary school classroom.* Pico Rivera, Calif.: Education in Motion, 1976. (P.O. Box 224, 90660. Excellent resource with background information on Asian-American, European-American, Native American, Afro-American, and Mestizo cultures. Covers holidays, people, art, cooking, games and songs, and a bibliography for each section. Multiethnic calendar is also included.)

264

Pasternak, M. *Helping kids learn multi-cultural concepts.* Champaign, Ill.: Research Press, 1979. (This book provides activities to help students develop increased multicultural and multiethnic understandings. The author's approach concentrates on developing a multicultural spirit to pervade the curriculum, rather than a few different cultures. A valuable list of resource materials and ideas for in-service training of teachers is included.)

Stone, J., and DeNevi, D. *Teaching multi-cultural populations: Five heritages.* New York: Van Nostrand Reinhold, 1971. (Articles deal with black, Puerto Rican, Mexican-American, Native American, and Asian-American populations. A most valuable feature is the extensive annotated bibliography, including references to classroom materials.)

Woodfin, M. J. (Ed.). *Books on American Indians and Eskimos:* A selection *guide for children and young adults.* Chicago: ALA, 1978. (This bibliography is designed to help educators make intelligent choices among the many book selections now available on American Indians and Eskimos. Each review summarizes content, comments on possible uses, lists strengths and weaknesses in writing and accuracy, and estimates grade level. Books are rated as good, adequate, or poor.)

Multiethnic bibliographies:

California State Department of Education. *Bibliography of Spanish materials for children: Kindergarten through grade six.* Sacramento: California State Dept. of Education, 1971. (Free. Educational Task Force, 721 Capitol Mall, 95814.)

Inland Library System. *Chicano: A selected bibliography.* Riverside, Calif.: Inland Library System, 1971. (Riverside Public Library, P.O. Box 469, 92502.)

National Conference of Christians and Jews. *Books for brotherhood for adults, young people, and children.* National Conf. of Christians and Jews, 1972. (Free.)

New York Public Library. *The black experience in children's books.* New York: New York Public Library, 1971. (Office of Children's Services, 8 E. 40th St., 10016.)

Oakland Public Schools. *The black Americans: Books for children.* Oakland, Calif.: Oakland public Schools, 1970. (1025 Second Ave., 94106.)

San Jacinto School District. *American Indians: An annotated bibliography of recommended resource materials: Elementary grades.* San Jacinto, Calif.; San Jacinto School Dist. (92382.)

Bibliography for Children

Bibliographies of multicultural children's books (books and periodicals):

An annotated checklist of children's stories with settings in cities outside the United States, 1960-1971. (Unpublished research paper, Catholic University, Washington, D.C., 1972. 50 pp.)

Cohen, D. (Ed.). *Multi-ethnic media: Selected bibliographies in print.* American Library Association.

Gonzales, E. M. de, & Pellowski, A. (Eds.), *Latin America: An annotated listed of materials for children.* New York: Center for Inter-American Relations, 1969.

Griffin, L. *Multi-ethnic books for young children: Annotated bibliography for parents and teachers.* Washington, D.C.: NAEYC, 1970.

Haviland, V. (Ed.). *Children's books of international interest* (2d ed.). Chicago: ALA, 1978.

Information Center on Children's Cultures. *Africa: An annotated list of printed materials suitable for children.* New York: Information Center on Children's Cultures, 1968.

Interracial books for children. (Bulletin of Council on Interracial Books for Children, Inc., 841 Broadway, New York, N.Y. 10023.)

Maryland State Dept. of Education. *Ethnic and cultural studies: A bibliography.* Maryland State Dept. of Education. (Single copy free.)

National Association for the Advancement of Colored People. *Integrated school books: A descriptive bibliography of 399 pre-school and elementary school texts and story books.* New York: NAACP, 1967.

Ullom, J. C. (Ed.). *Folklore of the North American Indians: An annotated bibliography.* Washington, D.C.: U.S. Government Printing Office, 1969.

U.S. Bureau of Indian Affairs. *Annotated bibliography of young people's fiction on American Indians.* Curriculum Bulletin No. II. Washington, D.C.: U.S. Bureau of Indian Affairs, 1972. (Office of Education Programs, 1951. Constitution Ave., NW, 20242.)

White, D. *Multi-ethnic books for Head Start children.* Part I: *Black and integrated literature.* Part II: *Other minority group literature.* Urbana, Ill.: ERIC Clearinghouse on ECE, 1969.

Children's books on general multicultural subjects:

Cole, A., et al. *Children are children are children.* Boston: Little, Brown, 1978. (Paper. Recipes, games, music, and crafts from many countries.)

Fiarotta, P., & Fiarotta, N. *The you and me heritage tree.* New York: Workman, 1976. (Craft projects from ethnic groups within the United States.)

Grunfeld, F. V. (Ed.). *Games of the world.* New York: Ballantine, 1977.

Books on Asian subjects:

Aruego, J., & Aruego, A. *A crocodile's tale.* New York: Scholastic, 1976. (Philippine folktale.)

Issa, et al. *"Don't Tell the Scarecrow" and other Japanese poems.*

Mosel, A. *Funny little woman.* New York: Dutton, 1972. (Japanese tale. Caldecott Award.)

Tuyet, T. K. *Children of Viet-Nam.* Berkeley, Calif.: Southeast Asia Resource Center, 1973. (Story and coloring book.)

Yashima, M., & Yashima, T. *Momo's kitten.* New York: Penguin, 1977.

Yashima, T. *Crow boy.* New York: Penguin, 1976.

Yashima, T. *Umbrella.* New York: Penguin, 1977. (Tale of Japanese people living in New York.)

Books on Latin subjects:

Bond, J. C. *Brown is a beautiful color.* New York: F. Watts, 1969.

De Poix, C. *Jo, Flo, and Yolanda.* Chapel Hill, N.C.: Lollipop Power, 1973.

Ets, M. H. *Gilberto and the wind.* New York: Viking, 1963.

Fraser, J. *Las posadas: A Christmas story.* Flagstaff, Ariz.: Northland, 1963.

Maury, I. *My mother the mail carrier/Mi mama la cartera.* Old Westbury, N.Y.: Feminist Press, 1976.

Schweitzer, B. B. *Amigo.* New York: Macmillan, 1973. (Tale of a dog and a boy.)

Serfozo, M. *Welcome Roberto.* Chicago: Follett, 1969. (A Mexican-Ameri-

Simon, N. *What do I say?* Chicago: A. Whitman, 1967.

Books on Native American subjects:

Baker, B. *Little runner.* New York: Harper and Row, 1962.
Beim, L., & Beim, J. *Little igloo.* New York: Harcourt, Brace, 1941.
Brill, C. *Indian and free.* Minneapolis: University of Minnesota Press, 1974.
   (Life on a Chippewa reservation. Photos from Red Lake, Minn.)
Jones, H. *The trees stand shining.* New York: Dial, 1976. (Poetry, illustrated
   with watercolors. Ages 4 and up.)
McDermott, G. *Arrow to the sun: A Pueblo Indian tale.* New York: Viking,
   1974. (Pueblo art. Caldecott Award.)

Books on black and African subjects:

Aardema, V. *Why mosquitoes buzz in people's ears.* New York: Dial, 1978.
   (Animal tale. Caldecott Award.)
Adoff, A. *Black is brown is tan.* New York: Harper and Row, 1973.
Aliki. *A weed is a flower.* Englewood Cliffs, N.J.: Prentice-Hall, 1965.
   (About George Washington Carver.)
Bond, J. *A is for Africa.* (Alphabet book, illustrated.)
Caselle, C. *Country of the black people* (Book One). Chicago, Ill.: Third
   World Press, 1975. (History of Ghana in pictures.)
Clifton, L. *Some of the days of Everett Anderson.* (Poems.)
Feelings, M. *Moja means one.* New York: Dial, 1971. (Swahili counting
   book.)
Giles, L. *Color me brown* (Rev. ed.). Chicago: Johnson (Chicago), 1974.
Hill, E. S. *Evan's corner.* New York: Holt, 1967. (A child in the city.)
Keats, E. J. *Goggles.* New York: Macmillan, 1969.
Keats, E. J. *Hi, cat.* New York: Macmillan, 1972.
Keats, E. J. *Snowy day.* New York: Penguin, 1976.
McGovern, A. *Black is beautiful.* New York: Scholastic, 1970.
McGovern, A. *Wanted dead or alive: The true story of Harriet Tubman.*
   New York: Scholastic, 1977. (About a runaway slave.)
Myers, W. D. *Dragon takes a wife.* Indianapolis: Bobbs-Merrill.
Smith, J. P. *Li'l Tuffy and his ABCs.* Chicago, Ill.: Johnson (Chicago).
   (Alphabet coloring book.)
Sutherland, E. *Playtime in Africa.* New York: Athenaeum, 1962. (With
   photos.)

Materials other than books:

Black ABC's (Set of twenty-six study prints. Available from children's Book
   and Music Center, 2500 Santa Monica Blvd., Santa Monica, Calif. 90404.)
Discovering the world. (Set of four filmstrips with four records or cassettes.
   Many aspects of different cultures. Full color. Comes with reading script
   for teacher. Available from Children's Book and Music Center. 2500
   Santa Monica Blvd., Santa Monica, Calif. 90404.)

Multicultural Materials

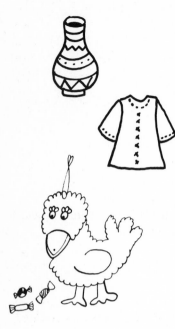

Filmstrips with cassettes. *One world* series; *Children everywhere* series. Lakeshore, 2695 E. Dominguez St., P.O. Box 6261, Carson, Calif. 90749.)

Multiethnic dolls.

Posters and prints. (Family-life scenes from other cultures; scenes of people from different racial and ethnic groups living and working together.)

Multilingual games. (Tri-Lang is a game in English, Spanish, and French. Monopoly and Scrabble are available in Spanish-language versions.)

African People 'n' Places. (Set of plastic pieces for make-believe centered on a game preserve in Africa. Human and animal figures, vehicles, and others. Ages 3 to 8.)

Navaho Curriculum Center, Rough Rock Demonstration School, Chinle, Ariz. 86503.

R and E Research Associates, 936 Industrial Ave., Palo Alto, Calif. 94303.

Southwestern Cooperative Educational Laboratory (SWCEL), 117 Richmond Dr., N.E. Albuquerque, N. Mex. 87106.

Trans-Ethnic Education Communication Foundation, P.O. Box 24740, Los Angeles, Calif. 90024.

Xerox Education Group, 1801 Avenue of the Stars, Suite 1052, Los Angeles, Calif. 90033.

Afro-American Book Store, 1708 Atlantic Ave., Long Beach, Calif. 90813.

American Indian Historical Society, 1451 Masonic Ave., San Francisco, Calif. 94117.

Appalachia Educational Laboratory (AEL), 1031 Quarier St., P.O. Box 1348, Charleston, West Va. 25325.

Central Midwestern Regional Educational Laboratory (CMREL), 10646 St. Charles Rock Rd., St., Ann Arbor, Mich. 63074.

Far West Laboratory for Educational Research and Development (FWLERD), 1855 Folsom St., San Francisco, Calif. 94103.

Ideal Printing Company, 649 S. Alderton Ave., City of Industry, Calif. 90033.

Inter-America Research Associates, National Resource Center for Bilingual/Bicultural Preschool Materials, 2001 Wisconsin Ave., NW, Washington, D.C. 20007.

Massachusetts Dept. of Education, Bureau of Curriculum Innovation, 182 Tremont St., Boston, Mass. 02111.

Mexican American Cultural Center, 3019 W. French Pl., San Antonio, Tex., 78767.

National Congress of American Indians (NCAI), 1765 P St., NW, Washington, D.C. 20036.

National Educational Laboratory Publishers, Inc., P.O. Box 1003, Austin, Tex. 78767. (Spanish-English bilingual early childhood program of 3-, 4-, and 5-year olds.)

The following book of black-and-white photos should be very appealing:

Raynor, D. *Grandparents around the world.* Chicago: A. Whitman, 1977.

Children's Book and Music Center, 2500 Santa Monica Blvd., Santa Monica, Calif. 90404, has the following "mural packets," or prints (by catalog number):

MC152. *Polynesia.*
MC153. *American dream.*
MC154. *I have a dream* (black American).
MC155. *Mexico.*
MC443. *Africa.*

Filmstrips, with records or cassettes:

Bowmar world culture series. (Peoples, their culture, and their music.)
Treasury of fairy tales. (Ten of the most familiar fairy tales.)

For multicultural videotapes:

UNICEF *Hi, neighbor* series (records or cassettes, available from Children's
    Book and Music Center, 2500 Santa Monica Blvd., Santa Monica, Calif.
    90404):
UNICEF #1. (Indonesia, Italy, Paraguay, Uganda.)
UNICEF #2. (Brazil, Ghana, Israel, Japan, Turkey.)
UNICEF #3. (Chile, Greece, Ethoipia, Nigeria, Thailand.)
UNICEF #4. (Guinea, India, Iran, Mexico, Poland.)
UNICEF #5. (Burma, Guatemala, Spain, Sudan, United Arab Republic.)
UNICEF #6. (Ivory Coast, Pakistan, Peru, Yugoslavia.)
UNICEF #7. (Jamaica, Madagascar, Ceylon, Philippines.)
UNICEF #8. (Colombia, Tanzania, Cambodia, Libya.)

Other records (available from Lakeshore; catalog number in parentheses):

African songs and rhythms for children. (FR7844.)
American folk songs for children. (FR7601.)
American Indian dances. (FR6510.)
American Negro folk and work songs. (FR7654.)
Around the world in dance. (XC542.)
Ballads of black America. (FR7751.)
Jambo songs and chants. (FR7661.)
Latin American children's games and songs. (FR7851.)
Music of the orient. (FR8745.)
We are America's children. (FR7666.)

Multicultural Folktale Involvement Kits from Lakeshore (each based on a cassette with a folktale on one side and description of the culture on the other):

SV1600 Eskimo Folktale Involvement Kit. (The sea monster and the fisher-
    man. Grades K through 3.)
SV1700 Indian Folktale Involvement Kit (How the procupine got his quills.
    Grades K through 3.)
SV1900 African Folktale Involvement Kit (How Talu the elephant got his
    farm back. Grades K through 3.)

Section 7
EDUCATION OF CHILDREN WITH SPECIAL NEEDS

We've provided this separate section on special education to stress the importance of this area, to stress the importance of thinking specifically about it, and to make it easy for our readers to find and use this material.

But special education—like multicultural approaches—is not something apart from the ordinary curriculum. "Mainstreaming" is possibly the most significant modern trend in special education. It implies that children with special needs are to be treated as far as possible like "normal" or "average" children—studying the same things in the same classrooms. Naturally, where a child with special needs is concerned there will have to be some modification of the curriculum and the environment; but if mainstreaming is to achieve its purpose, such modifications need to be as slight as possible.

We hope that teachers and caretakers will not set children with special needs apart—not physically, certainly; and not in their attitude toward these children. Our goal is individualized instruction for all *children, not just for those who are "special."*

Because we feel this way, we do not give specific activities in this section; instead, we provide some ideas and general guidelines under two major headings: (1) the educationally different; (2) the physically different. Following the ideas and guidelines, we give some helpful resources for special education.

The Educationally Different: Ideas and Guidelines for Teachers

Who are the "educationally different"? They are the children who differ mentally or emotionally from the norm, however the norm is defined. Educationally different children include gifted and creative children on the one hand, and educationally handicapped children on the other; by "educational handicaps" we mean learning disabilities, mental retardation, and emotional disturbance. Our ideas and guidelines, then, come under these headings:

Gifted and creative children.
Learning-disabled children.
Mentally retarded children.
Emotionally disturbed children.

Gifted and Creative Children

Here are ten general guidelines for working with gifted and creative children:

1. Encourage curiosity, exploration, and questioning.
2. Be willing to explore and to accept alternative solutions to problems.
3. Involve the children in special projects that will be of genuine value to them and to the school.
4. Don't feel threatened if you don't know the answers to their questions —be willing to help them search for answers.
5. Encourage the use of many resources.
6. Encourage higher levels of thinking.
7. Help the children to learn special skills having to do with research and references—such skills will always be useful.
8. Keep the children motivated and constructively creating.
9. Encourage the children to accept their gift as a responsibility. You may want to have gifted children tutor others—but only if this is really a learning experience for tutor as well as tutee.
10. Help the children develop a balanced self-concept and healthy social relationships.

And here are some specific ideas:

Provide a variety of resources: people, books, pictures, multimedia information.
Watch films; take trips; use television.
Let the children make films.
Teach the children to express their thoughts and feelings through art, poetry, writing and telling stories, movement, drama, and so on.
Find topics and set assignments which require analyzing, synthesizing, and generalizing.
Allow time for brainstorming. Encourage group discussions, debates, etc.

Accept the children's ideas and suggestions; accept the "wild" and the "wonderful." For instance: have a suggestion box; set up a court and hold trials; let the students make some administrative and pedagogical decisions; let the students take turns "teaching."

Learning-Disabled Children

When working with a learning-disabled child or children, keep these seven general guidelines in mind:

1. Place the child (or children) close to you, so that you can easily give extra help.
2. Minimize distractions.
3. Simplify the environment; restrict the number of choices.
4. Use concrete materials and provide experiences for all the senses.
5. Design tasks so as to ensure success and avoid frustration.
6. Have reasonable expectations.
7. Break the work into small segments.

Following are some specific ideas:

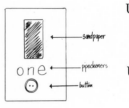

Use a multisensory approach to learning. For example, are the children learning about the number 5? Clap five times; eat five raisins; draw five circles; write "5" five times; "draw" a 5 in a salt tray; make (and eat) a cooky shaped as a 5; cut a 5 out of sandpaper.

Use plenty of "initial cuing." That is, help the children get started by reexplaining, restating directions, offering encouragement, saying "now" or "go," and smiling.

Play games. If you allow the children to play barefoot, they can use their soles as sensory receptors. If you alternate visual and verbal commands and signals, the children will learn different sensory cues. Remember that a quiet activity should follow a game, to calm the children down.

Use a multisensory approach when giving directions: tell, demonstrate, and illustrate, for instance.

Lead in gradually to some activities. For example, before throwing and catching balls, throw and catch soft objects such as yarn, fleece, or fur.

Play games to practice identifying body parts—"Follow the Leader" and "Simon Says" are both good. Don't use nicknames or baby talk for body parts.

For learning movement, allow free exploration. Have the children "overlearn" movement patterns. When you are teaching a skill such as dance or tumbling, hand- and footprints cut out of contact paper and stuck to the floor are useful as reference points.

Mentally Retarded Children

If you're working with a mentally retarded child or children, here are nine general guidelines to remember:

1. Be sensitive to the children's need for a sense of accomplishment—praise each child for completed work, no matter how small.
2. Demonstrate caring; but be firm and consistent.
3. Recognize each child's capacity and do not try to force achievement beyond it.
4. Whenever possible, teach by means of gestures and concrete examples.

5. Help each child to develop physical skills.
6. Use a multisensory approach to learning.
7. Learning should be progressive and cumulative—provide greater challenges in each succeeding lesson.
8. Require the children to make simple decisions.
9. Provide plenty of opportunities to learn and overlearn.

Here are a few specific ideas:

Provide activities which involve rhythm, basic movement, movement exploration, and other aspects of perceptual-motor development. Allow experimentation with different kinds of musical equipment and instruments. To help motivate the children, give them opportunities to demonstrate skills to others. Remember that physical activities can strengthen perceptual skills and concepts.

Relate visual input to kinesthetic feedback: for instance, use a mirror and a yardstick while the children do pushups, to show how straight the body is.

Use stories, plays, creative drama, and dramatic play. Tell stories which deal with familiar concepts, and then move on to stories which introduce new ones. (Remember to keep stories short.) When the children are learning new concepts, acting things out—actually participating—is very helpful.

To help motivate the children and focus their attention, use bright-colored objects or equipment.

Provide kinesthetic feedback by assisting each child as he or she goes through the movements involved in physical skills—until the child is ready to go it alone.

Use games. Be sure to include everyone whenever possible. Explain the rules carefully, and allow individual practice time.

Games should be noncompetitive—that is, each child should compete only against himself or herself ("Can you do better?" "How much can you do?" "Can you beat your own record?").

Emotionally Disturbed Children

Here are eight general guidelines for working with emotionally disturbed children:

1. Accept each child and try to build trust.
2. Reduce—if possible, eliminate—opportunities for failure.
3. Individualize instruction.
4. Try to identify situations that cause anxiety, so that you can reduce or eliminate them.
5. Be understanding; but set firm limits on behavior.
6. Provide stability: be fair, firm, and consistent.
7. Provide opportunities for autonomy and decision making, so that the children's behavior will become more mature.
8. Help the peer group to accept, influence, and encourage the emotionally disturbed child.

And here are specific ideas you should find helpful:

Help each child build a positive self-concept: give praise generously; vary activities so that all children will have a chance to succeed; give positive reinforcement for desired behavior; and be sure to include withdrawn children.

During physical activities, keep the children busy and make explanations clear, but brief.

Teach relaxation: try Yoga and breathing exercises.

Use rhythmical equipment, such as drums, whistles, shakers, and tambourines. Set slow tempos for more difficult movements; use faster tempos for easier ones.

Use aquatics; warm water has a relaxing effect. Remember to start with a set routine. To lessen fear of water, walk and jump in it. To help the children learn physical skills, manipulate their arms and legs; mechanical devices can also be helpful.

Use stories, plays, and dramatic play to encourage the expression of feelings—and remember to encourage the children to express negative feelings as well as positive ones.

The Physically Different: Ideas and Guidelines for Teachers

Who are the "physically different"? These are children with impairments of speech, hearing, or vision and children with orthopedic handicaps or chronic physical problems or diseases. Our ideas and guidelines for teachers and caretakers are therefore listed under these headings:

Speech-handicapped children.
Hearing-impaired children.
Visually impaired children.
Orthopedically handicapped children.

Speech-Handicapped Children

When you're working with children who are speech-handicapped, these nine general guidelines are important to remember:

1. Severe problems should be referred to a therapist.
2. Don't mention a child's problem in the classroom, particularly stuttering.
3. Help each child to relax.
4. Be aware of situations which aggravate the problem.
5. As soon as each child is comfortable, encourage him or her to participate.
6. When stress occurs, reduce the demand for speech.
7. Help each child to *hear* errors.
8. Provide a model for correct usage.
9. Help each **child** to produce correct sounds.

Some specific ideas follow:

Set a good example, and have the children play games involving imitation or impersonation. "Echo" songs are also good.
Sing and do choral reading.
Play rhyming games. Games in which the children are to complete rhymes are helpful ("Jack and *Jill* went up the _____").
To give the children practice in recognizing sounds, use puzzles, games, fill-ins, etc.
Read and reread familiar stories and poems, so that the children will become accustomed to sounds and usages.
Encourage spontaneous speech—use the sand table, the water table, puppets, dramatic play, movement, and snack time as opportunities for speech.

Hearing-Impaired Children

Keep these seven general guidelines in mind if you are working with a hearing-impaired child or children:

1. Seat a hearing-impaired child in the middle of the class, close to the front.
2. To facilitate lip-reading, keep the light source behind the child.
3. Get the child's attention; then speak clearly but without exaggeration.
4. Provide visual materials and instructions.
5. If a child has a hearing aid, be sure it is turned on and working.
6. Assign "buddies" to help each other find pages, follow oral directions, etc.
7. Create a tension-free environment with rich, stimulating interest centers.

We suggest these specific ideas:

Use activities that involve rhythm, basic movement, movement exploration, and perceptual-motor development. Use percussion instruments—these produce vibrations to which children can easily respond.

Use visual aids and tactile and light cues. For instance: use charts, graphs, and posters; use gentle touches; flash the lights on and off to get the children's attention.

To stimulate residual hearing and rhythmic speech, encourage participation in vocal music.

Play circle games in which you and the children face each other; point to the child you are calling on.

Have the children recite aloud or clap out a beat. Let the children place their hands on a piano or phonograph so that they can feel the vibrations.

Use games which emphasize visual cues—e.g., "Follow the Leader," "Jump the Brook," "Jump the Shot."

Use aquatics. Establish standards for signaling—e.g., splashing or hand waving. Set up a buddy system and enforce it. If there are children who shouldn't get water in their ears, modify strokes as necessary.

Visually Impaired Children

Here are ten general guidelines for working with visually impaired children:

1. Seat the children where they can easily see the board. Visually impaired children should have adjustable desks.
2. Be sure that the lighting does not create glare or cast shadows.
3. Use books with large print, magnifying equipment, and—if possible—a large-print typewriter.
4. Use materials which encourage tactile, auditory, and kinesthetic exploration.
5. Provide games and puzzles with raised surfaces.
6. Keep the noise level low.
7. If possible, assign a helper to tape assignments and give help with directions.
8. Provide unglazed paper, soft black pencils, and black felt-tip pens.
9. Use concrete materials.
10. Make contact by means of touch and voice.

And here are some specific suggestions:

For perceptual-motor development, use activities involving rhythm, basic movement, and movement exploration. Examples: have the children tap

278

to their pulse; use bright-colored tumbling mats; use continuous sound to develop the sense of direction; if necessary, use a leading pole.

Discourage unnecessary noise, and then use lightweight balls with a noise-maker inside.

Use plays, stories, and dramatic play—have the children imitate sounds they have heard or enact incidents they've experienced.

Use appropriate games. Mix visually impaired and sighted children on teams. Roll—rather than throw—larger-than-normal balls.

Use aquatics. Use a guide rope; use kickboards and floats. Use auditory clues whenever possible—e.g., have a child swim toward your voice.

Use "hands-on" devices whenever possible—e.g., have a child feel you doing a task.

Orthopedically Handicapped Children

Following are ten guidelines for working with orthopedically handicapped children:

1. Work out a carefully planned program to meet the needs of the individual children; and . . .
2. Obtain medical approval of the program.
3. During activities, let the children sit or lie down instead of standing.
4. Provide frequent rest periods.
5. Give kinesthetic clues—e.g., touch the part of the child's body that will be primarily involved in an activity.
6. Teach the correct way to fall.
7. Use lightweight equipment.
8. Promote self-acceptance and help instill confidence.
9. Help the children develop skills and talents that will compensate for their physical disabilities.
10. When a child has an obvious deformity or has lost a limb, help alleviate the child's fears about dressing and undressing with others.

And following are some specific ideas:

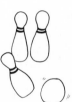

Use role-playing, dramatic play, and puppets. Assist the performers, and participate yourself. Make use of wheelchairs, crutches, etc., as props.

Use modified equipment and apparatus—lighter-weight objects (as was noted above), for instance, and larger balls.

Instead of clapping with the hands, teach the children how to beat time by tapping with a crutch.

Use isometric exercises when possible.

Teach the children how to balance on one crutch, so that they can throw and kick a ball.

For perceptual-motor development, use rhythm, basic movement, and movement exploration.

Teach aquatics.

Hold relay races in which children confined to wheelchairs and children on crutches play with unhandicapped children.

Resources for Special Education

Bibliography for Teachers

Complo, J. *Funtactics: Movement and speech activities for special children.* Belmont, Calif.: Fearon, 1979. (The aim of Funtactics is to encourage special children to express themselves through bodily movement and through speech. Emphasis is also placed on growth in concentration and problem solving. Activities are sequentially arranged and planned for a fifteen-minute period daily. They are clearly described and can be carried out by the regular classroom teacher.)

Fairchild, T., & Parks, A. *Mainstreaming the mentally retarded child.* Austin, Tex.: Learning Concepts, 1976. (2501 N. Lamar Blvd., 78705.) This book aims at helping the regular classroom teacher feel more comfortable with mildly retarded children in the class. It attempts to give a realistic picture of their capabilities, appreciation of their needs, suggestions for initial and ongoing assessment, and some practical ideas about how to work with them.)

Gaddis, E. *Teaching the slow learner in the regular classroom.* Belmont, Calif.: Fearon, 1971. (Practical ideas are included to involve the slow-learning child in learning, in social relationships, and in other aspects of the total classroom experience in the regular classroom.)

Gearheart B., & Weishahn, M. *The handicapped student in the regular classroom* (2d ed.). St. Louis: Mosby, 1980. (This book, revised after the passage of Public Law 94-142, the Education for All Handicapped Children Act, is based on the premises that there is no "right" method for educating handicapped children, that not *all* handicapped children belong in the regular classroom, and that those that do require individually planned programs. The focus is on "what to do" and "how to do it" for the regular classroom teacher faced with mainstreaming children with special needs. Sections deal with the mentally retarded; the learning-disabled; those with impaired vision, hearing, or health; children with speech problems; and "troubled" students. Appendixes provide valuable information on resources for working with these children.)

Geddes, D. *Physical activities for individuals with handicapping conditions.* St. Louis: Mosby, 1974. (This book provides activities and general and specific suggestions for those planning physical education programs for children with subaverage intellectual functioning, learning disabilities, visual or hearing impairment, orthopedic conditions, and emotional disturbances. Even those with no background in physical or special education can apply these suggestions and develop sound programs.)

Ginglend, D., & Stiles, W. *Music activities for retarded children.* Nashville; Abingdon Press, 1965. (This is an excellent resource to help teachers initiate a developmental music program for children with impaired intellectual functioning.)

Major, S., & Walsh, M. A. *Learning activities for the learning disabled.* Belmont, Calif.: Fearon, 1977. (Activities to aid specific learning processes are presented. Categories included are motor, perception, memory, language, mathematics, and conceptualization.)

McIntyre, B. *Informal dramatics: A language arts activity for the special child.* Pittsburgh: Stanwix, 1963.

Vail, P. *The world of the gifted child.* New York: Walker, 1979. (Part III of this book contains ideas and working with the gifted individually and in groups.)

Wedemeyer, A., & Cejka, J. *Creative ideas for teaching exceptional children.* Denver: Love. (This book provides sensory experiences to help the child with special needs develop understanding of basic concepts in language, mathematics, and sensory-motor areas.)

Wooster, J. *What to do for the gifted few: A handbook of strategies for differentiating instruction for gifted/talented students.* Buffalo, N.Y.: D.O.K., 1978. (This book presents options for learning experiences to meet the needs of the gifted. Ideas are included for varying the cognitive and affective areas, for collecting data about these students, and for classroom-management and teaching strategies.)

Journals:

Exceptional Children. (Official Publication of Council for Exceptional Children, 1920 Association Dr., Reston, Va. 22091.)

Focus on Exceptional Children. (Love Publishing Co., 6635 E. Villa Nova Pl., Denver, Colo. 80222.)

Gifted Child Quarterly. (Route 5, P.O. Box 630A, Hot Springs, Ark. 71901.)

Journal of Learning Disabilities. (Professional Press, 101 E. Ontario St., Chicago, Ill. 60611.)

Journal of Special Education. (Grune-Stratton, 111 Fifth Ave., New York, N.Y. 10003.)

Roeper Review: A Journal on Gifted Child Education. (2190 N. Woodward Ave., Bloomfield Hills, Mich. 48013.)

Organizations:

Alexander Graham Bell Assn. for the Deaf, 3417 Volta Pl., NW, Washington, D.C. 20007.

American Association on Mental Deficiencies, 520 Connecticut Ave., NW, Washington, D.C. 20006.

American Foundation for the Blind, 15 W. 16th St., New York, N.Y. 10011.

American Speech and Hearing Assn., 9030 Old Georgetown Rd., Washington, D.C. 20014.

Association for Children with Learning Disabilities, 2200 Brownsville Rd., Pittsburgh, Pa. 15210.

Council for Exceptional Children, 1920 Association Dr., Reston, Va. 22091.

Deafness Research Foundation, 366 Madison Ave., New York, N.Y. 10017.

Epilepsy Foundation of America, 1818 L St., NW, Washington, D.C. 20036.

National Easter Seal Society for Crippled Children and Adults, 2023 W. Ogden Ave., Chicago, Ill. 60612.

Bibliography for Children

Brightman, A. *Like me.* Boston: Little, Brown, 1976. (On the meaning of the word "retarded.")

California State Dept. of Mental Health. *Talk with me: Communication with the multi-handicapped deaf.* Northridge, Calif.: Joyce Media.

Fanshawe, E. *Rachel.* Scarsdale, N.Y.: Bradbury, 1977. (2 Overhill Rd., 10583. Tale of a girl who uses a wheelchair.)

Fassler, J. *One little girl.* New York: Human Sciences Press, 1969.

Fassler, J. *Howie helps himself.* Chicago: A. Whitman, 1975.

Gold, P. *Please don't say hello.* New York: Human Sciences Press, 1975.

Grollman, S. H. *More time to grow.* Boston: Beacon Press, 1977.

Kirchner, S. L. *Play it by sign: Games in sign language.* Northridge, Calif.: Joyce Media.

Lasker, J. *He's my brother.* Chicago: A. Whitman, 1974.

Levine, E. *Lisa and her soundless world.* New York: Human Sciences Press, 1974.

Litchfield, A. B. *A button in her ear.* Chicago: A. Whitman, 1976.

Litchfield, A. B. *A cane in her hand.* Chicago: A. Whitman, 1977.

Mack, N. *Tracy.* Chicago: Children's Press, Raintree, 1976. (1224 Van Buren St., 60607. Cerebral palsy.)

Ominsky, E. *Jon O.: A special boy.* Englewood Cliffs, N.J.: Prentice-Hall, 1977. (Down's syndrome.)

Peter, D. *Claire and Emma.* New York: John Day, 1977. (666 Fifth Ave., 10019. Hearing deficiency.)

Peterson, J. W. *I have a sister. My sister is deaf.* New York: Harper and Row, 1977.

Sobol, H. L. *My brother Steven is retarded.* New York: Macmillan, 1977. (Ordering address: Riverside, N.J. 08075.)

Stein, S. B. *About handicaps: An open family book for parents and children together.* New York: Walker, 1974. (720 Fifth Ave., 10010.)

Tomat, J., & Krutzky, C. D. *Learning through music for special children and their teachers.* South Waterford, Maine: Merriam-Eddy, 1975. (Paper.)

Wolf, B. *Don't feel sorry for Paul.* New York: Lippincott, 1974. (Artificial limbs.)

Learning Materials

Suggested Basic Materials

Constructive Playthings has several pieces of equipment designed, simplified, or adapted for children with special needs:

Adjustable chin-up bar.

Oversize playing cards.

Easy-to-grip scissors.

Super Saf-T Trike. (Catalog no. PC-382-301. Safe, padded, adult-sized tricycle.)

Special Education Rhythm Set. (No. RB-SE32. Rhythm instruments designed for special needs. Many are easier to grasp than those commonly used.)

These books come with 7-inch record:

Glazzard, M. H. *Meet Camille and Danille.* Lawrence, Kans.: H and H Enterprises, 1978. (Hearing-impaired.)

Glazzard, M. H. *Meet Danny.* Lawrence, Kans.: H and H Enterprises, 1978. (Multiply handicapped.)

Glazzard, M. H. *Meet Scott.* Lawrence, Kans.: H and H Enterprises, 1978. (Trainable mentally retarded.)

Glazzard, M. H. *Meet Scott.* Lawrence, Kans.: H and H Enterprises, 1978. (Learning-disabled.)

Also of interest:

Adkins, P. G. *A priceless playground for exceptional children.* El Paso, Tex.: Learning Resources Press. (609 La Cruz Dr., 79902.)

From Milton Bradley (Springfield, Mass. 01101):

Special education teacher's kit. (Mathematics, vocabulary, science, art, music. Over 1,000 ideas, all tested.)

Other materials:

And so they move. (Film, black-and-white, 20 min. Michigan State University, Audio-Visual Center, East Lansing, Mich. 48824.)

Mainstreaming children's games. (Record. Order from Children's Book and Music Center, 2500 Santa Monica Blvd., Santa Monica, Calif. 90404.)

Sources and Suppliers

Organizations:

Alexander Graham Bell Assn. for the Deaf, 1537 35th St., NW, Washington, D.C. 20007.

American Medical Assn., 535 N. Dearborn St., Chicago, Ill. 60610.

American Physical Therapy Assn., 1156 15th St., NW, Washington, D.C. 20005.

Information and Research Utilization Center in Physical Education and Recreation for the Handicapped, American Assn. for Health, Physical Education, and Recreation, 1201 16th St., NW, Washington, D.C. 20036.

National Therapeutic Recreation Society, 1601 N. Kent St., Arlington, Va. 22209.

Special Olympics, Inc., Eunice Kennedy Shriver, President, 1701 K St., NW, Suite 203, Washington, D.C. 20006.

Books on teaching the handicapped:

Bangs, T. E. *Birth to three: Developmental learning and the handicapped child.* Hingham, Mass.: Teaching Resources Corp. (50 Pond Park Rd., 02043.)

Burroughs, M. C. *Restraints on excellence: Our waste of gifted children.* Hingham, Mass.: Teaching Resources Corp. (50 Pond Park Rd., 02043.)

Fairchild, T. N. (Ed.). *Mainstreaming series: Understanding and teaching the mainstreamed child.* Hingham, Mass.: Teaching Resources Corp. (50 Pond Park Rd., 02043.)

Ketchel, M. F., & Marsh, S. R. *Changing the behavior of handicapped children: A guide for working with parents.* Hingham, Mass.: Teaching Resources Corp. (50 Pond Park Rd., 02043.)

Catalogs, handbooks, and resource books:

Beckley-Cardy. Catalog.
Children's Book and Music Center. Catalog. (2500 Santa Monica Blvd., Santa Monica, Calif. 90404.)
Constructive Playthings. Catalog.
Gearheart, B., & Weishahn, M. *The handicapped child in the regular class-room.* St. Louis: Mosby, 1976. (Excellent bibliography.)
Gillies, E. *Creative dramatics for all children.* Washington, D.C.: ACEI, 1973. (3615 Wisconsin Ave., NW, 20016.)
Handbook for teachers of the visually handicapped. Louisville, Ky.: American Printing House for the Blind.
McNamara, J., & McNamara, B. *The special child handbook.* New York: Hawthorn, 1978. (Reviews, ideas.)
U.S. Office of Education, Bureau of Education for the Handicapped. *Catalog of captioned films for the deaf.* Washington, D.C.: U.S. Office of Education, Bureau of Education for the Handicapped.

The following records, available from Beckley-Cardy, are recommended for special children:

Activities and songs for exceptional children.
Body space perception through music.
Musical fun with words.
Songs about my feelings.
Sound identification skills.
Special movement songs and games for special people.

Enrichment Materials

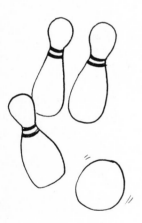

Special sports equipment:

Foam bowling sets and polo sets.
Adjustable basketball backstop.

Filmstrips for the teacher:

I'm just like you: Mainstreaming the handicapped. (Set of two filmstrips, with records or cassettes. Available from Children's Book and Music Center, 2500 Santa Monica Blvd., Santa Monica, Calif. 90404.)

Aids for the handicapped:

Three-way glassless mirrors. (Mirrorlite brand. For spatial awareness.)

Kits:

Kent, L. R. *Language acquisition program for the severely retarded.* Champaign, Ill.: Research Press, 1974. (2612 N. Mattis Ave., 61820. Designed for those with hearing-impaired, visually impaired, autistic, disturbed, and brain-damaged children.)
Linford, M., Hipsher, L., & Silikovitz, R. *Self-help instruction.* Part III of *Systematic instruction for retarded children: The Illinois program.* Danville, Ill.: Interstate, 1972. (1927 N. Jackson, 61832.)
Preschool children with Down's syndrome. (Dressing, dining, using the toilet, grooming. Behavioral analysis and management; detailed directions.)
Schaeffer, F. *Project "Me."* Glendale, Calif.: Bowmar. 1972. (622 Rodier Dr., 91201. Using audiovisual instructional materials in training the handicapped child; filmstrips shown on floor-based screen so that child will interact with a whole new environment.)

Tawney, J. W., & Hipsher, L. W. *Systematic language instruction*. Part II of *Systematic instruction for retarded children: The Illinois program*. Danville, Ill.: Interstate, 1972. (1927 N. Jackson, 61832. To increase language functioning level in retarded children. Controlled language statements are structured to higher levels. Highly structured program increases observable learning and behavioral control.)

APPENDIX

In this appendix, we provide some blank activity forms which can be duplicated for use in creating additional activities for each developmental area. You should find these forms useful as you design your own activities. augmenting those we have given in this book, to build your own file or collection.

The basic form we give here is appropriate for psycho-physical-motor, science, mathematics, language arts, and social studies activities; we also give one variation of it that is appropriate for art activities, a second variation appropriate for music activities, and a third variation appropriate for multi-cultural activities.

We believe that our models and sample activities are developmentally sound, form a logical sequence, and are aimed at clear and reasonable objectives. We hope that they will be helpful to you as you follow your own path in guiding young children's learning.

For psycho-physical-motor, science, mathematics, language, and social studies activities:

Description
Title (for children)
Curriculum area   **Age range**

What is our objective?
Key to table (area-level-objective)
What will we need?

How will we do it?
1.

2.

3.

4.

5.

What else can we do?   (Follow-up; variations; other activities)

For art activities:

Description
Title (for children)
Curriculum area   **Age range**

What is our medium?
Key to table (area-level-process)
What will we need?

How will we do it?
1.

2.

3.

4.

5.

What else can we do?   (Follow-up; variations; other activities)

For music activities:

Description
Title (for children)
Curriculum area   Age range

What will we experience?
Key to table (area-level-process)
What will we need?

How will we do it?
1.

2.

3.

4.

5.

What else can we do?   (Follow-up; variations; other activities)

For multicultural activities:

Description
Title (for children)
Curriculum area

What concept are we aiming at?
What will we need?

How will we do it?
1.

2.

3.

4.

5.

What else can we do?   (Follow-up; variations; other activities)

290